What people are saying about

A Spell in

The poet who reignites within us passion and wonder for the living world does as much for the healing of the planet as any ecologist. Roselle Angwin is one such poet.
Fred Hageneder, author of *The Spirit of Trees* and *The Living Wisdom of Trees*

Seeking the stories beneath the stories, the poet Roselle Angwin explores the forest of Brocéliande and the hidden mysteries of Arthurian and Celtic myth in this delightful immersion at the forest's heart, where its inhabitants, seen and unseen, have their own tales to tell.
Caitlín Matthews, Celtic scholar, author of *Diary of a Soul Doctor* and *Celtic Visions*

...a book in which to immerse yourself, letting go into the deep richness of the forest and its old tales...
Emma Restall-Orr, author on subjects such as pagan ethics and animism, one-time head of the British Druid Order, now managing a nature reserve and natural burial ground

Endorsements from course participants on Tongues in Trees
I have been following a rather wonderful online course, formulated and run by the remarkable poet, author and facilitator Roselle Angwin. The course is called 'Tongues in Trees' and invites us each month to observe a particular tree associated with the Celtic Ogham calendar. We are encouraged to relate in a creative way to the trees, through poetry, prose, folklore, land art and ritual. It is, in itself, a truly holistic introduction to each species... but I think the deeper knowledge and understanding

of trees and their huge importance in the life of our planet will take me a lifetime.

This course has been an absolute turning point for me. Roselle has brought to my attention the vast richness of the knowledge pertaining to both individual tree species but also the holistic understanding of the importance of trees in the ecosphere (which includes us!).

Roz Cawley

Taking part in this course has made 2019 extraordinary. I have always loved and felt connection with trees, but this is the year I have communicated with trees. I am deeply grateful to Roselle Angwin for her integrity, generosity and for sharing her fascinating writings. My internal and external landscapes have been profoundly enriched.

Leonie Charlton

'Mindfulness' is a buzz word at the moment but this course has enabled so much more – a sort of mind-allthesenses-spiritfulness and an enriched awareness of trees as the wonderful, sentient, numinous and giving entities that they are. Roselle's course modules are brilliant – full of information and suggestions while being open-ended, motivating and inspiring.

This is an update of something that I wrote near the beginning of the course. Since then the sentiment that it expresses has only become richer and deeper: I have never taken trees for granted. But this course has made me more aware of, as well as an aesthetic/spiritual connection with them, an almost visceral bond which I feel I have experienced before – either in this life or another, in this world or another.

Sheena Odle

'Tongues in Trees' has been an immersive, transformative experience. I can't recommend it highly enough. Roselle's sense of wonder and depth of wisdom have transformed my relationship with the Ogham trees and made me more open to the natural world.

Gabrielle O'Donovan

I had thought I was reasonably switched on, but this course has taken me way beyond that; still much more switching on to do but Roselle has gifted us a magnificent portal through which to dive deeper. I have individual trees I will engage with whenever I can and lots more to get to know – it has been truly marvellous and magical.

Ali Walters

PREVIOUS BOOKS

NON-FICTION
Riding the Dragon – myth and the inner journey
Element Books 1994, 978-1852305758

Creative Novel Writing
Robert Hale 1999 (hb 978-0709063445), 2002 (pb 978-0709070634)

Writing the Bright Moment – inspiration & guidance for writers
Fire in the Head (Arts Council England supported) 2005,
978-0954802707

FICTION
Imago
Indigo Dreams Publishing 2011, 978-1907401381

The Burning Ground
Indigo Dreams Publishing 2013, 978-1909357310
(both novels were shortlisted in the Cinnamon Press awards)

POETRY
Looking For Icarus
bluechrome 2005; Indigo Dreams Publishing 2015, 978-1909357884

Bardo
Shearsman Books 2011, 978-1848611634

All the Missing Names of Love
Indigo Dreams Publishing 2012, 978-1848611634

Trick of the Light, A – poems from Iona
Pindrop Press 2018, 978-0995680562

POETRY COLLABORATIONS
Hestercombe Prints and Poems (handmade artists' book with
Penny Grist)
genius loci, Arts Council England-supported, 2000, no ISBN

Hawk Into Everywhere, A, with Rupert Loydell
Stride Publications 2001, 978-1900152716

River Suite, with photographer Vikky Minette
Mudlark Press 2013, 978-0-9565162-4-4

A Spell
in the Forest

Book 1 - Tongues in Trees

A Spell in the Forest

Book 1 - Tongues in Trees

Roselle Angwin

MOON BOOKS

Winchester, UK
Washington, USA

JOHN HUNT PUBLISHING

First published by Moon Books, 2021
Moon Books is an imprint of John Hunt Publishing Ltd., No. 3 East Street, Alresford
Hampshire SO24 9EE, UK
office@jhpbooks.net
www.johnhuntpublishing.com
www.moon-books.net

For distributor details and how to order please visit the 'Ordering' section on our website.

Text copyright: Roselle Angwin 2020

ISBN: 978 1 78904 630 4
978 1 78904 631 1 (ebook)
Library of Congress Control Number: 2020941229

A CIP catalogue record for this book is available from the British Library.

Design: Stuart Davies

UK: Printed and bound by CPI Group (UK) Ltd, Croydon, CR0 4YY
Printed in North America by CPI GPS partners

We operate a distinctive and ethical publishing philosophy in
all areas of our business, from our global network of authors to
production and worldwide distribution.

Contents

The way we see the world shapes the way we treat it. If a mountain is a deity, not a pile of ore; if a river is one of the veins of the land, not potential irrigation water; if a forest is a sacred grove, not timber; if other species are biological kin, not resources; or if the planet is our mother, not an opportunity – then we will treat each other with greater respect. This is the challenge, to look at the world from a different perspective.
David Suzuki

Acknowledgements

From the first dedicated day course of 'Tongues in Trees', in November 2014 in Cornwall, emerged some beautiful pieces of land art and some fine writing. Thanks go to the participants, some of whom travelled quite a distance, for their participation, creative expression and encouragement of my work.

I'd like to acknowledge and thank particularly the first group of participants in my online yearlong 'Tongues in Trees' course. I can't imagine working with a more enthusiastic, inspired and committed group of people. Each of them in one way or another added to my own knowledge of trees, especially those people with whom I worked directly, and/or the Facebook participants who contributed so much.

My particular thanks go to Sheena Odle, for poems I've included in the book, and for her inspired book gifts, and Pat Childerhouse for her Hawthorn story and a poem, also here in the book. Sabah Raphael Reed made me smile with her tiny poem on Elder, reproduced under that tree's month. I would have liked to have included Ali Walters' beautiful photographs (some of which I'm lucky enough as now to shelve in my library, in her finely-bound artist's book), and many pieces and pictures by other participants. Thanks also to Roz Cawley, who has cheered my work on over the years, as well as through the 'Tongues' course.

As I write this, I'm partway through working with the second year's group. There are poets who are photographers and artists in this group, too, whose work is an inspiration. So far, this is also greatly enriching my own life with trees.

Carolyn Garry, I owe you thanks as well; not just for hosting the first 'Tongues in Trees' day-course in 2014, and a related yearlong series of workshops, 'The Wellkeepers', which will partly underlie my next book, but also for making your own woodland garden so freely available, and for your continuing support through many years.

Beatrice Grundbacher, I think you know that without you the first birthing of this book wouldn't have been possible. For that and for other things, thank you.

Chloë Balcomb, you asked the right question at the right moment, when I was wading through the mire of a boggily shapeless shoal of words, and it's because of you that the book has taken the final form it has, with a second to follow. Thank you.

Four writers in particular have been a source of inspiration: Peter Wohlleben, with his *The Hidden Life of Trees*; Richard Powers, with his Man Booker-listed *Overstory* (it should have won); Roger Deakin and *Wildwood*; and Robert Graves' classic and erudite work *The White Goddess*. I also have to mention Fred Hageneder, writer and musician extraordinaire, for his several inspirational tree books.

Thanks are due to my friend Kenneth Steven for his poem 'The Harp' from *The Missing Days*, and, too, to Paul Matthews, one of my favourite contemporary poets, for letting me use some of his words from *The Ground that Love Seeks*. Chris Powici gave me permission to reproduce two of his poems from *The Weight of Light* – thank you.

Clearly, a huge debt of inspiration goes to Forest: in the outer world and in our own imaginal life. I'm particularly entwined with a magical forest in Finistère, Brittany, likely a fragment of the old Brocéliande; and with its smaller cousin on Dartmoor, Wistman's Wood.

Tongues in Trees

First it was the big old fir in the orphaned
lambs' field at my cousins' where, astride
a curved limb, I learned to hear the whisperings
of cedar. That was before Uncle died.

Next it was the cherry; two, in fact,
making a fairy tale of a bungalow garden.
If in spring I climbed high enough
no one could find me for blossom.

Then, solitary adolescent with an old red
bike and a penchant for melancholia
and wild, I found the greenwood, and the ruins
of the hermit's chapel with its well and thorn tree.

At university, in the city, I filled the bath
with cut willow intending, I said, to weave baskets.
Instead, I let it sprout; lost and uprooted
as I was, willow was my green company.

Now, I walk out into this startling green blizzard
of chlorophyll each morning, every tree shouting
its jubilation of leaves. I know all their names,
though these days I prefer to let them be nameless.
Roselle Angwin

Introduction

The What, The Why, The How

Alongside the accelerating and unprecedented environmental destruction by our species that characterises our time, there is in parallel another and much more positive movement. This is a fast-growing international upsurge of interest in trees, accompanied by some astonishing science (of which more below).

What's also heartening is that the resurgence of interest in trees and forests isn't simply an interest in what trees might do for us, but in trees in and for themselves. In my view, one of the worst excesses of our time, encouraged by our Judeo-Christian heritage that stated that we had dominion over the planet and her species, is the viewing of the other-than-human as a 'resource', as if everything was put here for our benefit and control. This gathering shift in perspective is uplifting; it seems to me to be one of the most hopeful signs of change, or at least the potential for change.

Although it doesn't belong in this book, I'm also heartened by the swift-growing worldwide initiatives for forest gardens, which would transform our currently-devastating agricultural practices. Forest gardens allow us to replicate successful and biodiverse ecosystems that produce perennial food crops in symbiotic or at least synergistic layered vertical systems that will not only act as carbon sinks and habitat but also have a much lighter footprint than annual cropping, which devastates soil ecosystems and encourages erosion. Taking up a great deal less space to feed the people of the world means that our current population could co-exist alongside a serious and diverse regreening of our planet and a restoration of habitat, tree cover and species. Once you start to look into forest gardening and its companion, permaculture, no other method of food production makes much sense.

If you are reading this book, I guess you're already interested in trees. I'd love to think that this book might help entwine you ever more deeply with the other-than-human, in this case the tree community, and that this will bring your life into further harmony with the rest of this beautiful planet.

A crisis of meaning

In our past, not only our physical survival but some of our sense of meaning came from an awareness and direct experience of our connectedness with the land and the other-than-human. Animals, birds and plants, including of course trees were, I like to think, seen as marvellous companions, sharing with us our journey around our star; sharing in, perhaps, what we deemed to be sacred. At least, the rituals of our prehistoric ancestors, and the cave art they left behind, suggests that our view of flora and fauna was rooted in mystery and awe more than in the purely utilitarian.

At our current stage in history a great number of those species no longer exist, and our prey animals are largely shut away from our view in factory farms. At this point in the 21st century my guess is that more children *haven't* seen a cow, a sheep, a pig, a chicken 'in the flesh' than have. The *Oxford Junior Dictionary*'s recent excision of common nature words like acorn and conker tells us so much about our contemporary values. I also imagine that more children *haven't* built a den in the woods, or climbed a tree, or skinny-dipped in a river than have – probably by quite a long way.

Anyone who grew up with a cat or a dog, or a horse, will know that the kind of uplift and companionship offered by such an 'other' is unmatched by anything else. And trees have, or had, a strong presence in children's lives, and in the fairy stories that are so frequently rooted, at least in northern Europe, in woodland or a forest, with its secrets and terrors as well as its pleasures and enchantments.

The level of detachment from the rest of the natural world experienced in our Western societies is unprecedented. Alongside this exile – for exile it is – in a worst-case scenario, go our imaginative capabilities and a child's opportunity to learn about compassion.

While this is far from related simply to our deracination and disconnection from the other-than-human, I do believe that a lack of such natural relationships in our lives on a regular basis adds to a sense of meaninglessness, and certainly disconnect: we are isolated beings spinning around in space with sometimes no awareness of any kind of web of being in which we, too, are held.

Gifts of the trees

However, in addition to my proposal that the other-than-human also offers us both joy and a sense of meaning, for a moment let's recap what trees do for us on the physical level, giving their abundance so freely:

- Produce oxygen (during the daytime, anyway; and they produce four times as much as they need themselves)
- Sequester carbon dioxide, which clearly helps to mitigate climate change; or would do if we weren't logging, worldwide, around 18.7 million acres of forests annually, which amounts to 27 soccer fields every minute (2019 data). Trees are composed of between 75% and 95% carbon, which is absorbed from the air
- Prevent soil erosion
- Prevent flooding
- Offer shade and shelter
- Play a vital role in the harmony of the hydrological cycle, and ensure a supply of clean water
- Keep the air around and land beneath them cool
- Supply timber for all aspects of building houses, boats,

making furniture, fences, containers, fuel, woodchip, sawdust, mulches
- Supply food, medicines, fibres for clothing (viscose, rayon, bamboo fibres), dyestuffs
- Allow us to make paper

And for insects, animals, birds:

- Food
- Homes
- Shelter
- Protection from predators

Max Adams in *The Wisdom of Trees* has an ironic little passage called 'What Trees Do' in which he describes what engineers are currently trying to – well, engineer: a device that will harvest sunshine, capture carbon dioxide and not pollute the planet. 'The task is to construct a manufactory in which sunlight, water and air are harvested and sugars are produced and refined', with the potential for indefinite sustainability.

He then offers six specifications for the engineers to consider, and concludes that we already have such a device: a tree.

The healing power of trees

We know (perhaps have always known, consciously or otherwise, but science is just catching up) how simply walking in a forest can be healing for a human. Undoubtedly experiencing the presence of trees, and the colour green, in a broadleaf forest is in itself both uplifting and calming.

It's no surprise that walking in a forested area has an impact on the immune system that walking in an urban area doesn't. Leaving on one side the psychological effects, there has been a certain amount of scientific research that confirms that the phytoncides emitted by trees as part of their own protection system can lower blood pressure, lower the heart rate, lower cortisol or stress hormone levels and therefore reduce stress, as well as boosting a sense of wellbeing and also the immune system, which of course helps in the long term to reduce the chances of developing the diseases of our time, such as cardiovascular illness and cancer.

And it's not just phytoncides. Scientists tell us that when human beings see the colour green, particularly in a natural environment, our bodies manifest chemical and psychological signs of reduced stress and that too helps lower cortisol.[1]

We're only now beginning to rediscover what the ancients knew: how spending time among trees is one of the best approaches to health and healing. It's so significant that recently Japan spent several million dollars in a 'forest-bathing' ('shinrin-yoku') research programme studying the physiological and psychological effects of spending time wandering in a forest.[2]

Trees also act as mediators on a psychic level, once you learn to 'speak their language'.

To learn to cherish, I believe, in anything other than the abstract, we need to know that which we wish to cherish; we need to be familiar with its ways; we need to learn to understand and love it. It seems urgent that humans learn to really get to know, and really explore our interdependence with, other species, and recognise the significance and essential (in both senses) nature of a relationship of reciprocal affinity.

It's to this end that I take groups of people out to work in the woods. By introducing people to the experience of being with individual tree species and trees, I hope first to enable a deepening, and then perhaps to begin to shift participants' perspectives from the anthropocentric to the ecocentric via, in this case, the arbocentric. As we heal ourselves walking in the woods, so we can start to 'give back' and heal our relationship with the other-than-human.

The community of trees

We are only just now learning quite how many extraordinary processes go on out of sight, underground, in trees. Beneath our feet, invisible, is that vast web of interlinked mycelia that might perhaps be more 'forest' than the visible tribe of trees. A mature tree will have around five miles of root systems, but its mycorrhizal network ('fungal highways') could extend around the circumference of the planet. (George McGavin)

Recent research shows the extent of communication within the trees' root systems via the mycorrhizal networks that transmit messages, alerts, carbons and sugars between trees.

We know that trees live in an interlinked community that is more than simply many individuals existing in a forest. We know that they tend to thrive better in such communities. We know that trees can choose to 'feed' each other when one is weak.

In any forest, there are 'hub trees' or 'mother trees' that nurture their own young: they send excess carbon through fungal networks to their understorey seedlings and saplings, which they can differentiate from other species'.

We know, says Peter Wohlleben in his amazing book *The Hidden Life of Trees*, from work undertaken by Massimo Maffei at the University of Turin that trees can also differentiate between their own roots and those of relatives.

'Mother trees' will even reduce their own root competition to make room for their own offspring. When such trees are injured or dying, they can transmit carbon and defence signals to their own young, increasing their chances of survival.

And it seems trees will also help neighbouring trees of the same species if necessary, even if they aren't related: sometimes, for instance, you will see an old stump, even a centuries' old stump, sprouting green. Wohlleben tells us that this is because it's being fed sugars by others of its species nearby. When trees die, they seem actively to channel their own nutrients back into the collective 'placenta'. In other words, each tree nourishes and sustains the others.

Woodland, forest, strikes me as a perfect example of the individual and the community being gracefully, harmoniously and inextricably part of each other. Trees offer themselves so freely, so immediately, to the imagination, and to our responding with story, poem, and in metaphor.

The spiritual aspect

'...only people who understand trees are capable of protecting them.'
Peter Wohlleben

I believe that when we walk among trees, or notice a particular tree, a kind of exchange happens. As I have written elsewhere, in my experience trees love to be met. That might sound anthropomorphic – but it happens.

Trees have always figured in human awareness, in all cultures. (Think of the Tree of Life; the Tree of Knowledge; the Tree of Good and Evil. Think of talking trees, and of walking trees, in fairy and folk tales. Many dreamers have been 'taken' under a tree. Thomas the Rhymer is an example, taken to Faeryland when under a Hawthorn tree.) Our imagination is caught by trees, and we relate to them for more than the physical gifts they offer so freely. Wouldn't you say this is true?

I am thinking it might be useful to speak of my understanding of the spiritual aspect of relating to trees. What do I mean by 'spiritual'? In this context, an awareness of subtle dimensions of being beyond the physical/manifest. 'That which animates', is another way of speaking of it. Crudely, everything we might sense (intuit or feel) but can't perceive with our *physical* senses, although they may lead us there. A sense of a lively and different intelligence in the other-than-human world.

To unpack this a bit: the path I follow in my own life, and out of which has arisen this material, is a convergence of Zen mindfulness practice (being present), mysticism, and an earth-centred spirituality which draws on Bardic and Druidic wisdom teachings.

The reference point for my life, my practice and for the course from which this book arose is that there are non-material planes of being that manifest on the physical plane. Everything around us shares in the web of life, and contributes its own particular characteristics and qualities of energy to that web.

I begin with the belief that everything is sacred and worthy of respect and cherishing. (It's for this reason, by the way, that I have perhaps rather irritatingly, given each tree a capital initial, as if a proper noun: as a reminder. Fred Hageneder does that in his tree books; and I see that Glennie Kindred has done so in her own recent book too.)

According to this picture, on the densest plane, the physical plane, it may look as if everything is separate, as it appears in differentiated form. This is how we can create deep relationships – via an individual (human, animal, tree and so on). Yet through that individual we learn about the whole. And yet, if we shift our gaze from the one Silver Birch with which we have formed a bond and look beyond it, as it were, to Forest, already we start to see how the whole, the tree collective, has a different, connected, quality of being – trees working in community, in synergy.

If we imagine the soil beneath our feet, we now know what a vast interconnected network exists – not just of tree roots but also of a collaboration of different species, such as fungi, aiding each other's survival.

Beyond this again, beyond Forest, mystics have always known and scientists too are beginning to recognise, are the physical but also the energetic and invisible webs that link us all through different dimensions of consciousness. The concept that might best embody this invisible energetic spirit field is the Indian notion of 'prana'. Prana is that particular subtle energy, the life-force, that animates the universe and everything in it.

So when we connect with a tree, we're connecting not only with the biological organism: cells, xylem and phloem, roots, sap, heartwood, bark, trunk, branch, twig, leaf, fruit and so on, but also with a quality of energy that is unique firstly to the species, and secondly to that particular tree. A tree will be taking in air, light, water – and prana (as we all are). All of those qualities are transformed in a tree – or in any other being, and in one form or another are also transmitted, including to us.

When we walk in the woods and feel a particular sense of wellbeing, only some of that is attributable to, for instance, the phytoncides that the tree emits as part of its own immune defence system and which have a beneficial effect on us and our immune systems, and only some in relation to the colour green, as I mentioned above. Yet further, some of it is the experience of prana, in this case emanating from trees and taken in by ourselves and, by the same token, vice versa.

Each tree participates in a vast ecosystem of consciousness, in which we are all interdependent. Each tree 'tribe' and each individual tree expresses a specific quality of archetypal energy, its own 'take' on prana – hence the tree calendar alphabet with its depiction of archetypes.

In the moment when we pay attention to the being of the tree, we are also opening a channel for a reciprocal relationship between human and tree. Our job is to be awake to all this: to practise the art of tuning-in to these general and specific qualities; to try and be aware of the exchange of prana and the interrelationship of types of consciousness.

Waking up to this, and to how an individual – tree or human (or anything else) – manifests its own particular gift and qualities from its physical DNA and also its energetic blueprint – the archetype behind it – and to a recognition of how necessary each is to the whole, is part of the tacit underpinning of my work here and what I am putting to you, the reader. One of our practices is to 'tune in' to individual tree; beyond that, to individual species;

beyond that again to tree tribe; and thus to Tree. To bring back news of it.

And to remember – and feel again – the experience of unity that being in a wood or forest can inspire in us. In the simplest words, to slip the bounds of separative ego and *feel* oneself to be part of, not apart.

William Anderson in his inspiring book on the Green Man says it well:

> 'When an affection for a particular plant or tree is aroused in us we are linked through an emotional bond, more subtle and immediate than the effect of scent, to the greater world of vegetation of which the plant or tree is a part. It is a deep, wise, world, one to which we can only respond because we possess it in our own natures and in the instinctive symbolism of the soul, in the tree of life that forms the spinal column, in the roots of our feet and legs, in the branches of our arms, and in the flowering and fruiting of our thoughts and feelings in the crown of our head.'

And there is a further aspect. As humans, we are meaning-making, or at least meaning-seeking, creatures, and one of the ways we access the means of assuaging this need is through the imagination, and the symbolic life. This is where Soul finds itself most at home: that moist ground between physical being, feeling, imagination and meaning, all seasoned with something of the spiritual, the sacred.

Trees offer themselves so freely, so immediately, to the imagination, and to our responding with story, poetry and in metaphor. The course, and this book, rely heavily on that.

The Ogham tree calendar

Part 11 of this book focuses on 13 native trees, and their significance to our Celtic forebears (there are other sacred trees, too, but these are the ones I focus on).

The book's life sprang from two sources.

One was my personal experiences of and musings on trees, forest and the greenwood from my childhood and adulthood both, but in parallel much time spent over a few decades, initially occasionally but over the last few years frequently, in a forest in Finistère, Brittany, identified by some with, or at least as a fragment of, the ancient Brocéliande of the Grail corpus.

The second pathway is that for over five years now at the time of writing I've been leading workshops called 'Tongues in Trees' under the banner of 'The Wild Ways', a programme of outdoor courses with writing and other creative arts as means of reflection, exploration and expression. Initially these workshops were offered as day courses, and then as an online yearlong course. The aim behind them has been to enable individuals to reconnect creatively, practically and empathically with the other-than-human on many levels simultaneously.

The course has been rooted in what's known as the Celtic Tree Calendar and Alphabet associated with Druidic practices*.

It's hard to over-state the importance and significance of trees, tree-lore, and wood-lore to our Celtic ancestors. Many Celtic and Gaulish tribes were named after trees. Indeed, widespread in worldwide pre-industrial societies, including the Indo-European, was the belief the trees were our ancestral forebears, or that humans were created from trees. (It is still true to say that without trees, we are nothing. Tragically, in the world at present, we are on the inevitable trajectory, manifest most noticeably in climate change, of a scale of deforestation that could yet lead to our species, along with most others, being simply wiped-out.)

In Welsh, many words that concern wisdom, knowledge and consciousness employ the word 'wydd', meaning 'wood'; including the Welsh word for Druid, 'derwydd'. There are similarities in other European languages, where 'vid', or 'wis', connected too with wise, wit, and probably vision, (possibly even wizard and witch), also means 'tree'.

'Druid' might derive from the word for Oak, 'dru', or 'duir' (which has another meaning, too – as I suggest later in the chapter entitled 'The Wisdom of Trees'), coupled with 'vid', wise or wisdom.

There's a clear line to be found here. In proto-Celtic languages Oak was 'daru' or 'derwā'. A possible etymology for 'Druid' is most marked in the Brythonic family group of the Celtic tongue: the Welsh 'derwenn', the Cornish 'derowen' and the Breton 'dervenn'. The Goidelic branch offers words for Oak that are not dissimilar: in both Old and Modern Irish Gaelic the word is 'dair'; in Scottish Gaelic 'darach'. (Manx has 'daragh'.)

Throughout recorded history, and certainly at least since the time of Taliesin the Bard in the 6th century CE, the Bards of Britain have used the metaphor of 'wood' to describe words, especially poetry. Perhaps this is in part due to our human use of wood and bark for writing over such a long period of history, but it's more than likely that it reflects the value our ancestors vested in trees, for themselves, as presences, and so would naturally make trees central symbols in their worldview. No surprise, then, that trees might become glyphs, representing what we now know as letters, and also signifying months in a calendar.

There were certain trees that were sacred to our pagan ancestors of the Celtic lands, specifically associated, supposedly, with the Druids. Collectively, they became known as the trees of the Celtic (or even pre- or proto-Celtic) Ogham alphabet (sometimes mistakenly called runes), which was in use, some sources say, from perhaps as early as 2200 BCE; or perhaps from 600 BCE according to other sources, to around 700 CE (records vary).

Each of these trees marked a month of the turning year, and signified a letter, too, with individual trees being chosen for the way their natural qualities seemed to reflect certain metaphysical concepts which we could apply to certain times of year.

I want to stress that what I outline here is not intended to be either a definitive or scholarly contribution to any kind of 'truth' in relation to a Celtic Tree Alphabet/Calendar. It represents my own sense of an archetypal symbolic system that works for me on an imaginative level, that's all. I hope that readers will feel free to disagree with me and find their own tree-calendar, one that works for them.

I find Ogham to be a fine way of marking the months, with each tree representing a lunar month as well as a letter.

I have generally followed Robert Graves' system of tree-months and corresponding letters from his seminal book *The White Goddess*; even though this book has received a great deal of scholarly and not-so-scholarly derision, it 'feels' right to me, with some exceptions. However, sometimes I've departed from it, and generally I've made free with this calendar, as suits my imagination and decades of hands-on experience. I don't pretend this is in any way an academic book: it's intended more as a prompt to the poetic imagination.

There are many who follow different ascriptions from Robert Graves, and an altogether different number of trees and tree-species and different datings in the Celtic Tree Calendar. (There are many who dispute the veracity of any of this, too.) There are a number of different versions of the Ogham alphabet – the *Book of Ballymote* which, it is said, is a fourteenth century (or earlier) compilation of older texts, lists 150. Many of the better-known versions don't agree: on the trees included, the number of trees in a full alphabet, and the order of the trees and their letters.

We can't know at this late stage from a largely oral tradition exactly how the early calendar/alphabets were laid out; for me, though, the thirteen-month system for many reasons seems relevant. Graves puts forward fixed dates, whereas if it is indeed a lunar calendar (my own sense too), each month's, and year's, dates would shift as the moon's phases do – in other words, in our solar calendar the phases of the moon aren't a neat annual fit. I've stuck with Graves' dates though as it makes everything simpler.

* *The picture of what we know about Druidry, its history and its practices is confused and controversial. Much is a piecing-together of snippets; some is conjecture; some belongs to recent neo-pagan Druid Revivalism. Some people insist the Druids didn't ever exist. The evidence, and there's much of it, not least from Ancient Greek and Roman writers, is that Druidry and its practitioners most definitely did exist, though perhaps not in the romantic and also grisly way in which they're often portrayed. In any case, though, there are literal truths and there are symbolic truths. Whether or not we have an 'accurate picture' of Druid history is academic (in both senses) to me: what's relevant is that the symbolism of the Tree Calendar is a very effective way of deepening my spiritual practice tree by tree, month by month, year by year.*

See also the notes on the Song of Amergin in Part 11.

How This Book Works

'Tongues in Trees' until now has run as a hands-on outdoor workshop, under my guidance, and then an online course (both self-study and mentored), as I mentioned above. The remit has been simple but the effects often profound, with an early participant mentioning on social media that four years after she attended a one-day version of this workshop with me it has changed her relationship to trees entirely and permanently. At the end of 2018 I launched the yearlong 'Tongues in Trees' programme. This, alongside the time I've spent over a few years in a forest in Brittany, forms the roots of this book, which is written largely through the lens of my personal experience, coupled with study.

The book is in three parts. The first more personal part occupies itself with some aspects of what we know of trees, and their botanical, cultural and ecological history and mythological/symbolic significances as well as my more lyrical riffs on Forest.

The second is a more in-depth look at 13 particular sacred trees native to and embedded in the consciousness of the Celtic lands of Great Britain, covering a solar year through the trees representing, loosely, lunar months.

You may just want to read this book. But if you would like to approach it in a more experiential way, part three, the final short section, includes the briefs for inspiration and practice coupled with the symbolic representations of the individual tree-species' mythic qualities that I offer participants in the course programme for use as a creative process to bring about the deep immersion in the tree tribe. This part, and the book, closes with, I suppose, a look at the help we can give, as humans, on a practical level to trees and the planet, as a possible antidote to all the destruction at our hands.

The purpose of the creative aspect is twofold. One part is to feed your imaginal life and hopefully your creative and reflective writing so that new fragments, poems, stories, essays or prose passages might arise from your work over this year. I strongly encourage you to keep a 'yearbook' of this work in the form of a really nice biggish notebook in which to keep your notes and writings, any photographs or sketches, bark rubbings, pressed leaves, ideas and quotes.

However, a large part of my intention with such work is to re-envision and hopefully transform our relationship to the other-than-human, as I mentioned in the Introduction. *The earth does not belong to us; we belong to the earth.* The point of the book is to enable, in however small a way, a reader to become more intimate with the significance, and sentience, of the astonishing tree realm which not only shares our planet but also sustains our and other species' life on this planet.

You will, I hope, feel a deeper immersion in and relationship with trees, forest and all its inhabitants by the end of your year with trees, if you choose to follow this route.

PART I

THE FOREST

The Greenwood

Finally you open your eyes. The meadow's tall grasses curtain you; beyond, the blue hills rise. Emergent sun hazes their summits. You sit up. There ahead of you is the little path, and in the stone wall a small wooden gate.

You stand. Below in the valley swallows and martins skim the mist from the morning river. You stretch. The conversations of birds; the song of the water. Your hand lifts the old wooden latch. You step through. You slip into the green of the woods as into a silk dress.

The path rises gently, sprinkled with light. It's May and the land is alight with white blossom. The wood swims with the scent of bluebells; the air is lilac with it. A thousand wild bees drone. You're alone and it's the first day.

In the green glade pass the ruins of the hermit's chapel with its green dreams, the short walls grassed and blackbird-capped; the spring bubbling and chattering.

Follow the path in and out of sunlight. Oaks and ashes season the woodland; first bursts of honeysuckle; and look! – in the shade of this larch a host of goldcrests, a corona around your head.

Your feet firm on the good earth. Here there's no need for shoes, you can shake out the creases in which you hide; the truth is as it is, all around you, spread out.

The trees thin out, a little. In the undergrowth of campion, stitchwort, bramble there are rustles of lives going about their daily cycles. A wren skitters out; a bluetit. A very young vole, the length of your top finger joint, scurries across the path, over your feet, unafraid. In the distance a woodpecker knocks.

Soon, you will arrive. The green glade in the green day; summer still to come; and you are young, you are now, you are always. The threshold waits; and its guardian; and question and response will spring and be answered simultaneously, with no words. You pass through.

And there it is – waiting all your life for you, there before questions, before answers. You knew, and forgot that you knew.

The Forest

the old gods live   in stones   in trees
in mountains   rivers   earth and sea
we give each one a human name
and hope familiarity will tame
their raw primeval energy

our minds may settle not to see
beyond our rationality –
our hearts know better all the same
the old gods live

though locked away with reason's key
in waking hours, they struggle free
to seize our dreamtime and reclaim
their own – then it's a different game

the old gods live
Sheena Odle

I spend part of my year in a hamlet in a clearing in an ancient largely broadleaf forest in Brittany. A short walk away through the forest is a charming little town with its lake. The forest is populated by, among trees and plants, animals and birds, insects and humans, huge granite boulders like great sleeping animals, rock and tree cohabiting, adapting to and frequently fusing with each other. (In this way, it reminds me of my local Devon Wistman's Wood, on Dartmoor which, while being an enchanted fragment of ancient forest too, is on a much smaller scale than the wood in Finistère.) This is where I come for stillness, to write, to feel the expansive spaciousness that is ours when we stop cramming every minute full.

This is also where I learn from trees, though to start with I thought I was coming to learn *about* trees, not *from* them. This is where, too, I find green healing, remember the way a tree joins heaven and earth – arguably our task, also, psychologically, metaphorically, in our inner lives.

I walk the forest, listen for the birds, the rivers, the cascades, the stories of the wildwood that rustle in the leaves above me and the growth on every side, try and stay aware of the great interlocking network beneath my feet, the mycorrhizal web that keeps each tree in connection with the all, the forest, and carries its own stories of carbon, sugars, water, messages from tree to tree. How much we can learn from such an underground ecosystem – invisible, utterly interconnected, vital.

In the forest, I tread paths trodden since at least the Iron Age (the great oppidum, known as 'Arthur's Camp', crowning the forest, is mentioned in Caesar's *De Bello Gallico, The Gallic Wars*, and I like to think that it was the last village to hold out in the face of Roman invasion, as in Asterix the Gaul) and probably since the Bronze Age and the Neolithic before that; maybe even longer. (A kilometre or so away, no doubt part of the original huge megalithic site, is a rock 'abri'[3], where artefacts have been found that date the site to the Mesolithic.) The local prehistoric tribe, the Osismes, have certainly shaped the history, culture and stories in this land of Finistère. Finis-terre. The end of the earth.

In, as well as beyond, the forest, our ancestors live on visibly in the great structures they've left; structures whose purposes we're unclear on, but that they had purpose we can be sure. The area is dotted with menhirs, dolmens, tumuli – great longbarrows, allées couvertes, dating from the late Neolithic or the early Bronze Age, some standing for more than 5000 years.

One menhir stands right beside a hamlet: almost domestic in its benign presence, it has accumulated graffiti over the centuries: a curly-tailed pig, a donkey, a house. One very beautiful tumulus is in a carefully-tended meadow adjoining a small town and from its orientation and lack of trace of burials was probably used for ritual purposes. In the long allée couverte at Commana I smile at the inscribed pairs of breasts – the Great Mother – and the inscribed 'axes' that to me look much more like phalluses, but there – who am I to question the experts?

Next to the supermarket, where a road bisects what was clearly a significant prehistoric ritual site stretching over a large area, is a massive mushroom-shaped dolmen, four or five times the height of a human, still standing proud, if isolated, in its incongruous co-opted modern-day site.

Near my favourite pool is a stumpy little standing stone, or menhir, from the late Stone Age that went walkabout for a decade or two, then reappeared.

All of this seems to have grown out of the broadleaf forest that was itself probably once a symbolically, as well as actually, significant site stretching over a large part of Armorica, now Brittany.

Trees also somehow mediate between ourselves and a different reality, a different order of consciousness – pre-verbal, post-verbal, trans-verbal, non-verbal – I find it such a relief, often.

In the forest I step into a different kind of time. It's not simply that it – in human terms – so clearly stretches back so far into the past, but also that it allows me what Thoreau described as a 'broad margin' to my day, and my life. I love this; love the unaccustomed spaciousness where I'm not striving for anything, trying to complete anything, trying to get to the end of/get on top of anything; be responsible to anyone; I'm simply letting the natural rhythms of my day and night unfold in forest time. Everyone needs a broad margin to their day.

Entering the Forest

I'm fortunate enough to have, almost unbelievably, seven possible starting points for rambling in the forest where I might pick up scores of further paths, all within a few minutes on foot from my gate.

I have a favourite, though. Two minutes' walk from my garden is an ancient track down through a few firs into the broadleaf forest, past an old well and lavoir (an outdoor channelled but natural flow of water through one or two constructed stone chambers, where the local women [sic] would come to wash their linen – a kind of early launderette), and then a hidden spring that a local person told me was used in the Stone Age.

When I walk into the forest, I walk into a deep, receptive and attentive humming silence, a benign presence. I have walked here many times over many years now, long before I came to the cottage. Simply picking up this path raises a sense of anticipation and excitement. Everything about this forest stimulates my imagination. 'My' forest, the Forêt de Huelgoat in the Parc Regional d'Armorique, as I mentioned in the Introduction, is quite possibly a fragment of the legendary original Brocéliande of the Grail stories – which probably at one time existed in the outer world, and encompassed the whole of what is now Brittany.

What we do know is that the Forêt de Huelgoat is the remains of a truly ancient forest, though much of it was destroyed in tremendous storms at the end of the twentieth century. Once the whole of the interior of Brittany was blanketed with woodland, 'Une forêt mult lunge et lee', Robert Wace tells us in the twelfth century *Le Roman de Rou*: a very wide and deep forest.

That forest, Brocéliande, maybe, would then have included 'my' western area here in Finistère and the area now known as the Forêt de Paimpont, generally popularly identified with

Brocéliande, in the east of Brittany, and although it is no longer all the way forest from here to there, there's still a lot of forest. Once, the two forests would have been one. And another couple of little sacred woods from ancient times still survive in Brittany, that we know of – in fact one, really, bisected by a road into Coat an Noz and Coat an Hay.

Huelgoat Forest is much more modest than Paimpont, but utterly magical, with its own (admittedly slimmer) share of legends, Arthurian and mythological associations as well as ancient sites.

Despite its smallness, this forest has a quality of containment, depth and mystery, more low-key than Paimpont, that is richly concentrated, and not dispersed despite its obvious popularity.

It's also stunningly beautiful with its broadleaf woodland, its huge rounded granite boulders which co-habit comfortably with the trees, and the Rivière d'Argent and its dreamy pools named for fairies, or wild boar, the whole capped with the Iron Age fort named as 'Le Camp d'Artus' ('Arthur', supposedly – however I've discovered something more interesting about its name, to be recorded in a later book), refuge of the Gaulish Osismes tribe whose lands extended right up to the Baie de Douarnenez on the west coast.

But there are always two forests. And I don't mean 'Paimpont' and 'Huelgoat'. One is the physical wood and forest we encounter – or don't, but know they exist – 'out there'.

The other is the abiding forest of our imagination: a pristine (because unaltered – and unalterable – by humans) wildwood; the one we encounter in myths, legends, fairy stories. Of course, there is little 'wildwood' left on our planet now; but it lives on in our interior life, even if we weren't fed fairy stories as children. This Forest is magical, otherworldly, immense, scary, seductive and enticing. This is the Enchanted Forest. We could say that this is the true Brocéliande.

Bringing the two, outer and inner, together is a source of richness, nourishment, wholeness.

So Brocéliande is associated with the archetype of the Wildwood, that virgin and whole 'place' where innate wildness and natural principles combine to work in harmony and synergy ('the Tao'), beyond human interference.

It's not just the planet and other, wilder, species that need wild places, need the Wildwood; we do too. We need these places, and we need to be able to visit them, or their representatives, in the physical world as a way of restoring balance and harmony in the heart of the human species. We need to restore and familiarise ourselves with the Wildwood's correspondence in our inner lives; in making this living relationship we might have a chance of healing the wasteland, inner and outer, we've created in our deracinated industrialised world.

Entering the Wildwood is a step towards home.

'Entering into the forest is like going underground,' said the note beside one of the paintings by Marc Chagall in the enchanting (in both senses) summer exhibition at the Leclerc gallery in Landerneau a year or two ago.

Entering the forest is also like going underwater – entering a green watery realm: the fluid dance of light on and through leaves, the shush of breeze in the canopy so like the ocean and its waves. Going underground, entering the water – both, in archetypal psychology, associated with entry into the unconscious, the psyche, the emotional so-called feminine realm.

It's almost like swimming, and just as all-encompassing. I love that sense of deepening.

Whether underground or underwater, what it certainly is is a threshold – into a storied land. I already know many of the stories associated with this forest and other Brittany forests, and connected with forests generally. The Wood, archetypally speaking, has long been a birthplace for story: legends leak from every corner, one catches the whisper of story in the undergrowth, in the leaves, on the breeze.

As I enter the more open space above the river where the firs give over to beech, hazel and oak, I notice that I habitually hold my breath, as if crossing a threshold.

There are days here when I somewhat fancifully sense that I'm 'breathing in' myth, fable, poetry through my skin and the soles of my feet when I walk in this forest.

This wood seems even more than most to be a dwelling-place for magical tales. It invites a kind of listening; it offers a sense of enchantment in its winding paths, the rocks and the huge boulders, the streams that weave through it. Of course, the names that appear beside certain spots that seem to connect us to the tales of King Arthur (La Grotte d'Artus; Le Camp d'Artus), and others that conjure fairies, witches, devils, giants and wild boar (La Mare aux Fées, La Mare aux Sangliers, La Grotte du Diable) are part of the spell.

There are liminal places, thresholds into an experience of the meeting of the physical and the metaphysical, and times in which this sense is heightened and we're on the cusp of another reality hovering, waiting to be revealed – just a blink away, rather like walking in the forest, in and out of sunlight and tree shadow.

'To enter a wood is to pass into a different world in which we ourselves are transformed,' says Roger Deakin in his book *Wildwood*. '[The Greenwood] is where you travel to find yourself, often, paradoxically, by getting lost.'[4]

The Wildwood, any wildwood, is unfamiliar and uncharted, where anything may happen; where people go astray and might arrive somewhere distinctly other from everyday consciousness, and where the wild is what guides.

The wildwood is also the domain of those mythical beings who seem part human, part forest: dryads, tree-sprites or nymphs, elves, faeries, goblins, dwarves, Oak King, Holly King, Green Man, Green Knight, Wild Man; Robin Hood (Robin du Bois, Robin of the Wood), Maid Marian.

It's also where individuals have retreated for silence, peace, ritual and contemplation forever. (Think of the early pagan seers and sorcerers, the Druids, the later contemplatives and hermit saints.)

And for healing, as I am here now. In story, figures such as Merlin/Myrddin after the battle of Arfderydd in the Scottish borders in CE 573, and Suibhne Geilt in what is now Ireland after the battle of Magh Rátha in CE 637, both fled, mad with grief, to the forest to live in or among trees in their need for healing. The forest is a place of transformation, facilitating altered states such as shapeshifting (Suibhne supposedly flew through the treetops like a bird; Merlin in the forest of Celyddon, later known as the Caledonian Forest, rode a stag – or maybe shapeshifted into a stag).

The stories of an area grow out of that area and will be rooted in that land's character. 'Landscape informs the collective imagination as much as or more than it informs the individual psyche and its imagination,' says Sara Maitland in *Gossip From The Forest*.

It's not an accident that so many of our fairy tales, legends, myths and other ancient stories in Europe and the West in general, and some of our poems, too, incorporate entry into and a period in the dark forest (classic examples are also in the poetry of Dante Alighieri and Robert Frost). In the older tales, so often there is an intimate relationship between human and other-than-human concerns and cycles – the forest leaves one changed.

In one of the Grail stories, Parsifal is brought up in innocence, in a clearing in dense forest, away from other people and general human goings-on. His life is ineradicably changed when, for the first time, he witnesses outsiders: three knights from the court of King Arthur riding by on the edge of his and his mother's glade.

The knights in search of the Grail Castle have to ride through interminable deep forest to find the Castle – some, of course, never do. On this quest, some knights similarly are tested by their experience of the Val Sans Retour – a bewitched forested valley in which some seekers are doomed to ride round and round in circles forever.

And it's not just in fairy tales that one is abducted or obstructed by a forest. It's easy to go round in circles in a forest. Often nothing is what it seems, and we are disorientated – it's easy to mistake one place for another. And you know how so often forests have trees whose branches poke your eyes or grab your hair, or whose roots trip you up? – Well.

When I came to Brittany at a time of much grief and personal crisis (detailed in the later sequel to this book) and to write this tree book, for my first long, maybe indefinite, stay, I initially thought I'd be primarily learning and writing about the forest and its stories. What I didn't really realise until the Forest managed very successfully to first wound and then ground me – in the old-fashioned sense of immobilisation, as well as in the sense of bringing me to earth – is that actually my time here was also to be a time of stillness, deep grief and deep healing from the last decade of deaths, pain and loss and a very recent break-up. You can't do that when you're rushing around over-filling the cup of the days. (It turned out to be also a quest for the lost feminine: not only in my own past and present, but also in our culture and its last two millennia and more.)

I believe that our psyche knows what we need and where we need to be in order best to immerse ourselves in *anima mundi*, world-soul, with its capacity for healing, and, eventually, to contribute our own wholeness back to it; and if we ignore that our individual psyche, or soul, will deliver news of its needs more and more strongly until we can't avoid taking note.

Most commonly, we don't until our body stops us. Or at least, that's the case for me. I know this, and I so rarely take note if it means – as it invariably does for me – slowing up and letting go of all the *doing* that my enthusiasm for the world, all that's in it, and my familial, political, creative, environmental, earnings-related, animal and horticultural commitments involve.

I know for myself that when we are in a state of grief, exhaustion, or in the grip of what's called a 'peak experience', something in us often seeks out poetry, or story, in one form or another. It's as if we know that at such a time we need to drink from a deeper well than our contemporary materialistic culture or the more mundane concerns of 'everyday reality' can offer us. These are times when we might seek healing, or guidance, or understanding, or simply companionship on the journey.

Often, people also instinctively head out into the natural world. I've known since childhood that I might find re-alignment, inspiration, and uplift outdoors, when I cannot find it in.

There is a Welsh phrase: 'dod yn ôl at fy nghoed', which means 'to return to a balanced state of mind'. Literally, it translates as 'to return to my trees'. I find this beautiful. In English, we speak of returning to our roots, meaning a specific place; once again it's a tree metaphor.

As an adult, I've been able to dissolve almost any negative emotional state and return to equilibrium simply by walking out of my front door (given that my life has been almost exclusively rural). The bigger picture of the natural world in which we're such a very small, if such a very destructive, part has never failed me yet.

So I'm (also) in my Brittany forest for healing from such a time of immeasurable stress and grief in relation to traumatic family situations. The healing is there for the wanting, as long as I will turn to face the need for it.

Due to the tree roots, healing is also needed on an undeniably physical level since I now have a totally unusable, because fractured, writing arm – sheared right through at the top, just three days into my arrival for my protracted writing stay after my most recent trauma. But that too belongs in the book of my time there, the other book.

As I said above, it seems to me that the best thing we can do not only for ourselves but also for the planet is to tend our own wounds; then we are better able to help tend its needs for recovering from the terrible devastations we in our ignorance and greed are continuing to inflicting on it and our other-than-human relations. (It's never really as clean-cut as that – do the one and the other will follow. Sometimes the two work in synergy; sometimes there'll be fallow patches; sometimes we'll zigzag between the two, or even seem to backstep.)

In my woundedness, it seems natural to call upon the Forest to help. Although I have to walk gingerly, and usually with my (gifted) Irish hazel staff, so as not to jolt my arm (I've had dire warnings from the hospital doctor), I do still walk. What else can I do?

And what I will also do is pledge that I will continue to help to tend the wounds of the planet to my best ability. The trees listen; advise, guide.

The Dark Forest I

The path at first is wide, curving gently onwards to an unseen horizon that promises more of everything easy: joy, love, belonging... There are many branches and meanders, and mostly it's sunny. Sometimes rain comes in, makes the track and the snaky roots glisten; sometimes the wind keens in the trees like winter's voice, but soon enough the sun slides in again.

Eventually, of course, as in any fairy tale, we start to notice the far-off forest. On the horizon it's merely a shimmer, a shadowy mirage that maybe spells trees, and coolness.

One day, inevitably, it's a little closer; and then closer still. And now, frighteningly, the path fades out. Oh, how we party then, faces averted, looking back like Lot's wife to the sunny valleys and lush plains.

And again inevitably, later if not sooner, we arrive at where we had always been going by doing what we habitually do.

'Let us not speak falsely / For the hour is getting late', my friend Brian quotes to me, from 'All Along the Watchtower'.

And here is where the journey starts.

When our lives become too small, or our lies about who we are (whether to ourselves or to others) no longer hold, when we can no longer pretend we like what we don't, be what others wish or expect us to be, when can no longer live without what we need – in other words, take false trails (and who doesn't?), or stay with ones that merely lead in circles – then we will arrive at the very edge of the forest.

We're scared. What to do with a forest, a wilderness, when we fear it, or don't understand it? We torch it, we chop it down, we sell it off; or maybe we pretend, for as long as we can, that we haven't seen it, and turn back the way we came.

But there's only one way to deal with a dark forest, and that is to make a trail for ourselves, make our own way through it. We can look for an animal of the night, an owl or a fox, to guide us. We can put out a call to Those Who've Gone Before. But we still need to do it for ourselves. This is what makes us heroic; and how eventually we earn our own lives – to live rather than merely survive.

And the gift is that there in the heart of the dark forest is the treasure: the pure gold of our own soul.

Falling in love with it all over and over

When I enter the Forest, I seem to slip off a whole layer of skin. It invites me not only to shed my humanness but also within that to shed my naming capacities – one of the very markers of being human, making an identity. I pride myself on my knowledge of animals, birds, plants; and it is a way of offering them respect to recognise their individual identities. And simultaneously it's a way of remaining separate, reinforcing otherness. To name something is also to possess it, in a sense. The forest offers something different: a way of being kin to all that inhabit it; to walk among the all, to be alongside them.

Walking into an old-growth broadleaf forest seems to invite a response of slowing down and silence. In this slowness and silence a kind of stillness can emerge in which receptivity can be the predominant quality. Then we might 'become animal', to borrow David Abram's phrase; or, more, become what we are: the dreaming of earth.

As participant, I or we can receive, reinterpret and retell the stories of the earth's long dreaming, as they are expressed in rock, water, wind, tree, dragonfly, roe deer, buzzard. Or adder, thorn, hornet, rat, hurricane, cliff, whirlpool. Earth might speak through me – us – as if we are also the dream – which one might say we are. Our being here, our walking on this earth, is a co-creation, a mutual imagining. How to live, if not in reciprocal affinity?

My work with others in the outdoor or semi-outdoor courses and retreats by which I gain much of my living increasingly employs the entering of inner stillness by slow silent walking.

Supposedly I facilitate writing courses. In practice, they're holistic and about so much more than writing. As one participant said: 'I thought I was coming on a writing course. Now I see it's really about how we live.'

I notice that my preliminary focus, on almost all my courses and certainly all the outdoor ones, is about noticing: asking people to wake up, and relearn the arts of real looking, real listening, going deep; basically, how to pay attention, banal though that sounds. For many, they haven't noticed details like light bounced off leaves onto water onto rock since they were children.

For each of us, at some stage the ability to see the world as entrancing, as magical, and as the miracle it is, departed from our field of vision. In fact the ability to really look and so really see. As someone once said of the act of listening (or not): 'Mostly we hear what we expect to hear, and tune out the rest.' (Substitute 'see', 'smell', 'touch', 'taste' etc.)

You might ask – So what if people don't notice detail? And I might answer: What I want is for people to fall in love all over again. From this perspective three things happen that are of concern for me.

One is that really *seeing* the other – whether human or (and), as in this case, the land and all its other-than-human species – allows one to see deeply into the mystery of it all, and so come to cherish it. How can we know, come to love or value that which we don't notice?

Another is that, as meaning-making creatures, we start to notice connections and relationships, associations and similarities, the intertwining of everything. We start to feel affinity, commonality, with that upon which we gaze, and notice that, after all, we belong, here where our longing expresses itself, and where we notice that nothing is truly separate, nothing exists in a vacuum. Perhaps it all emerges then as a relationship of reciprocity: if all is consciousness, nothing is truly inert, and an exchange is an inevitability. There is a continual process of fluid migration: just as we cannot ultimately differentiate between particle and wave, so the wave that passes through me, the particles of which I appear to be composed, the atoms of the

'I' that thinks it is perceiving all of this 'outside' have before been mud, mouse, tree, rock, sparrowhawk, bear, fox, bramble, and so on.

The psychic equivalent of this is to be able to pass into another's reality; to take the shape of another, in the truest sense to 'walk in another's shoes'. This is an aspect of shamanism, or shapeshifting, and in Celtic mythology both Amergin the Milesian who colonised what is now Ireland in some time BCE, and Taliesin, the sixth-century CE Welsh seer-Bard, orate long poems tracking their various transformations in animate or elemental forms which begin with the phrases 'I am' or 'I have been'.

And thirdly – back to the question of noticing – for my purposes, once the imagination is drawn in, we can start to explore and express our experience through the creative arts, in my case most commonly writing, but also image-making and land art. Not only is this of inherent value, on several levels, to the artist or writer and perhaps also to an audience, but it's a way of continuing the earth's dreaming through a kind of recycling or restoring: a 'giving back' in the articulation.

There's a fourth, less definable, reason, and that's to do with the experience of the transpersonal, the transcendent; the deep and high experience of truly being part of it all; slipping the apparently separative limitations of humanness in a body. Experiencing that everything is sacred. In our culture, there are few ways in to spiritual experience and the sense of living an ensouled life, and this is one.

Apart from all this, and more pragmatically, we also feel good outdoors, especially in a broadleaf forest. I say broadleaf as coniferous forests, especially planted ones, don't have the same dappled and living quality, nor anything like the biodiversity. Having said that, I've never forgotten Laurie Lee's description of entering a pine forest in Spain, having spent long days walking across the hot plains, on his epic trek as a young man into that country during its civil war.

'...[B]y the next afternoon I'd left the wheat behind me and entered a world of Nordic pinewoods. Here I slipped off the heat like a sweat-soaked shirt and slept an hour among the resinous trees – a fresh green smell as sweet as menthol compared with the animal reek of the plain... and the afternoon sun sucked up the flavour of each tree till the whole wood swam in incense like a church.'[5]

The Wild Soul

Come into 'the brotherhood of eye and leaf', poet Wendell Berry invites us, in relation to the woods.

Trees in a natural forest (as opposed to conifer plantations) mirror and speak to something of the wild soul in a human. As we visit, we encounter and are supported by the elemental powers that reside in such places, and can reconnect with our own instinctual natures and the wild soul.

This wildness is not to be confused with a state of chaos, of being out of control, savage. It's more a question of relinquishing, at least temporarily, the ego's grip to larger natural rhythms, cycles, surroundings: an essential aspect of thriving. When one does this, one is more receptive to one's environment, physical or more numinous.

And simultaneously as we are drawn to the mystery of wild forests, we fear them – ancestral memories, no doubt, of their real dangers, culturally reinforced by our fairy and folk tales which have grown out of them and so often are set in them, at least in northern Europe (Sara Maitland points out that in a desert culture, the equivalent of forest would be desert: obvious once she mentions it, but something we might not normally think of).

In the forest, we lack horizons, perspective and light – it can be difficult to orientate ourselves, swimming as we do in the many shades of dappled green. It's hard to see any distance, and something in us is both excited by and fearful of what may lurk in those unseen shadowy places. In our so-called civilised culture we tend to eradicate such places and their inhabitants, routinely the other-than-human and in some places the human as well, without a second thought, for our housing developments and car parks, our factories and supermarkets, our reservoirs, dams and food supplies (especially our industrial-scale farming practices), our post-industrial-era wastelands.

Underneath that, though, I suspect a darker urge: we cannot bear the wild 'out there' because we cannot bear such unknown, uncharted – enchanted – territory 'in here', in our psyches. This is a disaster; a planet without the Wildwood will, after a while, no longer support other forms of life, including ours, and a life lived without soul will also not support any kind of meaningful life. There is great cost – personal, collective, intra-species, intra-planetary on many different levels – to this loss.

We could see forest as being a kind of mediator between realms; an entrance into Otherworld. 'The clearest way into the Universe is through a forest wilderness,' said the great conservationist John Muir. I think about this often. There's a lovely paradox in Muir's words: for clarity and entrance into the vast, take the way of darkness and confusion, where you risk being lost.

Our wisdom is found in, stored in perhaps, Tree and Forest. I'll return to that idea later. This is how we re-enchant our worldview, so empty and disenchanted in our materialistic and highly-technological society: by entering the Wildwood in one of its many guises; finding a way to allow ourselves to experience, to see, the beauty, depth and mystery in place and the natural world, in everything that surrounds us.

I've said it's about meaning. Soul, or psyche, loves such places, is rehydrated by the Wildwood.

Story helps, poetry helps, music helps, and art, and access to dream, memory, association all help. These are all ways of re-enchanting our view of the world. But there is still nothing like actually wandering beneath great and ancient trees.

It's true that some places lend themselves more readily to this enchantment. I'm here in the Forest of Huelgoat because it facilitates that entry so readily and easily for me. I've returned to 'my' Brocéliande many times in the decades since my first visit, never knowing that my life would take the turning that would bring me here more permanently, or at least, more frequently.

Each time I enter the forest, this forest, even in the tourist-dense summer when it shakes with human voices and is littered with clots of tissue and sweet papers, I know I have crossed a threshold, and the Otherworld is very close, just a step, a thought, away.

The Secret Lives of Trees

'To dwellers in a wood, almost every species of tree has its voice as well as its feature.'
Thomas Hardy

Almost all of us can feel, I imagine, a different kind of energy in the presence of trees: in broadleaf forest, there's a kind of calm radiance; but it's true that in conifer plantations, where little grows in the understorey, the atmosphere is totally different, and many people find it menacing. Beyond that again, once you've attuned yourself, not only is there a quality of energy specific to each tree species, but also a character unique to each individual tree.

Trees are conscious beings. Trees communicate. Of course they do, unless one takes the worldview that humans are the only sentient beings in a predominantly mechanistic world. It isn't either a surprise, nor new, if you are aware of subtle interconnections, and in particular of the sudden explosion of investigation into and writings about trees and their particular type of consciousness (that is, if one subscribes to the view that everything is consciousness in its own way).

What *is* new is our discoveries of *how* trees communicate. Richard Powers in *The Guardian* of Saturday 13th October 2018 writing about his book *The Overstory* (shortlisted for the Man Booker award 2018, winner of the Pulitzer prize in 2019) says this about trees:

'Once you begin to see trees, they start to reveal themselves as creatures with agency and intent. Recent research over the last several decades has discovered that trees are in fact immensely social beings, communicating with each other both over the air and through underground fungal networks.

And we humans have always been part of those networks. We've become what we are by virtue of what trees have allowed us to be... in a story much larger and older than the ones we usually tell about ourselves ... The truth is we're all in this business of life together. It's time to get to know the neighbours and to come back home.'

'...[P]lants have a sophisticated awareness of their environment and of each other, and can communicate what they sense,' said Anil Anathaswamy in the *New Scientist*.[6] 'There is also evidence that plants have memory, can integrate massive amounts of information and maybe pay attention. Some botanists argue that they are intelligent beings with a "neurobiology" all of their own... plant consciousness...'

If trees have memory – and it's clear they do – where do they keep it? Do we need to reassess our notions of what makes a brain, or a mind, or consciousness in general? And here's someone who looks at all these things and answers more questions than I knew I had: Peter Wohlleben, whom I mentioned in the introduction.

Wohlleben's *The Hidden Life of Trees* in its very fine translation by Jane Billinghurst[7] is that most wonderful of things: a synthesis of a number of groundbreaking scientific discoveries coupled with personal experience and observation, all put forward in an inspiring, conversational and flowing way that means that one rips through the 36 chapters with an idiotic sublime grin on one's face. (Or I did, anyway.) You'll never look at the trees the same way again if you read this book.

What Wohlleben brings to this is his long hands-on experience working with woodland and trees for the German Forestry Commission, his ecological thinking, and a poetic sensibility and empathy. Much of this thinking wasn't new to me, but it was still hugely inspiring, and I didn't know most of the scientific findings behind my own experiences.

One thing the book offers is a validation of what many of us know, have experienced and felt, or sense, is true of trees and our relationship with them.

As I mentioned above, some of Wohlleben's work draws on forest ecologist Dr Suzanne Simard's work on trees. (Much of what we now know about the mycorrhizal network is due to Simard's work.) Forest, Simard says, is a single organism made of many individuals, rooted in and communicating via a 'white web of mycelium', and below that the 'red and yellow horizons of minerals'.

Dr Simard tested her theory that individual trees, experiencing themselves as part of a single organism, share information and nutrition, carbon and sugars with others through their root systems. She worked with paper birch, Douglas fir and Western red cedar. Most commonly, the reciprocal affinity is between trees of the same species, though not always. To Simard's astonishment, it turned out through her experiments that birch and fir in this context tended to be interdependent, sharing nutrients both ways. She notes that when the birch trees were weeded out from forests clear-cut for commercial conifer plantations, the Douglas firs that remained noticeably declined in health and vitality. (Cedar, on the other hand, was 'in its own world' and not in communication with the other two.)

Science is providing evidence for what many people already sense: that there is an intelligence at work in plants and trees. We may need to redefine our understanding of intelligence. 'I've come to think that root systems and the mycorrhizal networks that link those systems are designed like neural networks, and behave like neural networks, and a neural network is the seeding of intelligence in our brains,' says Simard.[8]

Simard and her colleagues uncovered a 'massive below-ground communications network' exchanging carbon, water, nitrogen, phosphorus, chemicals, hormones, defence signals and other information. Mycorrhizal networks, 'fungal highways', are the means by which these nutrients are transferred. The editors of *Nature* in which Simard's paper was published called this network the 'Wood Wide Web'; a name so apposite that it has stuck.[9]

Nothing is free of political freighting in our species, including the language we use. In *The New Yorker*, Robert MacFarlane interviews the young plant scientist, Merlin Sheldrake. MacFarlane reports:

> 'A central debate over the Wood Wide Web concerns the language used to describe the transactions it enables, which suggest two competing visions of the network: the socialist forest, in which trees act as caregivers to one another, with the well-off supporting the needy, and the capitalist forest, in which all entities are acting out of self-interest within a competitive system. Sheldrake was especially exasperated by what he called the "super-neoliberal capitalist" discourse of the biological free market.'[10]

Needless to say, Simard's work and her descriptions of it lend themselves to the 'socialist forest' theory.

Whatever their own motivations plants, including trees, communicate by chemical compounds and by electrical impulses; by soundwaves, it turns out, at a frequency of 220 hertz.

As I say in the introduction, in any forest, there are 'hub trees' or 'mother trees' that nurture their own young: they send excess carbon through fungal networks to their understorey seedlings and saplings, which they can differentiate from other species'.

'Mother trees' will even reduce their own root competition to make room for their own offspring. When such trees are injured or dying, they can transmit carbon and defence signals to their own young, increasing their chances of survival.

And it seems trees will also help neighbouring trees of the same species if necessary, even if they aren't related: sometimes, for instance, you will see an old stump, even a centuries' old stump, sprouting green. Wohlleben tells us that this is because it's being fed sugars by others of its species nearby.

In his foreword to Pam Montgomery's book on plant spirit healing, Stephen Harrod Buhner makes this astonishing statement: '...plants [presumably including trees] can and will determine what particular chemical an ill member of an ecosystem needs, and further, they will then begin making it for them.'[11]

'Hub trees' turn out to be essential to the survival and wellbeing of a natural forest community. You can take out one or two without too much effect, but if you take out too many the whole forest starts to decline.

On the other hand, in plantations, generally coniferous, the trees behave like 'street kids': it's every tree for itself and no giving away what you want to keep for yourself (young capitalists in the making). Consequently, these trees tend to die younger – that is, if they're not logged first.

Lone trees, Wohlleben tells us, don't thrive as well as those growing together in a community. Similarly, contrary to most people's beliefs, trees usually do better for not being thinned out; strength comes from density. Every tree counts in its contribution to collective storm-resistance, to regulating the atmosphere for optimum moisture-content, for storing water and providing nutrients to the network.

Somehow, although it's good to have the science to back all this up, I suspect that many people will not be entirely surprised by these findings, though maybe our general awe and respect for the tree-tribe will increase. Let's hope.

In my waking dream

I am leaning my back against the lower trunk of a great tree. I think it's an oak. In my dream it is truly huge, and I am tiny: I could slip through the crack in just one of the deep fissures of its bark and walk between the worlds.

Above me, two buzzards flip and mewl and wheel in play. Around me is the forest's oceanic green; over my head the wind made audible by the leafy canopy is the forest's breaking waves.

My bare feet are sunk in the moss at its feet, and if I let them, they could sink right down through moss and leaf-mould, stone and bone, soil and root into the mycorrhizal network of the tree which, if laid end to end, would embrace the globe.

My whole weight is supported by the massive girth of the trunk: it is utterly secure, stable, sustained and sustaining. My arms and hands are spread out to each side of me and I can't now tell where skin ends and bark begins.

I am utterly held, utterly safe.

In my dream I know this is the World Tree, the Tree of Life, and that I might step through to the tree-behind-the-tree and travel simultaneously to past and future, to the Underworld and the Otherworld, and to the place where nothing and everything are the same, where there is no tree, no me, only the pure light of consciousness.

In time, I stand up. I am me and not-me.

'Join-up' with Trees

'The return to the green chaos, the deep forest and refuge of the unconscious is a nightly phenomenon, and one that psychiatrists [...] tell us is essential to the human mind. Without it, it disintegrates and goes mad. If I cherish trees... it is because of this, their natural correspondence with the greener, more mysterious processes of mind – and because they also seem to me the best, the most revealing messengers to us from all nature, the nearest its heart,' declares John Fowles in his long essay *The Tree*[12].

Our woodlands, Fowles continues, are the last fragments of 'comparatively unadulterated nature', and as such they provide the 'most accessible outward correlatives' of an ancient relationship, a feeling, a knowledge that we are in danger of losing. He describes our woodlands as 'the last green churches and chapels outside the walled civilization and culture we have made with our tools.'

When I facilitate outdoor workshops with the meditative component that is incorporated into them participants report a swifter than average sense of deep relaxation and profound restoration. Trees facilitate this dropping deep and deeper again into a state of unity – in itself, very healing for the human psyche.

If we were talking in horse-behaviour terms, we'd speak of 'joining up'.

But I'm aware there's a danger in this too – seeing nature as yet another resource, outside the human realm, put here for my or our benefit.

Our common contemporary worldview is that 'nature', divorced from us, is God-given (or a secular equivalent) for our use, a resource, and the rest of the natural world itself of only secondary importance, behind human concerns. With this view, the current and accelerating levels of destruction of land, displacement and suffering of peoples and animals, global ecocide, seem inevitable; the more so in a neoliberal capitalist approach rooted in the unsustainable concept of unlimited growth on a finite planet.

What increasingly concerns me in both my personal and professional life is how we can move from the anthropocentric to the ecocentric, and in so doing, recognise the crucial role of reciprocity; recognise our place in the web of co-existent relationships.

I think this has to start with a felt relationship with place, with the land, with other species and individual members of those species through direct experience feet-on-soil – maybe even bare-feet-on-soil: being outside at all seasons, in all weathers, at dawn and dusk, at night as well as daytime. Paying attention. This is how we learn to love, from knowing someone or something, and looking deeply.

Awareness continues from a felt experience of sentience in those Others with whom we share this outdoors, into reaching towards an understanding of what it means to believe, as I do, that all is consciousness, and that we are in continuous and interdependent relationship and exchange with all of that all. And then to apply that understanding, in practical terms, in how we live. Everything is essential to the web – and we as a species are destroying thousands of species and poisoning the land, waters and air, not just each year but in each moment.

How might I live, knowing that?

How might we recognise, re-envision and help restore the ancient mutual bond that ties us so irrevocably to this beautiful wild planet and its many inhabitants? How can I love and care for it all more actively, as the 'self', the one self, that actually it is, and we are?

The Wisdom of Trees

Writer and founder of the Dark Mountain network, Paul Kingsnorth, said that living without wild nature is like living without one of our senses or one of our limbs. Yes. How can we be whole, or have intimations of wholeness without regular access to at least some reminder of the ecosystem with which we share this journey through the cosmos?

We too are part of nature, of course. (How easy it is to see it as existing 'out there' only.) Our deep soul-life and the natural world seem to resonate in sympathy with each other. Bill Plotkin, founder of the Animas Valley Institute, suggests that both things working in tandem are needed to take us to maturation. Living as we do in the twenty-first century world, where for so many of us a divorce from both soul and nature has happened below the level of our conscious awareness, no wonder many people feel adrift. We forget our origins. In the forest, I am reminded, day after day after day. It can be humbling.

Trees are quite extraordinary beings. Quite apart from the nutrition, habitat and shelter they offer numerous species, including our own, as I mentioned in the Introduction they keep the rain cycle going so that earth remains moist enough for life, transpiring moisture out into the air through their leaves, and 'sucking' vast quantities of moisture from the atmosphere via the winds above the oceans, too, to recycle it, to keep the hydrological cycle going. They knit the soil together, thus preventing erosion.

Each year, the world's forests extract billions of tons of carbon dioxide from the atmosphere. That's an estimated twenty-eight per cent of all emissions, says M R O'Connor in an article in *The New Yorker*.[13]

They provide us with food, fuel and building materials, and act as the lungs as well as one of the major repositories of fluids of our planet, so protecting our water supplies, our soil retention, and cleaning and replenishing our air through ingesting CO_2, offering one of the most effective possible measures for combatting climate change.

They also offer us the main source for medicines in all eras including our own – a huge proportion of current pharmaceuticals, for instance, are or were originally sourced in the Amazon rainforest (and the appropriation of those by Big Pharma is another story).

Even now, there is still so much that we don't know about our neighbours the trees, and much that is being discovered, in part thanks to technology. M R O'Connor[14] speaks of how research scientists working as dendrochronologists can measure trees' daily rhythms, such as expansions and contractions of trunk girth, and how a tree can acquire millimetres of height in minutes, given certain conditions.

'One afternoon', wrote the author, 'a light rain became a torrential downpour... As the thunderstorm arrived, the plane tree's roots seemed to take a long drink: in a single minute, from 2:42 to 2:43 P.M., the tree's trunk grew nearly five millimetres. [At] 6:40 P.M., the rain seemed to fall horizontally, and the tree grew another three millimetres.'

The astonishing opening paragraph of O'Connor's article speaks of how the measured tree's expansion and contraction appeared to be affected not only by rain, and the rising sun, but by a nearby fish splashing, or frogs croaking. In the company of Jeremy Hise and Professor Kevin Griffin, and with the use of precision dendrometers that can convert physical motion into electrical impulses, O'Connor witnessed how it's now possible to measure the minutest changes within the trees in real time.

From this work we now know, for instance, that in the oak trees monitored in the USA at least, huge preparatory changes in the shape of cell division and radial stem growth begins two weeks before the leaves emerge. We know, too, that trees grow mostly at night; and that growth stops not in autumn, as one might predict, but in July, so that the trees, perhaps, can store carbon ready to lay down new wood during the second half of the year before the demands of spring.

And more

Arguably, much of our learning, at least in the past, was seen to come from trees: as far as we can discover, the Bardic-Druidic wisdom traditions that are the native shamanic practices of our islands seem to come directly out of the wildwood.

'[W]atching trees grow, remembering the trees that made me... words come flocking... A first sentence begins like a leafing woodland', writes Wales' former National Poet Gillian Clarke in her essay in *Poetry Wales*[15].

As I also mentioned in the opening to this book, there is much evidence to suggest that the word 'Druid' (or 'dru-vid) itself etymologically consists of words that mean 'tree', 'oak', and/or 'wood', and also 'knowledge', 'wisdom' or 'vision'. In addition to the direct Brythonic and Gaelic Celtic words there are very similar words in Germanic and Nordic languages (you'll remember I spoke of the Old English or Saxon word 'wis' above), plus root equivalents in various proto-Indo-European tongues and in Sanskrit.

What's more, 'Druid' or variants on it, including the name for oak, 'duir', in the Celtic calendar, likely also means 'door' – as in door to other realms, such as those accessed by a shaman. Some interpret it as meaning 'far-seeing'.

Similarly, but employing different root words: in both Welsh and Breton the words for 'tree' and for 'learning' or 'scholar' seem to be related. In Welsh 'gwydd', meaning 'tree', can also mean 'scholar', and 'gwybod' is knowledge. (It's likely that Gwydion, that most high Druid of Celtic mythology, takes his name from a word or phrase meaning 'wisdom of trees', or 'knowledge of trees'.) In Breton, a tree is 'gwez' and a scholar is 'gouez' (pronounced practically identically).[16]

And there are interesting elisions in Old English, too, where the word 'tree' shares its etymology with 'true' and 'truth', as well as with 'troth', as in 'betrothed', and 'truce'.

There's been a resurgence of interest in what are often called 'nature-based' and pagan spiritual practices the last few decades. One of them is Druidry, and it has much to contribute to our understanding of the web of life.

We know that Druids, as the priestly/shamanic caste of the late Bronze Age/Iron Age Celts, were charged with holding and continuing the wisdom of their culture. (What is less likely is that they were involved in human sacrifice, despite all the populist sensationalism attaching to such an idea. It seems increasingly likely that this was propaganda on the part of Caesar to discredit them and therefore justify their persecution.) A grove of trees was their outdoor sacred meeting place, the 'nemeton' (which word continues in various forms such as Nymet or Nympton in parts of the British Isles, notably Devon and Somerset, but also in other places in Europe).

We tend to think of these groves as being clusters of oak trees – we always associate Druids with trees, specifically oaks, and a common understanding of the word 'Druid' is 'some kind of pagan priest performing rituals in an oak grove'.

What we now know as Druidry, however, is largely a revivalist tradition from the eighteenth and nineteenth centuries. For our understanding of Druidry before that, we rely to a large extent on fragmentary written records by the Romans and Greeks, many of them collated by modern authors[17].

The Romans, of course, were writing as conquerors of Gaul (Celtic Gaul) and after their incursions into Britain, and their accounts as conquerors may be suspect, or at least partial (Graham Robb's book *The Ancient Pathways* sheds a great deal of light on the Gauls, showing them to be a highly-sophisticated people, with a well-developed culture and civilisation – from which, seemingly, the Romans frequently learned, rather than vice versa. Interestingly, Robb suggests that the famous Roman road was, in Gaul at least, built on pre-existent straight trackways.)

What we do know is that the Druids were a very highly-trained priestly class who were the keepers of the wisdom teachings, the cycles of the year and of time, the cosmology, histories, stories and mysteries of their culture. They were also poets, lawgivers and judges, and teachers.

Interestingly, it's said that their training took nineteen years – that's the length of a metonic cycle of the moon, and also, as it happens, of the number of stones contained in many Bronze Age stone circles in Britain. Esoterically, this possibly links both, whether or not connected historically, to a lunar-goddess cosmology.

Although both ancient and contemporary Druidry practices involve access to subtle planes of being through altered states of consciousness, theirs was and remains in contemporary practice a nature-based spirituality. It's at least in part through the Druids that we understand the depth of wisdom-teachings of trees and the wildwoods.

'If you would know strength and patience, welcome the company of trees,' said Hal Borland.

When I walk out into the woods now, all my senses are alert. I try to be aware of the individual trees, their individual species, and the great breathing body that is forest. Each tree has its own character, posture, temperament and tongue; the wind sounds different in each.

What have I learned from trees? I'm still learning.

It's something to do with learning to let go; to let be.

I'm learning to be wordless; at least, for the time I'm in the woods. 'No one really enters a wood unless they are prepared to give up their language', says poet Paul Matthews[18].

I'm learning how to hold still and let the world go by without fearing I'm missing something.

I'm learning to reach my crown to the sky, and my roots even deeper into the earth.

I'm learning just how slow tree-time is, and how very much goes on out of sight over many decades, or centuries.

I'm learning to remember that the natural exchanges of air, moisture, carbon and sugars, messages, happen without any effort, and will adapt as necessary without my having to drive it all.

I'm learning that I can survive. I'm learning how to host others; or rather, as I've always been quite good at hosting others, it's more to do with hosting others without it draining me. I'm learning how my deep nourishment comes from above and below, both; and that I can share it with others and yet not be depleted.

I'm learning about what it means to be both individual and community, family, without compromising either; though I already know how a parent, tree, animal, bird or human can also give up their own life for their offspring.

To be inextricably tied-in to a network; to be utterly interdependent with that network, even if much of its life goes on out of sight.

Trees Are Books

Leaves catching light
are the true scriptures

I'm freed then
from the need
to describe them

They describe themselves

They are their own
green messages

It is a book
which the wind is turning
from 'Green Theology', *by Paul Matthews*[19]

'He said once, that the stories of the Wood were as numerous as leaves on the trees,' writes the monk who, according to John Matthews' engaging retelling of the story, acted as scribe to Taliesin[20].

Over the last few decades there has been a resurgence of interest in trees, and what 'tree consciousness' might mean.

Author Nigel Pennick in his book on the Ogham alphabet[21] suggests that trees are (also) a metaphor for human consciousness, and that this is most visible still in the Welsh language (as we have seen above).

Picking up and progressing my earlier motif exploring the etymology of 'Druid': humans have long associated trees with knowledge, wisdom and consciousness. Think of the Tree of Life, the World Tree (well-known in Europe as the 'Yggdrasil' of Norse mythology), the Tree of Knowledge (in the Bible it became the Tree of Knowledge of Good and Evil, adding a dualism because of a value judgement that is elsewhere absent).

All early knowledge, says author Fred Hageneder,[22] is connected with trees: all ancient cultures have acknowledged the power of trees to elevate, or mediate, human consciousness to higher planes of perception.

Interestingly, Plato in *Phaedrus* tells us that the first prophecies were the words of an oak.

The Buddha, Siddhartha Gautama, found his enlightenment and the source for the 2,500-year journey of what is now Buddhism under the Bo, or Bodhi, tree.

And then there's Hinduism. The Vedas, the Hindu sacred scriptures, were considered to be leaves from the Tree of Knowledge – leaves as letters of the ancient sacred alphabets.

There are links in the word 'veda', etymologically, with the proto-Indo-European root word 'weid', which means 'to see', 'to find' and also 'to know'. This word has its echoes in the proto-Indo-European Celtic tongues as 'fidh' (variants 'vid' or 'veid', plural 'feadha'), which can mean both 'tree' and 'wood'; and also carries the idea of 'knowledge'. As it happens, the individual 'letters' of the Ogham alphabet are known as 'fidh'. In shamanic tradition the tree, as spinal column of the world if you like – think World Tree as axis of the earth – is an entry-point into subtle realms, both 'above' and 'below': that is, the shaman in spirit-journeying might descend into the roots as well as into the upper leaf canopy in his or her search for wisdom, information, or healing from the spirit-world.

There is Moses' Burning Bush – burning, but not consumed. This, symbolically, is to do with illumination, revelation, wisdom – the perennial fire of spirit.

Similar to this, and to my mind a very powerful symbol, is what is known as the Green and Burning Bush of Celtic mythology.

The motif comes from the story of Peredur in the Welsh

Mabinogion, that ancient collection of magical tales. (Peredur is perhaps better known in his incarnations as Perceval or Percival, and Parsifal, of the later mediaeval Grail legends.)

Some of the tales related to Peredur's quest to heal the suffering king of the land involve various motifs that suggest the natural state of unity between the apparent pairs of opposites. In a steep-sided wooded valley and on the bank of a river (trees and water often seem to enhance and amplify each other's powers) Peredur 'saw a tall tree: from roots to crown one half was aflame and the other green with leaves'. Here, we could say that the green of the leaves represents the life in matter (the soil-nutrients, water and sap in the tree) and the (fiery) life in spirit, which are ultimately indivisible.

Interestingly, this 'green and burning' tree is identified by R J Stewart as a Hawthorn[23] a tree of initiation and commencement, whose calendar month kicked off my own time here in Brittany. Others say it's an evergreen, probably a Yew.

As for the connections between the sacred, wisdom, and the power of trees, you can barely enter the Forest here at any one of its entry-points without a sense of the undercurrents of an ancient spirituality.

Woods retain their power to entrance; even greatly-diminished woods. Perhaps we all half-hope, entering woodland, to see a white hind, or a stag, antlered deity of the greenwood, or some other magical creature like a unicorn – for itself, but also because of our half-remembered childhood understanding that animals, like trees, do have a magical side; are representatives of something we both know and don't know at all.

The Dark Forest II

So, by and by, in the heart of this dark forest, you see – miles away and close at hand – The Tree. Call it the Tree of Life; call it the Tree of Knowledge of Good and Evil; call it the World Tree.

Its branches are ablaze with all the birds of the heavens; in its roots, the animals of meadow and woodland make their homes.

You can climb in its branches to the heavens; but first you need to climb down its ganglia of roots, into the Underworld heart of the dark earth with its dreams and memories, ancestors and becomings.

Every threshold is guarded. Here, on the descent, you do battle with your fears, your regrets, your unmet hopes and dreams, your past, your future, the ways in which you've messed up, been unkind, acted out of ignorance and thoughtlessness.

There will be a question for you.

You have to loosen your pride.

You have to let go of all you know.

You have perhaps already let go of your youthful innocence, your sense that your little life is a vast unending canvas that stretches to the stars.

And now, at last, you can ease your rucksack off your shoulders, and leave it here propped against the tree. In the realm of the Underworld you won't need all the things that seem so essential in the world between heaven and earth.

But you will need to sacrifice something in order to cross the threshold – perhaps that which is most precious to you. (And you'll have to do that again climbing back up before the ascent into light – but that's another story, and your most precious thing may no longer be the same thing as before.)

And then you can let go; in fact, there is nothing else you can do if you wish to find the Pearl Beyond All Price that is your own soul.

The Sun-God and his Letters

There are many ways to make and mark a journey, and/or to mark a year and our passage with it and through it. For me, the changing faces of the trees in the Forest, and the quality of each species and its individual trees, have become ways to note and respond to phases of my time here.

In my life, for many years now, I've marked the months by way of the Ogham tree alphabet and calendar. In this calendar, each letter of the old Celtic alphabet is associated with a certain tree, and each tree with a certain month, as well as quality.

One of the major finds of my student years was Robert Graves' astonishing and iconic work *The White Goddess*, a (much-disputed, as I mentioned in the Introduction) presentation of Goddess-centred spirituality via Bardic and Druidic philosophy and teachings from pre-Christian Britain. I suppose I'd have to say that this book has played an important part in shaping my adult life, all my adult life.

As stated above, Graves is largely responsible for what we now know as the Celtic Tree Alphabet, or 'Ogham'. He draws in part on the long Celtic poem the 'Cad Goddeu', apparently truly ancient but preserved in written form in the *Book* (or *Song*) *of Taliesin*. There is a story that the *Hanes Taliesin* was first recorded by a Christian monk who was befriended by Taliesin of the Radiant Brow in the 6th century AD (though most of our extant texts date from the Middle Ages). This contains references to the attributes of different tree species from the original Druidic and Bardic oral tradition.

Graves combines this with the 'Song of Amergin', all heavily spiced with his own interpretations and conclusions. I find the whole thing utterly entrancing. The 'Song of Amergin' is even older than the *Hanes Taliesin*: it is said to date from the settlement of what is now Ireland by the pre-Celtic Milesians some time between 1600-1268 BCE – which adds a possible Ancient Egyptian twist to the sources of this alphabet.[24] (Some have thought that the Milesians were Iberian Celts; it's most likely that they were Phoenicians, who came across the Mediterranean from Asia Minor, the region that now primarily encompasses Turkey, Syria and the Lebanon, and then via the Iberian peninsula into Ireland, predating the Iron Age Celts.)

Unfortunately, the only version of the Song that now survives is a translation from the Old Goidelic into colloquial Irish, but there is still a great deal to interest us in it.

Quite apart from its helpfulness as a source of poetic inspiration, I find this idea of alphabet and calendar invaluable as a way to work with the trees and their individual qualities on a symbolic and poetic level. Learning their language is a way of attuning myself to the turning year and the quality of each time-period, in order to work in harmony with the cycles of the earth made visible, and with the greater cycles of the cosmos.

The Ogham alphabet was a way, supposedly, of Druids communicating and memorising significant wisdom teachings without having to write anything down, and would not be understood by others who were not initiated. It was also a way of marking the turning points of the year via trees, so a calendar, in addition to an alphabet.

Some say that our ancestors took their original inspiration for Ogham from the twisted branches of old Oaks.

It is more commonly recorded in the literature that Ogma, the sun-god from the mythical Tuatha Dé Danaan race and noted for his eloquence and poetry (Ogmios to the Gauls), created the Ogham alphabet from watching the flight of that magical, secretive bird sacred to the Druids, the crane, in flight (Mercury/Hermes was also supposed to have created the Roman/Greek alphabet from the same phenomenon). Seemingly the letters were 'written upon the sky' not only by the birds' legs and wings, but also from their flight patterns and the way they changed when the tired lead bird swapped with another.

Migrating cranes, to the Celts, were significant birds. Associated with the Triple Goddess, they were also connected with both divination and madness – probably the kind of madness that appears to co-occur with prophetic insight. Merlin in his madness after the battle of Arfderydd, retreating to live wild in the Forest of Celydon with only a piglet for company, prophesied, and also read the 'letters' written by cranes in the sky. These birds are connected with the Ogham script – as well as with prophecy, divining and madness.

The sun-god and his letters

Out of primal sound came the sounds we know as letters, and out of primal light their shapes. Then came the first word ('In the beginning was the Word').

Alphabets of whatever nature are potent. Since whenever it was that we learned, historically, to shape sounds into letters and words, all cultures have valued words. The use of words, at least partly by virtue of their ability to travel through and transcend time, is a primary act of magic.

The Ogham 'letters' are horizontal or diagonal strokes on a vertical line: to the right of it, to the left of it, or right across it, in groups of five. The vertical line was carved into stone or wood; or a kinetic version was on the shinbone or nose (attached to the living person!), the *fidh* or *feadha* made by one to all five of the digits for another to see but briefly, as the communication wasn't always intended for public consumption.

In his magnificent re-creation of *The Song of Taliesin*, mentioned above, John Matthews[25] narrates his story about the finding of the sacred letters by Ogma, with whose name 'Ogham' is associated. So here is yet another version of how the Ogham alphabet was created. Ogma, also known as 'Sun-Face', may have been an incarnation of the great sun-god who appears in so many of the global myths about the origins of our world. Some scholars connect him with Herakles, another sun-god[26]. There are texts that also connect him with the god of poetry – apposite indeed given his association with the origins of the sacred alphabet.

Ogma dreamed, 'bound upon the Wheel at the hub of the turning stars, while all around him the tides of fate swept in and out like oceans in endless flux', in Matthews' lyrical words. Ogma in his dream saw himself as 'the bright-faced wanderer who made songs that mankind could hear, so that all might understand, at least a little more, their place in the pattern of creation'.

As he thought about humankind's need of a sense of meaning and insight, so he struggled against the bonds that tied him to the great Wheel.

From his place at the hub of this wheel in his struggles he noticed the spokes radiating out from this Wheel, and he saw a sign carved upon each of the twenty-five spokes. He observed, too, that each of the spokes was made from a different wood.

Ogma's journey was long and arduous. Eventually, when he broke free of the Wheel, Ogma came upon a well radiant with light. Within that light were twenty-five fragments of wood, each carved with one of the signs he'd dreamed. He reached out to them and was given them, placing them in a leather bag at this waist. (I like to imagine that this was the craneskin bag of Celtic tradition: a most magical object, containing keys to the mysteries of the worlds.)

After he had travelled the world for age upon age, Ogma came at last to a place where the trees had been cleared. There he planted his twenty-five staves, so that eventually they would grow into a great forest. 'Many names it had, but to those who serve it now it is called ... Brocéliande.'[27]

... or the moon-goddess...

Here, we might move into lunar time, which brings me nicely to a thought: if Ogma was the sun-god, then what he may have been delivering was, in nice balance, lunar, or feminine, wisdom.

Ogma the sun-god delivered twenty-five spokes, Ogham staves, or trees, to the world. Personally, as I mentioned above, I find that Robert Graves' thirteen rather than twenty-five 'feadha' (the plural of 'fidh', meaning 'a tree', and the name for the Ogham glyph we'd call 'letter') resonates with me and my relationship to specific trees, though in my version below we miss out the vowels.

Graves suggests that the tree-calendar is lunar rather than solar, and offers thirteen trees for thirteen consonants and thirteen 28-month lunar days, with one day, the unnamed day, left over, so to speak, for the winter solstice (though Graves marks it as being 23rd December, not 21st). He suggests that a further five vowel-trees mark the solar quarter-date 'stations' of the turning year (the solstices and equinoxes), and Samhuinn or Samhain, now Hallowe'en, that gateway between the worlds and the beginning of the new Celtic year.

Rather than the quarter-dates, some associate the vowels with what are known as the cross-quarter dates that sit midway between solstice and equinox: Imbolc or Candlemas on February 1st; Beltane or Mayday, May 1st; Lughnasadh/Lughomass or Lammas, August 1st; Samhain or Hallowe'en, November 1st; and the fifth here being the winter solstice, that time out of time, when the sun appears to be at a standstill for three days before resuming its journey back towards the east.

The number five, as in the vowel-trees, and its pentagram is traditionally sacred to the Goddess. We know, too, that Taliesin called the Cauldron belonging to the Great Goddess in her incarnation as Ceridwen the Mother Goddess 'Sweet Cauldron of the Five Trees'. (The Cauldron, among other things, symbolises Her womb in which all life begins or is restored.)

Graves' thinking on it all, and his writings, as I suggested in the Introduction, have been treated with derision by a great many academics and scholars; but far more people have been inspired by his ideas. There are literal truths and there are symbolic truths, and we need both, and tend to interpret the latter according to our own psychological disposition, the prevailing culture, and the phase of life – some might say incarnation – in which we find ourselves.

For me, as a symbolic system with which my imagination can engage, it's unrivalled. What I put forward from here is only my own way of working with the tree months and an alphabetical notion that I find speaks so richly to my imagination. What matters to me is whether it deepens my sense of connection to the tree and the forest, and of their connectedness to everything else.

Numerous versions, and letter-counts, of this calendar alphabet exist; who is to say which – if any – is 'right' or even 'true'? There is much disagreement over how many trees there are in the alphabet (the range is from 12 to 25 or even more), which months they represent, and whether we're talking solar years, lunar years, or some altogether different ascription. People get very heated about it (two of us who espouse the thirteen-month system were given a very stern talking-to on a Facebook group dedicated to a twenty-tree system. But no matter. *The Book of Ballymote*, a relatively ancient Irish source, lists one hundred and fifty.)

Of apples, Eve, and what to do about Q

In Part II of this book we will be looking closely at thirteen trees, and at what they might symbolise in our lives.

There is a difficulty, though, in following Graves' alphabet, which is the one on which I've based my own: he leaves out the one tree that, to my mind, absolutely cannot be left out of such an alphabet. Apple is not included in the Brythonic, or 'P' Celtic, alphabet that Graves uses (the Brythonic tongues are Welsh, Cornish, Breton and originally Manx), even though the Apple is hugely significant in so many of our Brythonic Celtic myths and legends. You will remember, for instance, that the dying Arthur was ferried by priestesses to the island through the mists, to the sacred Isle of Avalon, Avellenau, whose very name means 'Apples'. In this Brythonic Celtic tongue Apple is also apfal, aval, afall, apfallen; and many other recognisable versions of this word, all beginning with A, occur in other Indo-European languages. In Graves' version, though, the vowel A is carried by Ailm, usually seen as Silver Fir, or by some sources Wych Elm.

In Irish versions of the Ogham alphabet we have the Apple as Quert, since Goidelic, or 'Q' Celtic languages, Scottish and Irish Gaelic, both include Q and Quert for Apple. In my version, Apple as Quert replaces Ivy for the eleventh month, late September and into October.

After a great deal of reflection, I've also replaced Reed with Blackthorn for the twelfth month. Initially, in my work, Hawthorn and Blackthorn, which are 'sister' trees, both ruled the month that includes Beltane, or May Day, in the month before Oak. I've good reason for this shift, however, as I now believe that Blackthorn, the 'dark face' of Hawthorn (which is also known as Whitethorn), governs our entry into the dark part of the year (in the northern hemisphere) at Samhain, known in our current calendar as All Souls, or Hallowe'en.

As late as the 20th century and even into our own, some of these trees still prompt(ed) superstition in people, a result of either misunderstanding how our ancestors viewed trees, or possibly negative publicity on the part of the Church. I'm thinking of how, for instance, the Yew in churchyards is seen as 'the tree of the dead' – a vast over-simplification – and treated with some apprehension; or how the May (Hawthorn) blossom shouldn't be brought into the house or it will bring bad luck (the Hawthorn is a tree sacred to the Great Goddess and it is true that, as a faery tree, it needs to be outside; my own sense, though, is that it was abjured by the Roman church due to two things: one, it was very significant as a tree to our pagan ancestors, and probably connected with the May Day fertility revels which the church would have found so abhorrent; two, its flowers are perceived to smell of female sexual secretions, which a patriarchal tradition would have condemned as whorish).

And look at what happened to the Apple, supposed agent of the Fall out of the Garden of Eden, alongside of course the serpent who 'tempted' Eve to seduce Adam; and all three (Apple, serpent, Eve) have been blamed ever since.

What if, in fact, esoterically speaking, the Apple was an agent of transformation into a higher level of consciousness, prompted by the serpent of wisdom which is interchangeable with the dragon in our mythology, and the serpent-dragon that gives us our ley lines mapping the land, and also the kundalini energy that in Eastern mysticism sits coiled at the base of the spine until awoken, when it will rise to the Crown chakra of the head in an enlightened being? (Think about the topknot on Buddha, the halo around Jesus' head.) What if Eve represents an aspect of the Great Goddess, charged with initiating a man into the subtle consciousness of the awakened heart?

Waking up in the Dark Forest

The wheel of the year turns. You wander on. You've come so far: '– been down so long it looks like up to me,' tra-la.

But things are different tonight. What you thought was outside turns out to be inside; what you thought was inside is outside; and strangest of all, each is also the other.

Above you is the full moon. As if in response, in the depths of the dark forest there glows a small light. At this turning point of the year, as the first rays make themselves felt, anything seems possible to you now.

What matters is keeping your eyes on that small fire – you know that everything in the universe, from the blue whale in the icy depths to the dance of mayflies, or linked particles, resonates with everything else, speaks one to the other and on. You also know that keeping that fire in sight, keeping that fire alight, is crucial.

There's a kind of song, too, between the fire and the small lantern you carry, lit from the last hearth. Carrying fire to fire is, you know, the way forward; a way of tending the world's fires and the fires that burn in the heart.

It's been an arduous dark journey, a twisting turning road that has cost you almost all you have, and you long to rest, to warm yourself at the hearth.

As you approach and the light increases you can now see the further obstacles in your path. They are the same old same old – the thickets of thinking, the walls of fear that divide and separate, the treacherous pits of illusion and disillusion, the seductive side paths that will lead you only around in a circle.

This time you see them in advance of stumbling blindly on into them. 'When we see things as they really are, then all obstacles disappear and nature becomes our collaborator,' he had said*.

You've been through the cleansing fire that burns away what is not true Self, you've been tried by the waters of the heart, you've climbed the mountain of singlemindedness, you've learned how to make your own wings to soar like the buzzard who's circled you now and then on this lonely journey. You know you will be tested again and again, that there are more layers to be stripped or burned, scrubbed or washed away, and that that's simply how it is. You no longer wish it to be different. Now, you can hear. Now, you can see. Now, you know that nothing is worth the sacrifice of stepping aside from your own path towards that glowing fire that is home.

Now, the forest and its 10,000 inhabitants are your collaborators, your guides and companions. Now you can never be alone.

* *Joseph D D'Agostino,* Tarot – the royal path to wisdom, *with reference to the Wheel of Fortune.*

Forest Otherworld

I enter the green light of the forest and I am in the Otherworld.

Wren speaks in my chest; I feel the rush of wind in the wingpits of my buzzard self.

As wild St John's Wort I hold my many faces to the sun. I am the green thought driving the idea of bilberries towards their fruiting.

I'm the leaning rock and its twin towards whom it leans, my feet deeply buried in the good soil. As moss, my green pelt gently coats the stone.

Am hazel. I exhale in spring and my thousands of leaves open. Through summer's dreaming I let my fruits swell into slow new life. I inhale in winter, give away the fruits, let drop all my leaves back into the rich earth.

I spill with the waterfall into the little pool; I become body of otter, fish, dragonfly, deer, badger, boar who lap, breathe, sip, lick, suck and drink me in. Drink us all in.

I spin through the canopy with my fellow goldcrests.

Movement. A flicker of lightdarklight. Sniffing the air, I freeze, then bound with my kin up the steep track to the lost glade. I breathe out the breeze; I breathe in the small summer rain.

I am here, now, and I've always been here, or there
or everywhere.

PART II

TONGUES IN TREES: THE TREE MONTHS

The Song of Amergin

It's impossible to work with the Tree Alphabet Calendar without saying something about the Celtic magical tradition that underpins the tree-months. So here it is: 'The Song of Amergin' that adds its mystery to what we know of the origins of the Ogham alphabet calendar.

Each tree in my 'canon' has a poetic line in the title section that describes something of its month, or its mythological associations. Each has a particular correspondence in Celtic culture and story. Sometimes a connection between the month, the tree and the line is clear; very often it is not at all without an understanding of the original texts and culture (and frequently not even then).

However, even if it seems at a tangent, it will, perhaps, cast new light on that month each time; or at least offer another image. What I suggest to course participants is that they notice their own response to the line.

These lines are closely associated with the 'Song of Amergin'. I don't know at what point in history they were adopted into the Ogham alphabet, or if they were always the guiding principle.

There are very many different versions, however, and I have made free from my own long knowledge of this mythological tradition, of the trees, of different monthly attributes and of astrological signifiers to 'name', if you like, each month. (Each month's 'keynote' has a mythological connection, though some of them remain, at the moment, obscure.)

I've drawn on various versions, but used my own experience and intuition, mixing, matching, merging and sometimes departing altogether from the traditional translations (which should really also be called 'versions') when I have good reason to. What I offer, below, is by no means definitive, and is a poet's rather than a scholar's version. I've rooted the lines in Robert

Graves' translation but also taken great liberties.

The best and most beautiful version I know is Gabriel Byrne's, available on YouTube read in the Irish and then in English by Byrne from his own translation.

The Song is, and quite rightly, one of the best-known texts from what is now Ireland. It's a spell-like sacred incantation with profound ecological, shamanic and shapeshifting resonances attributed to Amergin, or Amhairghin, a legendary Bard and chieftain of the Milesians who landed on his second attempt on Irish shores between 1700 BCE and 1000 BCE (one record is more precise, dating Amergin's arrival to between 1287 and 1286 BCE. Robert Graves gives an even more exact date: he says 1268 BCE.) Like many cultures, Ireland had a rich oral tradition of wisdom teachings, the contents of which were preserved in poetry, song and story and usually transmitted by the highly-trained Bards and Druids. This was only much later committed to written texts, so we cannot be sure of the originals.

Amergin's name supposedly means 'born of song'. Amergin was of the 'seventh and final' race of people, the Milesians, or Sons of Mil Espaine, who took possession of the island. Whether this is a race memory of a prehistoric people travelling the Atlantic seaboard northwards from the Iberian peninsula ('Espaine') and settling Ireland, or whether we read that as meaning Milesians colonisers from what is now Asia Minor, probably Turkey or the Levant (there was much trade by sea in prehistoric days from the Phoenicians of what is now known as the Lebanon and its adjoining areas), or whether indeed the name is purely mythological (rather in the vein of the ancients scribing 'Here be dragons' on maps for the areas they hadn't yet recorded) isn't important here.

Amergin and his tribespeople displaced, according to the pseudohistorical 'High Kings' list of Ireland (believed to date from the eighth century CE) the Tuatha dé Danaan who, despite what I wrote above about the seven races, are mythologically seen as the original people of Ireland. The Milesians are said to be the ancestors of the current Irish.

The Tuatha dé Danaan, usually translated as 'people/tribe of the goddess Dana' (or Danu), are the Otherworldly race in Irish mythology, of whom Manannan Mac Llyr, the sea-god, is one of the best known of the Children of Llyr/Lir (from whom we have King Lear). The Tuatha dé Danaan constitute a pantheon whose figures and their attributes appeared in a number of forms all across the Celtic world, notably in the Welsh *Y Mabinogi*. They probably represent the main deities of pre-Christian Gaelic Ireland.

The Song of Amergin
My version

Dec. 24-Jan. 20 B (Birch/Beth)
I am a stag of seven tines in the midwinter birch wood

Jan. 21-Feb. 17 L (Rowan/Luis)
I am the mist over a wide river-valley

Feb. 18-Mar. 17 N (Ash/Nion)
I am the wind on deep waters and the returning tide

Mar. 18-Apr. 14 F (Alder/Fearn)
I am the song of a shining tear of the sun

Apr. 15-May 12 S (Willow/Saille)
I am the Hawk of May, balanced above the cliff

May 13-Jun. 9 H (Hawthorn/Huath)
I am the most radiant among blossoms, the Flower Maiden

Jun. 10-July 7 D (Oak/Duir)

I am the oak-king who sets the head aflame
I am the god who crowns the waxing year

July 8-Aug. 4 T (Holly/Tinne)
I am a battle, the spear and the god who wields the spear
I am the god of the waning year

Aug. 5-Sept 1 C (Hazel/Coll)
I am a salmon's wisdom in the pool of inspiration

Sept. 2-Sept. 29 M (Vine/Muin, or Bramble)
I am a hill of poetry

Sept. 30-Oct. 27 Q (Apple/Quert/Apfal)
I am the island of apples and eternal life

Oct. 28-Nov. 24 St/Z (Blackthorn/Straif)
I am the black bough, the Cailleach

Nov. 25-Dec. 22 R (Elder/Ruis)
I am the faery tree and I am a wave of the sea

Dec. 23 (no tree) (Yew)
I am the waves' eternal return
The grave of every vain yearning
I know the secret of the three moons
And the secret path
And my dwelling place is the wind on the sea, the dolmen on the hillside, the rock in the river.

13 Sacred Celtic Trees, Month by Month

Including their History & habits, Gifts from, Mythology, Symbolism

B for Beth: the Birch Tree

Betula pendula
December 24th–January 20th
The Poets' Tree
Inception, initiation & rebirth

I am a stag of seven tines in the midwinter Birchwood

BIRCH, BETH

The Celtic calendar and alphabet begin with Birch, Beth, or Beith, for B, that solitary dancer-on-the-edge. Beth is the harbinger, we could say, of the returning light: the tree guarding the gate of the year.

The winter solstice – a word which means 'sun standstill' – takes place on 21st December, and there are then three days when the sun appears to rise and set in exactly the same place. After the winter solstice, Birch speaks of the sun's return: of birth and rebirth, of the arrival of the new or reborn. We know that the earth, however imperceptibly, now starts to turn back towards the longer days, and Beth steps forward, leading us through the doorway. Traditionally in Celtic culture, this gateway was also into the Otherworld that lies parallel to this – across the waters, hidden in mists.

Supposedly, Birch is ruled by Venus. This doesn't correlate with other astrological teachings, but it does with the appearance of this tree. If your birthday falls within Beth's dates, take extra notice of her properties and qualities.

Birch is one of the prettiest trees, almost ethereal, a faery tree.

Max Adams says it's a poet's tree: if ever it were threatened, it would be the poets who would defend it. In Druidry, the Birch is the tree that 'adopts' the Bard.

The Druids' name for Birch is reputedly 'White Lady of the Woods', and in Celtic lore she may also represent the slender graceful maiden form, sometimes known as Bride, of the Great Goddess 'the White Lady' Ceridwen, who in another form is Elen of the Ways. Birch is also associated with Grainne of Irish legend.

Often, I've noticed, a thrush will choose a Birch tree to perch in, singing its rainsong.

In Europe, our most common Birch is the silver Birch, *betula pendula*; extra beautiful for the grace of its weeping branches.

On the edges of Dartmoor near where I live, above the river Dart at the edge of the tree line, is a tree I think of as the Queen Birch. I look out for her as I ascend to the high ground. Slender and elegant, white lady, she has a double trunk that shines, as Birches do: moon-white. She's a grand old lady now. Nearby, often, there is a herd of cattle grazing under commoners' rights that includes two white cows, each with black ears, rather like cattle out of Celtic myth. As I pass the tree and the cattle, I know I'm entering the Otherworld of the moor.

As with so many trees, Beth is revealed with the undressing of winter: once its delicate yellow heart-shaped leaves have let go (often the Birch leaves are on the tree for as many as ten months in twelve in Europe), the silver bark becomes more visible, shining in the forest, and the magenta canopy of branches more obvious. The magenta darkens through the late winter, and the more mature trunks are tarnished, like the metal silver, with black cracks and fissures; this commonly happens as a Birch tree ages.

Birch is one of the earliest signs of spring's stirrings. Because of this, it was known as the tree of renewal, rebirth and inception to the Druids. It's also a tree of initiation.

I look for the crowns of the Birches turning magenta-purple as the cells start to fizz with anticipation in late January or early February, adding tone and hue to the drear of winter. (If it happens that there's also willow in the vicinity, there's a visual treat as willows' branches wear their flaming orange best around this time too.) Birch holds on to her leaves late, and is in leaf early again, often the first. Her gold-green catkins can appear as early as mid-February, at least in the Westcountry; not long after the crowns turn a deeper magenta. Look out for both in the late winter.

Holding the Edge: the Birch Tree

Bone-white under the moon
her trunk is made of rock
and the poor soil under the rock
her branches of owl-call and distance.

Out there where the hare crouched
that time, out beyond the edge
of the forest is where you'll find her
holding herself a little to one side

braving the unknown uplands
in her dream of perpetual becoming
the imperative to travel, to make new –
creating and recreating Forest.

In time they will flock after her
but for now she can do only
what she must – her slender
white body, mulberry-dark hair

with its autumn flakes of gold

bringing light to the arid hillsides
proclaiming the possibility
of growth, of continual return.
Roselle Angwin

In the Americas and Canada, the commonest Birch is the paper Birch *(betula papyrifera)*. This one is often whiter still in her satin-smooth bark than the weeping silver Birch. And so sensual. I was writer-in-residence at the National Trust property Greenway, the former home of Agatha Christie. The little poem below I perched in the fork of a paper Birch from a 'Literary Trail' I created.

paper birch
your thin skin
always peeling

Birch history and habits

About 11,000 BCE, after the slow retreat of the glaciers, Britain once again became hospitable to trees. Oliver Rackham in *The History of the Countryside* tells us that the trees that, during the Ice Age, had retreated southwards now started to migrate to more northerly latitudes. 'The first to colonise our tundra were birch, aspen and sallow... relatively arctic trees.'

The silver Birch dances on the edges; is a tree of beginnings. Birch seeds and the fine pollen from the catkins fly far from the original tree to make new forests. Fearless coloniser of new ground, Birch is what they call a 'pioneer' species, establishing tree cover on wasteland and scrubland, re-establishing itself after changes of climate, and is comfortable on the margins. It doesn't require rich soil, nor is it a prima donna about conditions. It pushes on, solitary, self-reliant and self-propagating, looking for the new, moving through the uplands, re-treeing what was otherwise all gorse and bracken in places like Dartmoor, Exmoor, in Wales, Scotland and Cumbria, in Brittany, throughout northern latitudes. (Finland, of course, is famous for its Birch woods.)

Wohlleben tells us how Birch's pioneering solitary habits cost it: it outgrows its strength, burns out, often dies young. That's the price you pay for living on the edge, and for growing up to three feet in any one year: the isolation of breaking new ground, and the growth spurts, in the end cost your vigour. Birch, however, in its lifespan does better in not-too-intimate company, but in any case not many other species will follow into the wilder edge-places – at least, not for a little while. This pioneer species can create a small forest in a decade.

These trailblazers, of course, eventually open the way to others; others that will eventually supplant the pioneers by competing for light, space, nutrients. These slower-growing trees thrive, as saplings, in the dappled shade cast by the Birch, but as the Birch begin to weaken a little the latecomers are growing stronger and taller, and eventually outstrip their hosts and quite literally overshadow them, for trees like Birch don't do well in shade.

A pioneer tree is more vulnerable to predation by rabbits and deer, especially as a sapling, out in the open on its own. The Birch guards against this by toughened bark, and also by its production of betulin, which not only gives the bark its whiteness, and acts as a kind of sunscreen for the trunk, but also tastes foul to any herbivore looking for a snack. Betulin is both antiviral and antibacterial, which not only helps a tree that is generally not protected and aided by its fellows, but also offers help to humans.

The gifts from Birch

Birch bark canoes date back a very long way, and through many cultures. In northern latitudes particularly such as parts of Scandinavia (notably Finland), Birch bark has long been used for making baskets and even water containers, and making and waterproofing boats, due to the fact that the bark and the tar are waterproof (hence its usage in canoe-making). It's also been used as glue.

Birch twigs were used as besoms, brooms; and are still sometimes used for the rural custom of 'beating the bounds' on New Year's Day, a way of remembering the territory within which a community lives.

Historically, Birch bark has been used for millennia for writing – the ancient Indian Vedas were scribed on Birch bark. There are still extant various inscribed scrolls of Birch bark.

Birch gives us a delicate sap, subtly uplifting to drink. In Scandinavia Birch wine is made from this; I made some once and it was sublime, though I felt bad about tapping the tree for its sap.

Birch-tar (resin) has been used for centuries as an antibacterial and antiviral ointment to treat skin complaints, and in shampoos. A decoction of the bark can help relieve aching muscles.

A homeopath friend tells me that a homeopathic dose of Betula alba will alleviate symptoms of allergy.

One of its most useful gifts to humans is that it makes wonderful kindling for fires, thanks to the oils in the bark. Max Adams in *The Wisdom of Trees* describes travelling with a small, lightweight and precious bag of Birch bark as tinder for his campfires.

Its mythology

An ancient tree of beginnings, both literally as above and symbolically at the turning of the year, Birch guards, we could say, the threshold and, living as it does on the cusp of wildland and upland, old year and new year, has been considered to be a tree of initiation.

It is seen in shamanic cultures as a tree that will allow the shaman safe passage into the Otherworld, and some say the Siberian shamanic culture sees it as the World Tree.

This is interesting, as beneath the Birch often grow fly agaric mushrooms: those red caps with their loose white spots that are known for being highly toxic. Shamans in the Arctic Circle and Scandinavia know that the hallucinogenic compound found in fly agaric, once it has passed through a reindeer, can be ingested by drinking the reindeer urine: the other toxins are rendered harmless by the passage through the deer, but the hallucinogen is preserved. (There is a lot to say about this, but not here.)

Fred Hageneder, who has written several books on the more esoteric and mythological meanings of trees, has this to say about Birch, quoting George Calder, Celtic scholar, in 1917:

'In Irish mythology, the first Ogham signs were carved into Birch, to warn the light god, Lugh, that his wife (she of the Birch tree) was about to be kidnapped by the underworld: "... on the Birch was written the first Ogham inscription that was brought into Ireland, to wit, thy wife will be taken from thee ... unless thou watch her. It is on that account b is still written at the beginning of the Celtic alphabet".'

I imagine it was to do with the winter solstice, point of maximum darkness (and entry into the Underworld), and that Lugh's wife (whose name we are not told: Beth/Birch?) is about to be abducted by the god of the Underworld in the way in which Persephone was abducted by Hades. Lugh as a fire-god loses the battle for light at this point – though of course it returns as the earth spins, and the abducted one re-emerges as the Maiden in early spring.

In old Scandinavian myth and folklore, we can find the predecessors of the better-known Cinderella in the 'Cinder-eaters': young people who slept between the hearth and the raked-out piles of ashes down the middle of the old longhouses, Robert Bly tells us in *Iron John*. It is my sense that they are mirroring a state of hibernation before being initiated into a new phase. They are also inner-hearth-tenders. The reason I mention them is that Cinderella wore a dress of Birch-bark. There are many gaps in information about such ritual behaviour; but much on which to speculate in terms of the symbolism of all this.

I am a stag of seven tines in the midwinter Birchwood

And the 'stag of seven tines'? In Celtic lore, a full-grown stag from the Otherworld ('a roebuck of seven tines') crashes through the Birchwood at the winter solstice, pursued for three days by the midwinter hounds of the dying year. Carrying on his back the spirit of the new year, he bears the returning sun between his antlers ('sun' becomes 'son' in Christianity; and before that, it was the time of the eternally-returning Son, Mabon, or The Mabon, in Celtic myth).

There are parallels in other cultures to this idea of a stag bearing the new sun, the new year, into life between his antlers. Meinrad Craighead in her *The Sign of the Tree* tells a small tale of the First Buck, A First Nation creation story in which, on the first morning of creation, standing at the centre of the earth and baying at the heavens and so calling all life into being, is a stag. His voice echoes around the void, and at the sound, the Tree of Life springs from his antlers.

Symbolism of Birch

Birch is a tree of new beginnings, and is the tree par excellence for symbolising renewal and regeneration. Birch can also symbolise clarity, courage, boundaries and also extending oneself beyond the familiar boundaries, and the importance of solitude, of being able to strike out alone when necessary.

The Birch-Tree At Loschwitz

At Loschwitz above the city
The air is sunny and chill;
The Birch-trees and the Pine-trees
Grow thick upon the hill.

Lone and tall, with silver stem,
A Birch-tree stands apart;
The passionate wind of spring-time
Stirs in its leafy heart.

I lean against the Birch-tree,
My arms around it twine;
It pulses, and leaps, and quivers,
Like a human heart to mine.

One moment I stand, then sudden
Let loose mine arms that cling:
O God! the lonely hillside,
The passionate wind of spring!
Amy Levy (1861-1889)

L for Luis; the Rowan Tree

Sorbus aucuparia *(rose family)*
January 21st–February 17th
A Faery Tree: Lady of the Mountains
Guidance, guardianship, protection

I am the mist over a wide river-valley

ROWAN, LUIS

Rowan is the tree that continues the Celtic calendar and alphabet and takes over from Birch as we approach the cracking open of the earth and emergent new life and move towards the festival of Imbolc, Candlemas, in which, in the northern hemisphere, the snowdrops, pollen-laden catkins and the first lambs appear. Janus the twofaced god, the January Man, who looks to the outgoing year and the incoming year simultaneously, is beginning to fade back into the past.

Rowan is a magical tree, guardian to and dweller in both this world and the Otherworld. All the trees of the Ogham alphabet are sacred trees, but Rowan has something particularly special about it.

I say 'it' as, Lady of the Mountains though she might be archetypally, I find her shape-shifting gender quite frequently, and some Rowan trees have a distinctly masculine, albeit gentle, quality to them. Many others seem gender-neutral; androgynous in spirit, which reflects the fact that the trees are hermaphrodites. (This is my experience: your own perceptions may be different.)

Incidentally, the spirit of all the trees sacred to the pre-Christian pagans in Britain was seen to be feminine: the gender of the dryad that inhabits the tree*. However, to me, there are tree species that are most definitely masculine in energy: Oak, for instance; and Holly too.

Rowan was sacred to Bride/Brigid, or Brigantia, the Great Goddess, also sun-goddess, to the Celts, who in Maiden form is also the Lady of Imbolc. At the bottom of the little red Rowan berry there is a five-pointed star, or pentagram, as there is at the base of an apple which, like the Rowan flowers and also five-petalled dog rose or any of the *prunus* family blossom, is a symbol of dedication to the Goddess.

At this dark time of year, the sun's fire is sleeping in the cave of the heart, soon to stir to warm up the soil for new life. The berries of Rowan remind us of this fire. By the time we move out of Rowan month, the earth is more than midway between winter solstice and spring equinox, and the days are noticeably lengthening. We think of February as being a harsh month in the northern hemisphere, and sometimes there are hard frosts, and snow. But here in the Westcountry, February is often mild enough for us to sit outside, briefly and well-wrapped, in watery sunshine, and listen to the birds trying out spring songs.

We can carry some berries with us to remind us of Rowan's protective fire burning within us, to see us through this (and any) dark time.

Near here there is a traditional storyteller whom I see walking the lanes sometimes in his old-fashioned rural outfits, white whiskers and all. I went to hear him once, and he began a session by pulling out a small glass vial with three dried rowan berries in it – more powerful a gesture than I can rationally account for. (I sometimes find myself collecting three berries in autumn to carry with me.)

I love the Rowan tree, Luis. I look out for it wherever I go; and there's something particularly magical about its joyful presence in hilly and often bleak areas.

My favourite is one with three intertwined trunks. She is definitely a she: the Three Graces. I found her close to Samhain at Blackdown Rings in South Devon: a very beautiful Iron Age fort in line with various other forts and beacons, as well as with the rather magical Hound Tor on Dartmoor. In one corner there is a distinctive mediaeval motte; the Rowan, however, guards the opposite bank of the earthwork, overlooking a field with a big grey horse in it. (It's been my impression that Rowan has an affinity with animals generally; I suspect it's reciprocal.)

* 'The relationship between tree spirit and wood was thought to be similar to the relationship of the human mind and body, although the dryad might sometimes leave the wood and walk around.' (Fred Hageneder) As it happens, the perception of an indwelling spirit of a tree occurs throughout the world.

Rowan history and habits

Like Birch, Rowan is really another uplands tree, so is not as common in lusher lower lands. It might be that you will find 'yours', depending on where you live, as a cultivar in a park or a garden. It may particularly welcome, therefore, human attention. In places like Dartmoor, Wales, the Scottish Highlands, Rowan may be found following the footsteps of Birch up a hillside, or a stream. Stands of Rowans can be found at some altitude in mountainous areas. A hardy little tree, it is nonetheless not generally long-lived – forty-five or fifty years is its general lifespan, though there is one in Scotland that is known to be over a hundred.

Rowans live lightly: they don't over-shade the ground beneath them, so that other species can flourish, and their demands of the soil are slender. Sometimes, they seem to grow on bare rock.

Most of us, when thinking of Rowan, probably picture the berries, so copious in late summer that we'd think that time to be Rowan's.

August
and summer has spread
all across the bright moor
her red

rowan berries
Roselle Angwin

It might seem odd then that Rowan, with its associated shock of red berries, represents the winter, the dark face of the year, and it's not an easy tree to distinguish when bare, being understated in character (apart from its fruiting habits, which are wild and glorious) and not terribly tall.

Its bark is silvery-grey, not gleaming silver-white like Birch, and not as matte and dappled licheny grey-brown as Ash (despite Rowan's other name, Mountain Ash, it is not related to Ash as in *fraxinus excelsior*). In colour, the trunk sits somewhere between the two. It has yet another name: the Quickbeam, from the Old English cwicbeam ('cwic' as in 'quick', meaning alive, or conveying life). Its leaves are similar to Ash with parallel pairs lining the twig, tipped with a single leaf, but slightly finer and faintly serrated.

The name Rowan may come from the Norse 'ruan' meaning 'tree'; or it may be linked with the Old Icelandic 'runa' which can mean secret, or to whisper, as well as meaning a charm; and the Sanskrit 'runa', with the meaning of magician. This in turn probably links with 'rune' (properly, not the same as Ogham), and Rowan was used to carve rune staves, or sticks.

The gifts from Rowan

Rowan generally produces copious berries, welcome food for the overwintering resident and migrating flocks of thrush and blackbird, redwing and fieldfare in the cooler parts of our temperate zone.

For humans, the berries of this fine tree make a beautiful clear red-amber jelly. The berries contain a bitter alkaloid, parasorbic acid, that is not good to eat raw as it can cause digestive upsets, but they're OK cooked, and despite what I just said, the dried leaves and berries both can help with gastritis, diarrhoea and general cleansing of the kidneys and digestive system. It's powerful medicine, so you don't need much. (You can eat the odd berry raw from the tree: just one is quite thirst-quenching when you're hiking.)

Cook them up with crab apples too and you have the sun in a jamjar to store for the winter; or add elderberries to deepen the colour. They're quite tart in taste, and you will in any case have to use enough sugar to preserve the jelly (between 100% and 150% the weight of the fruit), but I like to keep the brew sharpish as they're better with savoury dishes than as a jam substitute.

Traditionally, they're eaten with strong-tasting game like pheasant; I eat them with vegan bakes and beanburgers. They're good alongside cheeses. I used to make a fine rowanberry wine, pale golden in colour.

Rowan wood was traditionally used for spindles and spinning wheels (presumably with invocations to the Goddess – it being associated with Brigid's arts of being muse for poetry, art, spinning and weaving).

Its mythology

Rowan, like several trees in this calendar, has connections with faery. It has always traditionally offered protection and guardianship to humans and domestic animals alike against the powers of darkness and the malevolent aspects of sorcery, or the so-called 'evil eye'. Although it is primarily the twigs that are used, sprigs of leaf and blossom, or sprays of berries, were also put into hatbands, hung above hearths, lintels, stable doors and barns, and even tucked into the headcollars of horses, or tacked above the manger of horse, cow or goat.

People wish on the rowan tree: at some level we know that it may give us entry into the Otherworld. In upland areas, old farmsteads often have a rowan near the house, or the gate. It's traditional to whisper them secrets, ask their protection out loud, and – on rare occasions (see the story below) – curse someone on the rowan tree.

Known also, like Birch, as the Bard's tree, in its history Rowan has been one of the most venerated trees. In times past, no one was allowed to use its timber, bark, leaves or flowers for other than sacred ritual (which could include, nonetheless, the placing of twigs above doorways and in stables and stalls against misfortune).

A Rowan twig was found in in a small bag in a Bronze Age burial tomb in Sweden – invoking safe guidance, safe passage, perhaps, to the departing spirit as it travelled between the worlds.

Rowan was seen as a mediator between this world and the next; or between quotidian reality and the Otherworld. It's perhaps for this reason that it was also used at Mayday, Beltane, one of the important seasonal festivals to our ancestors, both as mediator and as an inner and outer cleanser.

As a Faery Tree it was reputedly beloved of the Little Folk, Royal Race, the Good Neighbours who live in the hollow hills or near the ancient wells and sacred springs; this may be why people would whisper secrets to it.

Story

There is a modern-day myth, one could say – one of those rather tragic but true romances – relating to Rowan in the life-stories of Gavin Maxwell, author of *Ring of Bright Water*, and poet Kathleen Raine (Maxwell's book was titled from a poem of hers; one imagines written for him. As an aside, it was the reading of this poem, 'The Ring', aged 11, that set me on the course of becoming a poet.) The story as I tell it below is put together, very much abbreviated, from *The Saga of Ring of Bright Water*, by Douglas Botting.

Although Raine and Maxwell discovered, on first meeting each other, that they had places and ideas in common, their resulting friendship was extremely tumultuous, and ultimately destructive. Maxwell had a tremendous impact on Raine, and she fell inexorably in love with him. Maxwell was rather cavalier about people's falling in love with him; it seems it happened a great deal. However, he was basically homosexual, though Botting, his biographer, also calls him 'confused'. Whatever, Raine's love could not be returned as she would have liked; by all accounts, Maxwell rather used her.

A few days after they first met, Raine had a kind of vision of a Rowan tree covered in white blossom, and within its branches perched a blackbird. There was a boy of about twelve asleep at its foot. 'Tree, flower, fruit and bird, the very flow of life into and through the tree, was in the mind of the sleeper at the tree's foot – "his dream raising the tree and its flowers continually into being".' In her 'Northumberland Sequence', she wrote of this waking dream.

Amazingly, miles away from her, Maxwell had written a poem that in the sequence of images depicted her vision of the tree, though in his there was no sleeper and the blackbird had become an ousel (which I think is a related bird).

Just as amazingly, she didn't at that point know that Maxwell had a Rowan tree between the bridge and his house; a tree he was fond of, and which later became very important to her too.

Clearly, a poet might consider that this could only deepen, confirm, consolidate and affirm their relationship.

Maxwell had the greatest respect for her intellectual powers. As an older woman and a published poet he looked up to her, and began to believe she had special powers, magical powers, that set her apart from others.

Then one day he allowed her to stay at his beloved Camusfeàrna, or (properly) Sandaig, on the Scottish coast. Even though he wasn't there, she was, it seems blissfully happy, delighted too to discover and sit with her back to Maxwell's Rowan tree: 'What a miracle, what unimaginable blessedness, to be here and now at the place on earth I most desire to be; by

Gavin's rowan.' (He also noted that she'd sat beneath his Rowan tree.)

She felt that it was a calling for her to 'enrich and transmute for him his world into poetry' – which she did.

Not long after, Raine was given a lift by Maxwell from London to Cumberland; he was travelling back to Sandaig and she was going to stay with a friend, the painter Winifred Nicholson, but they were caught in a snowstorm in the Borders and decided to make an overnight stop in an hotel.

This involved a contretemps that was the beginning of the end. Raine, presumably in an attempt at intimacy, showed Maxwell diary entries about him and his sexuality, which both impressed and incensed him. That night, in an incident that he described as 'appallingly embarrassing', she tried, unsuccessfully, to seduce him. He repelled her, and she sat up most of the night writing him a lengthy letter.

That night, she also had a dream about Sandaig, in which the house and the Rowan tree were barred to her by a high wooden fence, and all the beauty of the place destroyed.

Later again, the friendship patched but only patched, Raine was staying at Sandaig while Maxwell was away for some weeks, to look after his beloved otter Mij. 'Like some shrine I tended his house,' she was to write, decorating it with sea shells and wildflowers. When Maxwell returned, however, with a male friend, he was outraged to find Raine still there, and thundered at her, throwing her out.

Distraught, she fled the house in floods of tears. Halfway between the bridge over the burn and the house was the Rowan tree. As Botting records it:

'Beside herself with anguish and weeping aloud, she laid her hands on the trunk and called upon the tree for justice. "Let Gavin suffer in this place, as I am suffering now!" she cried. She was calling for the loosing of the lightning from the magic tree. To Kathleen, this was not so much a curse as a "desperate heart's cry for truth".'

But the incident has gone down in the history of Gavin Maxwell as a curse laid on him by Raine on the Rowan.

Raine did return to Sandaig some time later, and was shocked to find the house, and the Rowan tree, enclosed by just such a fence as she had dreamed of those years before, and she felt repelled by an 'intangible negative force'.

She confessed to Maxwell in passing that she had cursed him on his Rowan tree, and Maxwell was aghast and distraught, for he was sure she had genuine occult powers, and was in fact a witch (of the malevolent sort). She had asked him to marry her, but nothing would have persuaded him.

In fact, her curse – or plea – to the Rowan tree did seem to announce the beginning of a series of extreme misfortunes in Maxwell's life, from the illnesses and deaths of his otters, to his own car accident and the burning-down of his house at Sandaig; and then his final illness.

Although there was contact between them, initiated by Maxwell as much as Raine, and they even tried sharing the house, they could not move beyond the friction that arose every time they were together. 'You are a destroyer, Kathleen', he'd said to her, and he continued to 'disown and deny any participation in a relationship I had thought mutual', as she wrote.

But the thread wasn't severed. Once he knew that he was dying, he wrote to her, saying: 'I am just asking you to accompany me in spirit', and received in return a letter expressing the depths of her love for him. He asked for poems, and she sent him, among others, one of the most beautiful and moving poems she'd written, for the occasion and for him. Though they wouldn't see each other again in this life, some sort of reconciliation had happened, and Maxwell had by his bedside in the hospital a collection of her poetry; one of only two volumes he read while in there.

Kathleen was among the friends who returned to the bulldozed blackened remains of Sandaig where Maxwell's ashes were scattered.

I am the mist over a wide river-valley

Apart from the fact that in our part of the world misty mornings over the brook in the valley are a frequent characteristic of this time of year, in my imagination this phrase has to do with penetrating the veils between this world and the Otherworld, entering the mists that hide Avalon from our everyday sight. Remember how King Arthur, dying, was conveyed in a barge on the wide water by nine priestesses through the mists to Avalon?

Symbolism of Rowan

As a powerful talisman, we could see Rowan as a guide when we journey into the unknown, and as a protector of our home, and our being in general.

With its roots in the Otherworld and branches in this, so to speak, Rowan can help us draw back the veils of unknowing so that we might see more clearly, especially when we feel we are straying in the dark, and understand the purpose of our journey here from a subtler perspective. Rowan can help us reconnect to our higher knowing and purpose.

Rowan protects, guards, guides and cleanses us on many levels, and connects us too to sources of inspiration. Remember its connection with Bards, music, poetry (via its link with Brigid) and divination.

Rowan

Lost on the moor
in a Grimpen Mire fog

wandering like orphans
you, dell-dweller, called us

we fell into the soft green
bowl of turf that held you
in this stony place
and now palmed us

you, rowan, blazed
your red berries
like eldritch fire
that lit us not after all

into the bog
but instead pointed
the way home
the way we'd almost forgotten
Roselle Angwin

N for Nion (Nuinn): the Ash Tree

Fraxinus excelsior
February 18th–March 17th
The World Tree/Queen of the Woods
Connection, relationship, inspiration

I am the wind on deep waters and the returning tide

ASH, NION

The Celtic calendar and alphabet continues now into its third lunar month with Ash, Nion or Nuinn, for N.

'The ash grove, how graceful, how plainly 'tis speaking
The harp (wind) through it playing has language for me...'

At this point, I should say that – bearing in mind that anything to do with Celtic Ogham calendar-alphabets is speculative, as we don't know for certain – some (later) calendars reverse the positions of Ash and Alder, as Alder grew more important in Celtic mythology. However, I've always known this as the Beth-Luis-Nion calendar, so for the moment at least I'm staying with this order.

Ash is a beautiful, graceful tree, known in the past as Venus of the Woods. Its leaves are paired rather in the way that Rowan's are, but there are fewer on a stem, and they're slightly larger and not toothed. The branches are arranged opposite each other.

One of the things about Ash that pleases me every year at around this time is the fact that I can use the phrase 'apical helisphere', to describe the growing tip, most noticeable in the Ash when it is tipped with the prominent sooty-black pointy swelling that will open into early magenta and yellow flowers, followed by the feathery leaves.

The Ash, as a light-loving tree, also lets sun and air through its canopy. Elegant and ethereal, her delicate leaves nurture a host of species of flora and fauna. To sit beneath one on a summer's day is a very calming experience, in the dappling grace of its leaf-light.

Ash takes us almost up to the vernal equinox. If Oak is the king of the forest, at its zenith on the summer solstice, Ash has to be the queen. The more you look for these two trees, the more you notice that they often occur paired. Arguably, they are the two most iconic species of the UK.

While the Oak has a wide, sturdy, spreading habit, Ash tends to height (up to 45 or so metres) and slenderness; it's a *neat* tree, although an older and coppiced Ash can be twisted, gnarled and hollow, at which point it will also likely be hosting a full and well-developed ecosystem. It doesn't become fully-grown till it's about 100 years old, and can thrive for several centuries after that. An older Ash may have branches that are downward-curving, with a bit of an upward flick at their ends, rather like a cat's tail.

Britain has something like 80 million Ash trees (or at least did have in 2012, before Ash dieback had really taken a hold) and counts don't generally include the extremely-numerous and probably very ancient coppiced Ash-stools in hedges and woodlands.

Sadly, as you will know, Ash trees all over the country in the UK are suffering from Ash dieback, where the leaves start to disappear from the crowns. Some arborists suggest we might lose 80% of this ancient and iconic species to the wind-borne fungal disease. The Government has acted far too late to ban the import of foreign Ashes apparently responsible for bringing in the disease from Eastern Europe – some would say completely unnecessarily anyway, given how well the Ash tree grows, or has grown, here, and how prolific it is – at the moment.

We have several that have succumbed on our land; a

nurseryman friend tells us not to cut them down, however, as we don't yet know which will recover and continue to produce strong and resistant offspring.

And it seems there's little that can be done. All we, the public, can do apparently is to wash our hands after visiting woodland in order to try and halt its spread. (It's rather reminiscent of the Government's instructions for the event of a nuclear disaster in the 70s/80s: paint yourself white and hide under the kitchen table. But it may, may possibly, help halt the spread.)

A year or two ago I wrote:

'Because of the time of year here in the UK, I've been noting with joy a kind of green aura around each of the young Ash trees in the avenue along the brookside path below our house (I say 'aura' because they are not in any visible way actually leafing, but from a distance there is a very distinct green tinge to the whole stand, as well as each tree).'

Now as I walk through, I speak to them, I tell them I care about them, wish them vitality and longevity. What else can we do? As we are interconnected, then it may be that at some level they 'receive' the care we put out, and are affected by it, as we are reciprocally by them, whether or not we're conscious of it.

Ash history and habits

Ash trees can be male, female or hermaphrodite, botanically-speaking. They can basically grow anywhere, although they prefer limestone soils to acidic ones, and are one of our commonest, and oldest, tree species.

You may see in the hedges enormous old spreading 'stools' of Ash, where they've been laid, or steeped, or coppiced in the past, but continue to put up runners. Many hollow Ashes still survive, and continue to provide habitat for other species. The poet John Clare called these 'dotterel ashes':

how oft a summer shower has started me
to seek the shelter of a hollow tree
old huge ash dotterel wasted to a shell
whose vigorous head still grew and flourished well
where ten might sit upon the battered floor
and still look round discovering room for more...
John Clare, ca. 1825

One of the latest trees to come into leaf, they can still be fairly readily identified in the spring by their fat sooty-black buds. They will continue to bear their clusters of keys from the previous season like bundles of pygmy bats, or leftover musical notes. Or, said a friend of mine, like left-out punctuation from a James Joyce novel.

Their bark, though smooth, is often flecked with subtle colour: pale gold, pale green-grey, grey-white. Very often they will host mosses or liverworts.

The gifts from Ash

As a species, we've used Ash for a long time. Ash timber was found as a component of a Neolithic trackway in Somerset, dating from about 3800 BCE.

The countryman's staff was his Ashplant. As they grow fast, straight and true, Ash sticks have traditionally made rafters in ancient roundhouses, been cut for staves, for tool handles, for arrows, for spear shafts, for axles, for spindles, for hoops binding barrels, and more. John Evelyn in 1664 in his book *Sylva* describes how Ash was used by 'Carpenter, Wheel-wright, Cart-wright, Cooper, Turner and Thatcher' and for 'Carts, Ladders' and more; and William Cobbett in 1825 declared that 'We would not well have a wagon, a cart, a coach or a wheelbarrow, a plough, a harrow, a spade, an axe or a hammer, if we had no ash.'

Its straight grain, pale colour and high tensile strength and flexibility make it valuable for furniture. I remember watching a cabinet-maker friend heat the off-white Ash wood in a steam cabinet to bend into exquisite chair-backs, and for other furniture. I have a round table that he made me from Ash – pale and beautiful it is.

Ash has always provided good fodder for herbivores, notably cattle. Its branches were routinely cut, in effect pollarding the tree, to feed fresh or dried, rather like hay, in the past. It's said that this practice dates back to Neolithic times.

For humans, its minor healing powers are associated with digestive and kidney problems, gout and rheumatism, with the bark of the root being the most potent.

Ash leaves form a rich humus, nourishing the soil where they fall, and are less acidic than Oak.

Its mythology

For the Celts, Ash is a tree of returning, (re)making relationship between the unconscious mind and the conscious, between inner and outer, so that spring (in the northern hemisphere) might flow again through our veins.

Ash also, to the Celts, was considered to exert power over water. Traditionally, the Celtic peoples would incorporate Ash timber into their boats to prevent their sinking.

In some cultures, Ash was feminine; in others, masculine. For instance, in Old Norse mythology, in the *Eddas*, which are both poetry and prose accounts of 'In the beginning', Ask and Embla were the first created human beings, like Adam and Eve in the Garden of Eden. Here, Ask is the man, and Embla the woman, both created out of tree trunks that the gods, while strolling by a river-lake, lifted from the shoreline. Ask is an Ash; Embla we're not so sure about – it might mean Elm. The Vikings were known as 'Aesling': 'men of Ash'. (I need to say here, though, that in Celtic mythology the first man was probably Alder, the first woman Rowan.)

If you have read A S Byatt's magnificent and intricate book

Possession, you might remember that an important conceit was the creation by the fictional Victorian poet Randolph Henry Ash (NB) of a body of work, in poetic form, of the story of Ask and Embla. Embedded within this is a kind of declaration and plea to his contemporary poet-friend Christabel LaMotte, in which Ask and Embla represent, among other motifs, the possibility of a pure and pristine love relationship as befits a Garden of Eden story.

Druids' wands were sometimes made of Ash, so there was a less utilitarian or aggressive quality to the wood in addition to its being used for tools or spears. The sea-god Manannan's trident, like that of Manawyddan or Poseidon, was constructed of Ash. This links both the creative force of the solar willpower associated with spears and arrows, magically speaking, with the receptivity of water, the ocean, the feminine.

Its Old Irish name *nion* links it with Nodens, or Nuada of the Silver Hand, a king of the Otherworldly race of the Tuatha dé Danaan, first inhabitants of what is now Ireland.

Odin, perhaps one representative of the Hanged Man of the tarot, was hanged from the World Tree for three days and three nights – a story of initiation through transformation rather than death *per se*. (Some accounts say nine days and nine nights.) The Ash is Odin's tree – but it's also the tree of his wife, Frigg.

For nine days and nine nights
I hung on the windswept Tree.
I was struck with a spear and given
to Odin – myself given to myself.
(from the Eddas)

And Yggdrasil is the World Ash, the World Tree – though before this the World Tree was, conceivably, a Yew. This transition may mark a movement away from the 'old' ideas of the Neolithic to a more worldly outlook that arrived with the late Bronze Age and early Iron Age: it seems that Iron Age warriors preferred Ash to Yew for their weapons, too, according to tree expert and author Fred Hageneder.

I am the wind on deep waters and the returning tide

The phrase 'I am a wind on deep waters' has tremendous poetic resonance for me; of all the key-phrases in the Song it is the one, for me, with the most charge; the most profound and potent. However, it doesn't immediately give up its meaning; I'd be hard put to explain it, intellectually.

Here's an attempt. It's worth bearing in mind that, archetypally speaking, Jung suggests that air (wind) is 'masculine' in tone where water is 'feminine'; air representing the intellect and the thinking function, water the emotional and feeling aspect.

Historically, some of our human creation stories start with the wind-god making love with the sea-goddess, impregnating her.

In some cultures, it was believed that mares – themselves companions and symbols of the Goddess – could be impregnated by the wind, usually the east wind.

The image of wind, or a breeze, occurs occasionally in the arts to symbolise inception/conception/impregnation:

– a wind ruffling the table cloth outdoors at the very opening of the film *Amélie* supposedly symbolises her conception
– at the beginning of the film *Chocolat*, Vian and her daughter Anoukh are borne on the (north) wind into their new life and home.

We could see this keynote as a depiction of the meeting between masculine and feminine, out of which much that is creative can arise. It's also the case that the sun is born – rises – in the east (air, in some medicine wheels, including my own), and dies –

sets – in the west (water). Between the two is the spectrum of day.

'Returning tide'? As spring is ushered in, we are moving towards the tide of green coming to flood the land: the 'life' aspect again, after winter, of what Clarissa Pinkola Estes reminds us is the continuing cycle of life/death/life.

The Ash in Davy Hallett's Hedge

This old ash is tired of the wheelings
of the Milky Way. It's seen five thousand
moons climb up its blotchy trunk; witnessed

enclosures, the slow erosion of the land, the exiling
of badgers, foxes, countryfolk. It's kept its own
counsel about the hoard of history, the loamy

bundle of coins buried at its feet. It hasn't
counted the generations of farmers taking shade
at lunchtime; watches impartially over barley failure,

mellow years. It bears a crop of initials, men
and women long gone in the tide, the letters
each year stretching further. It's host to birdsong

and the exuberance of spring. From the limb
on which the tyre now swings, plaything
for Davy's children's children, once a man

hanged himself.
                    The ash is tired.
Half its limbs have shed themselves; each year
the twigspread's thinner. Now it's fading,

dying gently from the crown. Still, though,
scraps of sky snag in its branches, and at night
stars dance in the gaps like messages of hope.
Roselle Angwin

Symbolism of Ash

I've always had the sense that Ash might be a boundary tree. Somehow it seems to epitomise 'right relationship', 'right connectedness', and so on – not too distant, not too close. (I personally experience an Ash boundary through the fact that I find Ash a little slippery to engage with: slightly aloof, almost; impersonal. It might be different for you.)

If it is about right relations, it is also about finding balance – balance between intimacy and solitude, between feminine, masculine and the synthesis of the two.

As we emerge from winter storms towards the spring equinox here in Britain the weather veers between wild winds and gentler days. The Ash stands steady, canopy yielding gently, roots well planted, as the earth prepares for the flood of returning spring to come in.

Ash is also an opener tree: into the realms of inspiration.

F for Fearn: the Alder tree

Alnus glutinosa
March 18th–April 14th
Alder King as Bridge
Balance, magical transformations, mystery

I am the song of a shining tear of the sun

ALDER, FEARN

In my Celtic calendar and alphabet, we move now into the fourth lunar month, with the time of the Alder tree, F for Fearn, Alnus glutinosa, a member of the Birch family. (If you see Alder and Birch side-by-side you can see the similarity.)

To me, the Alder is a secret (not quite secretive) tree, and has an air of self-containment and mystery about it. When you walk through a cluster of Alder trees there is a feeling of something otherworldly, and somehow populous, about the grove.

I have found that the Alder has crept up on me. Alder is overlooked by many people, myself included. Until the last decade or so, Alder rather eluded my interest until I started to notice that around this time of year (from January onwards) there was a thread of trees alongside the brook in our valley who, like the Birch, also started to bear reddy-purple crowns, with a greyish cast.

Investigating further, I realised that these trees with their feet in the water and whose branches were decorated with tiny dark cones (unusually for a deciduous tree, of course) even as they were beginning to sprout new lime-green then reddish catkins were Alder. The cones are the female parts of the tree, the catkins the male. It's the older catkins, along with the twigs beginning to wake up to leaf buds in the late winter or very early spring, that give the tree their reddish tinge.

I have come to very much appreciate Alder. I enjoy being in its company, but I'm respectful of its self-containment, and its magical properties. (NB this is my experience: yours might be quite different.)

Alder history and habits

Like the Oak, it seems that the Alder tree arrived on our British shores in about 8000 BCE.

As with the Willow, another inhabitant of wettish places, Alder carr offers good habitat to many members of the ecosystem, and biochemically changes the ground, fixing nitrogen and creating a nutrient-rich environment for other trees to follow after; so Alders are trees of transformation in a literal sense, as well as in their metaphorical context (more below).

Alders are relatively fast-growing, but are not especially long-lived – they thrive for about 75 or 80 years, on average.

Their leaves are oval, slightly pointed or sometimes with an indented tip, and leathery; not dissimilar to either Beech or Hazel but tougher than Beech, smoother than Hazel, and darkish green.

The gifts from Alder

To the Hopi, Alder was a sacred tree. Different parts of it produced the dyes that together form three sacred colours for the Hopi: red, yellow, black.

Here in Britain, it's mentioned in the Welsh Triads that the red sap was used as a dye by 'sacred kings and warriors of the alder cult'. It also gives a green dye, which is said to produce the Lincoln green used for the garments both of Robin Hood and his Merry Men, and for the faery folk (think leprechauns). In both cases, the green helps to conceal the wearer from unwanted eyes.

I am the green that tints the clothes of fairy folk and forest
folk
of those who hide from human eyes and live where humans
seldom go
I am more than just a colour   I am a way of being
more than chlorophyll and light   I am a way of seeing
Sheena Odle

In European culture Alder was used to make bridges (being somewhat rot-resistant), to make boats, and also to make shields, and spears, as well as clogs. Apparently, parts of Venice and the foundations of several mediaeval cathedrals were built on Alder pilings or foundations. More ancient are the foundations of the little crannogs, stone 'islands' built by Neolithic humans in the Scottish lochs; of Alder in many cases.

Being very fine-grained, it was also an excellent wood for charcoal, and was used extensively as charcoal for gunpowder in various historic battles.

The bark of Alder, like Willow, contains salicin, the active ingredient for salicylic acid, an analgesic from which aspirin was derived.

Rather more poetically, it is said that a whistle made from green Alder wood will call up the winds, or air sprites (sylphs) and water sprites (or undines).

Its mythology

In an Irish legend, the first man was made from Alder, and the first woman from Rowan.

In Celtic mythology, the Alder is very much linked with Bendigeidfran, Bendigeituran (which means 'Blessed' or 'praiseworthy'), or Brân, whose magical tale appears in the Mabinogion. As one of the Children of Llyr, an Otherworldly race, he was known too as Brân fab Llŷr. Yet another name is Brân of the Singing Head. Brân, whose name means (and who is symbolised also by) 'Raven' or 'Crow', is known as the Alder King.

Robert Graves translates the crow or raven as 'sea-crow' in relation to Brân. This is interesting, as the sea-crow is presumably the chough: a cousin to the jackdaw, but a slimmer acrobatic bird with red legs and a red beak. Found on the sea-cliffs of Ireland, Wales and Cornwall, it would once have been abundant near Caer Brân, the Iron Age hillfort associated with Brân, and the most westerly caer on the Atlantic coasts of Britain.

The chough is strongly linked with Cornwall and occurs on the Cornish coat of arms, and frequently in other Cornish heraldry. There is a legend which says that if the chough dies out, the Celtic Cornish nation and its language will too. A few years ago, both seemed true; but there are now a few breeding pairs of choughs re-establishing themselves in Cornwall, and the Cornish have once again (April 2014) been officially recognised as a minority nation, and with a growing number of Cornish language revivalists.

It was said that choughs, like ravens, were to be found also at the Tower of London; for the relevance of this, see the story coming up below.

Although it's not certain why Brân was connected with the Alder tree (the relevant details may have been lost after the oral tradition came to a close), Jacqueline Memory Patterson has this to say: 'Such was the reputed harmony of the music played on Alder pipes that the topmost branch of the Alder tree became known as the 'oracular singing tree of the raven god Brân...'.

In other accounts, it's because Alder was sacred to the Druids and is associated with protection and oracular powers, both of which were attributes of Brân. On the living tree, omens were read in the way the branches moved in the wind, and heard in the rustle of its leaves; in other words, its 'head' was oracular as, after his death, was the head of Brân, the warrior god whose totem tree it was. We might say, esoterically, that the singing 'head', or crown, of the tree, like the singing head of Brân, could represent the opening of the crown chakra in a human.

It may also be that Alder was the totem of a particular tribe, and associated with this king or god. (Throughout the Celtic and Gaulish worlds tribes often took the names of trees, as they did too in Teutonic and Nordic cultures.)

Here's my telling of Brân's story; it comes from the second Branch of *The Mabinogion*, that collection of early mediaeval Welsh magical tales (through which I had the pleasure of stumbling in Middle Welsh for my degree course).

Brân, King of the Island of the Mighty and a giant of a man, whose name means Raven or Crow, was asked one day by the Irish High King, Matholwch, for the hand of his sister, Brânwen ('White Raven' or 'White Crow'), in marriage. Brân was pleased to agree (his sister, of course, had no say in the matter), and to forge strong alliances between the two kingdoms.

At first, everything seemed fine. However, the marriage was rather doomed from the start when Efnisien, half-brother to Brân and the other Children of Llyr, brutally cut off the ears of the horses of Matholwch in revenge for the High King not having also sought his permission for Brânwen to marry.

All seemed to be healed, however, when Brân in appeasement offered Matholwch the marvellous cauldron, known in myth as Ceridwen's Cauldron, one of the wonders of Britain, in which dead warriors could be placed to return them to life.

For three years everything seemed quiet and peaceable.

One day, however, Brân received a visit from a chough, who made a point of landing on the king's shoulder and drawing attention to itself with ruffling feathers and many variations of song and chacking. At first, the king didn't perceive him, the bird being the size of a flea to Brân's enormity. Then, to the king's astonishment, something started to speak his name in a high voice, over and over. It was the chough, and Brân, turning his head, noticed that the bird had, bound to its wing, a letter.

The letter was from Brânwen, telling how she'd tamed the bird under cover of darkness, and taught it how to find her brother. Her letter spoke of the cruelty of Matholwch: that she had become a scullery-maid, had to cook for the court, and was regularly beaten. She begged that Brân might come and rescue her, bring her home.

Brân, incensed, called his army to him.

Brân was a huge man, and lacking ships big enough to carry him he merely waded across the Irish Sea, with his armies and his pipers on his shoulders.

As he neared the Irish shore, men ran to the king, saying that they had seen a forest on the sea, where there had never before even been a tree, and that in that forest they had also seen a moving mountain.

The king asked Brânwen, the queen, what she thought it might be.

'These are the men of the Island of the Mighty,' she responded, 'who have come hither to protect me.'

'But what is the forest?' the king's men asked.

'The yards and masts of ships.'

'And what is the mountain by the side of the ships?'

'It is Brân my brother, coming to the shallows and rising.'

'What is the lofty ridge with the lake on each side?'

'That is his nose,' she said, 'and the two lakes are his fierce eyes.'

The High King of Ireland found himself somewhat afraid. Pointlessly, considering that Brân had crossed the ocean by wading, he commanded his men to tear down the bridge that crossed the wide stretch of the River Shannon between the shore and the palace. To Brân, of course, it was barely even a minor inconvenience: he laid his own body down so that his men could treat him as a bridge that would allow them all to come to the aid of his sister.

Brânwen, and her young son, Gwern, were rescued by the company; and it was the turn of the High King of Ireland to offer appeasement. Because of Brân's size, no one had ever built a house that could fully contain him and also give him space, so Matholwch commanded his best builders to make that house.

But trickery was at work, and luckily Brân's suspicious half-brother found it out in time. In the great hall of the house, a hundred leather bags were hung, supposedly containing flour. Efnisien went round the hall putting his enormous hand (for he too, of course, was a giant) into each bag and crushing the skull of what was actually one of Matholwch's armed warriors within.

Nothing is ever simple, is it? Feeling himself insulted by the High King's actions, Efnisien once again took revenge, this time by killing Matholwch and Brânwen's son, Gwern. At that, a serious battle broke out.

Efnisien made amends to Brânwen: noticing that the High King was sensibly restoring his dead Irish warriors to life in the famous cauldron he lay down himself among the dead warriors, and was thrown into the cauldron. He was able to break the cauldron once and for all from the inside, and sacrificed his own life by so doing.

Brânwen, however, saved from her sad life, died of a broken heart at the loss of her son.

Seven men only from Brân's huge army, drawn from all of the 54 *cantrefs* of mainland Britain ('Ynys Prydein'), survived the conflict, Brân among them, but he had taken a poisoned dart in his foot and knew he would die.

He instructed his men to cut off his head once he had died, and promised that he would be with them, talking and singing; and so he was, through seven years in Harlech, and eighty on an island off the coast of Wales; eighty-seven years of forgetfulness, feasting, singing, merriment, and no one ageing.

But Brân had told them that, of the three doors in the hall on the island, they mustn't open the door that faces West, and Cornwall (Kernow). Eventually, of course, one of their number did so: and suddenly all the misfortunes they'd suffered, all the sorrows and tragedies of the world, all the ageing that hadn't troubled them to date, poured in and they could not stay.

Brân's final instruction to them was to take his head to the White Mound, Bryn Gweyn, in London (Caer Llyndain), upon which the Tower of London now stands; and to bury it there, looking out to Gaul. He would continue to sing, he promised, and his eyes towards Gaul would ensure no invasions from that direction.

As long as his head remained buried, and ravens still lived in the Tower, Britain would be protected, goes the story.

And Cornwall? In the far west, looking out over the sea in almost every direction, as I've mentioned is Caer Brân, a magical circular hillfort, said to be a benign place of refuge as well as the place where the *pobel vean*, the 'little folk', reside. I know the place well, and I have the distinct sense, each time I'm there, that a protective masculine energy presides over and guards the land below: the various barrows and tumuli, the beautiful Iron Age courtyard village of Carn Euny, and especially Sancreed well in the valley.

In Sancreed church there are three carved crows, or ravens (or, according to my theory, choughs) hosting Brân's spirit.

I also have a sense, correctly or otherwise, that the name Sancreed might point all the way back to the Brythonic Mother Goddess Ceridwen, she of the Cauldron of Eternal Life, mentioned in Brân's story. (The well, of course, is cauldron, Grail, and womb all at once; and mythologically such a well will have regenerative powers.) If so, this is a beautiful pairing, Brân as protector of the feminine in the valley. (Madron Well is supposed to be the original 'Mother Well' of Cornwall, as the name suggests, but I believe that Sancreed is a more powerful place, and the well there the original omphalos.)

I am the song of a shining tear of the sun

Here is the fiery sun-god shining through, and there's the raindrop that represents, we could say, water and the goddess. If we met the opposites in Ash, now we are bringing them together.

Symbolism of Alder

Alder, with its roots in water and the reddish colour of its upper branches in spring, has been seen as resonant with both the feminine element of water, and the masculine element of fire, reflected in its bearing of male catkins and female cones on the same tree.

Alder, like Brân in the myth, forms a bridge between the masculine and the feminine, its time spanning the spring equinox when the pairs of opposites – earth and heaven, night and day, dark and light, moon and sun (symbolically if not actually), and masculine and feminine – are held in perfect balance for just a little while. (Alder, from its growth habits, also connects earth and water, of course; two aspects of the feminine, just as air and fire are two aspects of the masculine.)

In the ancient Brythonic poem, the 'Cad Goddeu', or 'Battle of the Trees', the Alder was named as the first tree, the 'battle-witch tree of the woods'.

These two words together hint at how the tree was seen, archetypally: as a tree fit for battle (its wood was used for shields and spears both, being light and durable), and a tree with otherworldly powers. There is also this:

> The high sprigs of alder are on thy shield;
> Brân art thou called, of the glittering branches.

> Sure-hoofed is thy steed in the day of battle:
> The high sprigs of alder are in thy hand:
> Brân thou are, by the branch thou bearest...
> from *The White Goddess*, Robert Graves

In the myth of Brân, we remember that the Alder King also champions the feminine, the Queen Brânwen, his sister, whose name means 'White Raven' (with the previous caveat). Alder, then, can represent the warrior within, the inner king who will fight to protect the feminine and the feeling nature, as well as bridging the energies of masculine and feminine, head and heart, fire and water.

His song is perhaps an invocation of higher nature, higher powers.

Alder reminds us of the potency and essential qualities of the inner worlds; that we need to return to them often, and to bring them together with the outer.

'The battle-witch tree.' Alder will enter conflict when there is no alternative, and fight on. Alder also encourages visionary qualities and helps the development of psychic shields.

S for Saille: the Willow (Sallow) Tree

Salix
April 15th–May 12th
The Musician and Seer's Tree
The intuition, the unconscious, the emotional & dreaming life

I am the Hawk of May, balanced above the cliff

WILLOW, SAILLE

Down By the Salley Gardens

Down by the salley gardens
my love and I did meet;
She passed the salley gardens
with little snow-white feet.
She bid me take love easy,
as the leaves grow on the tree;
But I, being young and foolish,
with her would not agree.

In a field by the river
my love and I did stand,
And on my leaning shoulder
she laid her snow-white hand.
She bid me take life easy,
as the grass grows on the weirs;
But I was young and foolish,
and now am full of tears.

In the 1880s, Irish poet William Butler Yeats wrote the poem above, better known now as a folk-song. The 'Salley' in the title is the then-contemporary Irish name for the Saille, or Willow tree (and from which we also get Sallow, a Willow variant).

This has particular resonance for me as when my mum had Alzheimer's one of the few things left that we could do together was sing this song, which she loved.

Willow takes us from the stormy promise of spring towards summer. In the old calendar, it would be high summer, and Willow's time includes the old midsummer day of Beltane. There is a great deal to say about Willow, and I find that, like the physical tree itself but also what I have to call its vibe, it spreads and spreads, and words can rather emulate that and become somewhat rambling.

Willow is, after all, a tree of great sympathy with water, which left to itself is uncontained and spills everywhere, knows no boundaries (hence its connection with intuition, the dream life and the subconscious, all of which transgress the boundaries of the rational mind), and leads us dreaming by the hand (I have a favourite old Willow down by the brook in the valley which curves out just so, making a seat over the water: I think of it as my 'dreaming tree').

Willow, which is most frequently found growing by water and is much more 'watery' in its nature than the also-water-loving Alder, propagates itself of course by the female blowsy seed heads of catkins blowing away on the breeze, but also by dropping its twigs into the water.

If you've ever tried to grow Willow, you will know that a cut twig stuck into the ground will grow so easily and quickly that before you know it your garden will be dominated by a full-grown tree. In the days when I was a shoemaker, working out of the National Trust workshops at Francis Drake's old home, Buckland Abbey in Devon, my next door neighbour, who was a basketmaker, cut me a Willow pole which he drove into the ground to form one end of a washing-line in my garden. Within 18 months, I had a fully-fledged tree, home to various tits as well as willow warblers.

If it's the indigenous White Willow, *salix alba*, this tree could reach 25m, about 80 feet, in height.

Most of us are familiar with the Weeping Willow, or with the Goat Willow, better known as the Pussy Willow, which is properly a Sallow, in fact. (There is – in a complete disregard for boundaries – a great deal of hybridisation that goes on in the Willow family.)

Willow history and habits

Washing lines aside, my own history with tree nature began with Willow.

Some time back in the last century, I conducted a transatlantic interview for a leading mind, body, spirit magazine with Eliot Cowan, author of *Plant Spirit Medicine*. That interview changed my understanding of our relationship with plants.

By the time I did the interview, I'd been working myself with plants for a very long time: as foraged foods, as medicines, as dyestuffs, as the ingredients for the ceremonial incenses I used to make and sell. I knew the plant world, especially the wild and herbal plant world, well. But this was something else: both a quantum leap and also, it seemed, drawing to the surface something I'd always known but forgotten. My connection with plants and trees was amplified by 100, 1000, times.

I had favourite trees. Like many people of a romantic disposition, I'd focused in particular on the Rowan tree, that elegantly robust little survivor on our uplands, with its magical reputation and its cluster of jewel-red berries lighting the shoulders of Dartmoor or the hillsides of Scotland, presaging the end of summer.

Always in my consciousness has been both the Silver Birch and also the Hazel, another magical tree to the Celts with, like Willow, its affinity for water (Hazel was, and still is, commonly used for dowsing) and all its connotations of wisdom.

Not long after the plant spirit interview I'd taken a week off to go to West Cornwall, renting a small place within the sheltering arms of a triple earthwork – iron age fogou included – near Lamorna, with the intention to explore plant spirit medicine more thoroughly.

I knew the area, and had imagined I'd spend time investigating the bond between me, human, Rowan, Birch and Hazel, so having dumped my stuff I went off for a stroll on the land, assuming I'd encounter some of these trees.

Immediately, however, I found my awareness hijacked by a particular tree, a Willow, in a grove of Willow carr. The tree was friendly but extremely insistent, in a way that I'd not known a tree could be; and for the rest of that day, and indeed the whole rest of that week, I spent much of my time near that Willow, which had turned out so quickly to be my plant ally. Alongside this tree, I had some strange and particular inner-world experiences, sometimes of an out-of-body nature.

This whole thing took me by surprise, and unsettled me; not least because I'd taken little notice of Willow before, despite using its pain-relieving properties for humans and animals in my family. Also, I was rather taken aback that such a gentle-seeming tree could be so – well, forthright and demanding.

Ever since then, though, I've been aware of it and its whispers. Back in Devon as I look down the little lost valley its stand of Willows I notice even before the huge and stately old Oak: the dozen or so of them swaying in the breeze in their slender tall *willowiness*, for Willow when it's not been coppiced or pollarded (usually as an osier or withy for basket-making, hurdle-making and the like) is both tall and elegant. They stand out, too, for the silvery underside of their leaves, distinctive from a distance. And there is nothing like a stand of leafless Willow in late winter blazing their red-gold trunks and stems to lift the heart in the apparently unending drabness.

When I was a child growing up on the banks of the Caen

Stream in North Devon (on which Henry Williamson set his classic book *Tarka the Otter*), myself and my sisters used to cross the stream and slip into the small park where the Weeping Willow sobbed its way right to the ground. We had enough cover under its sheltering tent to believe ourselves to be completely invisible to passersby whom we would, we hoped, surprise by our soft songs and whispers emanating apparently from the tree.

The gifts from Willow

Willow supports a vast number of insect species (and thereby the birds that feed on them), and its male pussy willows and female catkins provide an early source of pollen and nectar for bees.

It is one of the trees that has offered most to humans. In wet countries like Britain Willow has been the main material for making baskets, stock fences, containers of various sorts, the wattle in wattle and daub huts, and even coracles, as well as besoms or brooms. On Shetland, a Willow basket from the sixth century showed that the technique we use currently is not too different from that of fifteen hundred years ago. Astonishingly, still extant is a fishing 'net' woven from Willow way back in around 8300 BCE.

Willow is also widely used for decorative sculptures (as well as living bowers). If you drive up the M5 north towards the junction for Wells and Glastonbury an enormous woven Wicker Man is poised mid-stride at the edges of the Somerset Levels, widely-known for their basket-makers and Willow trees. On the A303 heading east through Somerset a small Willow deer is poised, leaping out of a hedge.

And there is a beautiful Willow stag in the woodland sculpture walk at Calgary Bay, Isle of Mull.

Willow is used for cricket bats (usually the white Willow, *salix alba*) and – the musician's tree – harps; and in the construction of double basses. The finest artists' charcoal comes from Willow.

Willow-beds, like reedbeds, can be used as water-purifying systems as an ecological approach to dealing with grey water and sewage.

Currently, woodchip from Willow is being formally trialled as a potential controller of apple scab. Watch this space.

Perhaps the most significant use of Willow, though, is its pain-relieving properties. Willow contains salicylic acid, from which was synthesised back in the C19th what we now know as aspirin. Also found in meadowsweet and to some extent in Alder, it's an effective anti-inflammatory and general analgesic, and taken in herbal form, most commonly as an infusion of the bark, doesn't affect the stomach in the same way that aspirin can (if you want to use it in this way do check out doses, etc.)

Willow

24th January, 5am, faint shine of streetlight and frost
glazing the black bark and half the eastern sky cradled
in its thin branches, my neighbour's bare wee tree's
become a star-cracked vase brimming with night
and god knows what nebulae and rush
of strange dark matter trembling on the lip
Chris Powici, This Weight of Light, Red Squirrel Press, 2015

Its mythology

Willow is very much associated with the watery emotional nature, and therefore also archetypally with the feminine principle and the intuition. It's also connected mythologically with both Brigid, and Hecate, Goddess of the Moon, thresholds and crossroads. It's a tree associated with vision or seership, with poetry, and with music.

Folklore suggests that Willow can uproot itself and follow unwary travellers. My own sense is that its 'psychic net' stretches a long way; and I have found it to be benign if, as I wrote earlier, insistent.

In Britain, there are 16th- and 17th-century records of abandoned lovers wearing a kind of crown of the flexible Willow twigs and leaves; and you might remember that Ophelia is depicted by the Pre-Raphaelites as drowning beneath a Willow tree.

From my own experience above, I can confirm that Willow can confer or enhance seership and vision. To aid your dreaming life, you might want to put a short length of Willow twig under your pillow.

I mentioned that Willow wood was, and is, used for harps. Harp music has a poignant, plangent sound, and was often used for singing laments. Perhaps for this reason, and also the weeping tendencies of some of its kind, it is associated with loss and grief, where once, however, it was seen as a tree of celebration.

The original Weeping Willow, probably salix babylonica, was perhaps associated with Psalm 137:

'By the rivers of Babylon we sat down and wept when we remembered Babylon.
There on the willow trees we hung up our harps.'

I love this poignant little poem by my friend Scottish poet Kenneth Steven:

The Harp

Under the burning crumble of the peat
Last spring, they found the harp.
A thousand years and more it lay
Unsung, the chords taut in buried hands
Of Celtic Bards. The music curled asleep,
Its strings still resin, left full of woods
And sea and birds, like paintings in the earth,

And only curlews mourning in a bleary sky above.

They lifted out the harp, a dozen heads
All bent and captured, listening for the sounds
That might lie mute inside – the bones of hands
That once had strummed for kings. But all around
Were broken promises, the wreckage of the Viking lash
Across their history's face. The harp still played –
Remembered how to weep.
Kenneth Steven, The Missing Days, *Scottish Contemporary Poets, 1995*

Willow's month straddles Beltane, 1st May, the old midsummer festival in the northern hemisphere. Beltane's name derives from Belin, a Celtic sun-god whose name in turn derived from Bel, the Sumerian Willow god. (Bel supplanted Belilis, the earlier Sumerian Willow goddess.)

The Gaulish god Belenos was also a sun-god; and it's likely that 'bélier', 'ram' in French, which gives its name and symbol to the zodiac sign of fiery Aries, has the same root.

I am the Hawk of May, balanced above the cliff

This keynote, adapted from Graves' version of the 'Song of Amergin' and his notes, is the one that has caused course participants the most confusion. I can understand. *What?* Why for *Willow?*

The original significance of this keynote, like some others, is elusive. Anything I say here is feeling around in the dark for pointers.

Perhaps we should look towards shamanic interpretations of animal, plant, tree-lore: if the hawk symbolises the ability to pick out detail, significant detail, from the perspective of height, then maybe it's a kind of 'remedy', animal-medicine: when swamped by watery Willow (the feeling nature, emotional reactivity, the kind of muddle where you – and I use this phrase advisedly – 'can't see the wood for the trees'), maybe a hawk's eye view can help. On the medicine wheel, the hawk is a powerful ally, offering the ability to see our life in perspective, to enable us to free ourselves from unconscious baggage. He can also help us to connect to ancestral roots.

The hawk, esoterically, is seen as royal. Hawk or kite, Graves tells us, was a symbol for the Egyptian royal family, connected with Horus. Esoterically, and from the perspective of archetypal psychology, Horus/the hawk represents the Higher Self, that aspect of our consciousness that is concerned with the transpersonal, that which can rise above the petty concerns and desires of ego, moving us away from the swampy territory of the ego.

Cliff? This may symbolise, like the hawk itself, the bigger wider perspective of the life-death-life nature.

However, here's another attempt. Gradually, as I work with the trees, I feel I am gaining further different and deeper perspectives. Sometimes they seem to go against more traditional teachings. What I say here is *my perception*, and it may seem left field. There is more to be developed here, but for now, this is my thinking.

S, Saille month, Graves tells us, 'is the month when birds nest'. Above the cliffs here, in Devon, you can see peregrine falcons; they're frequently seen at nesting-time, which is just about now in Willow time (though often earlier too).

The Welsh word for hawk, Gwalch, in mythology, was a mystical prefix for the Welsh names of two significant figures, Galahad and Gawain. The figure we know from Arthurian Romance as Gawain is probably Gwalchmai from the earlier Mabinogion. 'Gwalchmai', it is suggested, could mean 'Hawk of May'.

Gwalchmai, Gawain, is Arthur's nephew. Unlike for most

of the questing knights the Grail, representing among other possibilities the deep feminine, is not Gawain's obsession. The reason for this, I suggest, is that *he is already in touch with the feminine nature.* Indeed, Gawain is not only a champion of the feminine and the Goddess, but may also be Her representative. Gawain's shield bears the pentagram and an image of the Goddess in her later incarnation as the Virgin Mary above it, on the inside, where he will be continually reminded of his commitment to Her.

Why Willow? Well, the Goddess is often seen as Brigid in Great Britain, and Willow is Brigid's tree. That, at the moment, is the closest I can get.

Symbolism of Willow

Willow helps us access our dream life, our intuition, our unconscious imaginal and emotional life.

It can remind us of the importance of allowing and protecting what we might call the qualities of the deep feminine, and the intelligence of the heart, to balance our reasoning mind.

Willow reminds us to 'go with the flow', and offers a perfect example of flexibility and the utility of that. It also teaches us the lessons of expansion, and confers the confidence to expand.

H for Huath, the Hawthorn Tree

Crataegus monogyna
May 13th–June 9th
Queen of the May: the faery tree
Guardian of the doors to the Otherworld (promise, initiation, entry into the mysteries, fulfilment)

I am the most radiant among blossoms, the flower maiden

'H, which starts in the second half of May, is the season of flowers, and the hawthorn, or may-tree, rules it. Olwen, the daughter of "Giant Hawthorn", [had] hair as yellow as the broom, her fingers pale as wood-anemones, her cheeks the colour of roses, and from her footprints white trefoil sprang up – trefoil ["three-leaf"] to show that she was the summer aspect of the old Triple Goddess. This peculiarity gave her the name of Olwen – "She of the White Track". Trefoil was highly-praised by both Welsh and Irish Bards and Homer, who called it "the lotus".'
from *The White Goddess*, Robert Graves

HAWTHORN, HUATH, is the portal to midsummer 'proper'. Its leaves appear first around the spring equinox, and then its blossom, usually in late April or May.

I've departed from some writers in giving Hawthorn's sister-tree, Blackthorn, its own place in the year, and the month diametrically opposite Hawthorn. I say this so that the two, when you come to Blackthorn, are considered in tandem. In this world, things appear to occur in pairs: night follows day, winter follows summer, brightness needs its shadow.

As sister trees, the May or Whitethorn (other names for Hawthorn) symbolises the peak of the light time, and the

Blackthorn the dark; faces of the same principle, and between them they map the journey of the Maiden of Imbolc in early spring to the Mother of midsummer, followed by the Cailleach, the wise crone, who ushers in winter at Samhain, which used to be the old Celtic new year – after which the Maiden is once again reborn.

Hawthorn leaves are lobed. In part because of this, the thorns are easily told apart, since Hawthorn's leaves will be on the trees before Blackthorn's, but Blackthorn's blossom before Hawthorn's. (Having said this, here in Devon on the Dartington estate a Hawthorn hedge was showing a few leaves and one tiny blossom in January this year – unheard of, almost.)

Hawthorn history and habits

When I was five, we lived for a while high up on a hill – the last house in the village – overlooking the wild Atlantic at Saunton Sands in North Devon. Because of the prevailing southwesterlies, the few taller bushes in the hedges that survived the salty onslaught were mostly old solo Hawthorns (they can reach an age of a few hundred years).

I remember being entranced by them: the wild and witchy shapes they made, all their twiggy branches streaming northeast, utterly reshaped by the winds, bent to the winds' demands. I'd stare up at them, their carved or sculpted forms perched high on the high Devon hedges: to a child they looked portentous (not, of course, that I knew that word) even though they were probably shorter than my dad. I knew even then they were magic trees; the more so when one winter they turned sharp black against the high white snowbanks stacked in the narrow lane where normally no snow was ever seen.

If you have ever travelled on the Levels in the Summer Country, Somerset, in the UK, in April or May or later you'll have seen how the land is stunningly white with blossom, as if bridal. It floods the eyes, and feels very potent. There is no room in your sight for anything other than this flower-sea of white. This is Hawthorn at its most potent.

Have you noticed how it is that in some years, presumably due to weather conditions at a certain time, a hawthorn tree that is normally white may instead bear rose-pink blossom? (It happens to buddleia, too, but in reverse: normally purple blossom can instead be white.)

It's not for nothing that the Hawthorn, five-petalled like the rose to whose family it belongs, is also named the May tree, and that we still have the festival of Queen of the May, that honouring of the feminine principle, fecundity, and the faint but sustained echoes of the days of the Great Goddess. As it's in full blossom, generally, on May Day, Beltane in the old calendar (for the sun god 'Bel' or 'Belenos'), it's traditionally venerated then. (May Day was once determined by the first flowering of the May.)

Beltane, Hawthorn month, ushers in summer (in fact Beltane, May Day, marked midsummer in the old Celtic calendar), and the cattle, penned in for the winter, were traditionally set free into pastures or onto the hillsides at this time. The rituals around this time of year are very much to do with fertility, with the land at its freshest and lushest.

On May Day the May Queen, crowned with blossom, was accompanied by the Green Man, whose head would bear a crown of twigs and leaves, among them Hawthorn. In rural Britain, it still happens that schools or colleges pick out their May Queen each year from among the pupils, and parade her through the streets (I had that honour as a college student; no doubt some would say it turned my head, and explains my interest in things fey or fay).

With the current pagan movement these festivities have been re-established; and in fact have never completely disappeared, anyway, as seen above in relation to May Day festivities. The dancing round the maypole is very clearly a continuation of a fertility rite involving a phallic symbol; as is the 'Obby 'Oss festival that has continued in Padstow, Cornwall. The Floral Dance in Helston, also in Cornwall, while altogether more sedate, is another continuing public ritual.

In pre-Christian times, it seems that couples chose each other, jumped the Beltane (May) fires together, and were 'married' for a year and a day on Mayday. Perhaps this is a vestige of long-ago-forgotten rites to do with the King promising to husband the land in its real sense, in marrying the Queen (more below).

Christianity needed to diminish the hold the Old Ways had on people, and one of the ways was to demonise trees. The most obvious way to dethrone trees and lessen the respect the people had for them as sacred symbols was to associate those with thorns, anyway, with the crown of thorns of Jesus. The thorns took it hard, and it has been seen as unlucky to bring may blossom, Hawthorn, into the house for centuries now, and the tree was shunned. (Some say the scent of its blossom is redolent of female secretions, which can't have helped its case.)

It's hard to imagine how anyone could experience the Hawthorn as anything other than fertile, generous and life-giving, benevolent... and yet, and yet – the thorns are prickly; there is another side to all this exuberant joy. Still, sitting near or beneath an old Hawthorn in her full dress is a sublime summer experience, leading to a trance-like tranquillity. No wonder she was seen in the past as guarding the entrance to Faery.

The gifts from Hawthorn

Physiologically, apart from providing food for animals and birds, Hawthorn is a potent remedy for the heart, normalising and regulating its rhythm and blood pressure, and restoring heart-strength. It's been a potent medicine for me. (You can eat the leaves in sandwiches, and a few berries, but any further dosing should only be done under the supervision of a qualified herbalist.)

The berries provide wonderful and essential food for birds

through the winter. The hedges, especially if they're intertwined with Blackthorn, offer nesting sites and protection to birds and animals, as well as safe wildlife corridors.

Psychologically, its symbolic 'meaning' is as an 'opener' tree, also a heart-healer; an enabler and initiator. It brings the heart, in every sense, back to balance, and can help in dissolving boundaries as well as setting them. Hawthorn can encourage and allow the heart to release stress; it also allows us to trust again, and to let go of fear, says Glennie Kindred.

Its mythology

Hawthorn is a tree of initiation and commencement, says R J Stewart. He mentions that Hawthorn is one of a triad of sacred trees in oral tradition, representing a gate between the worlds (the other two being the oak as a major guardian tree, and the ash as a mediator).

The Hawthorn tree is an iconic species in Devon and Cornwall; on the moors, as in the coastal hedges of my childhood, it's often solo, ancient, and twisted into a pennant-like shape, streaming away from the direction of the prevailing winds, as I mentioned above. You often come across Hawthorns by stiles, those threshold places.

It's a smallish, tough, resilient tree, rather like the native people of those counties (I speak as one myself).

The thorns, especially the Hawthorn, mark the faery paths and spirit tracks of our land.

Significantly, almost every holy well I know in the Westcountry has as its guardian a Hawthorn, and it's believed that when well and thorn appear together, one of the entrances to the Land of Faery, or the Otherworld, is there or close by (as, in fact, you'd expect anyway from a holy well).

Both thorn and well work in synergy, each enhancing the power of the other. These well-trees in parts of Britain are also 'dressed' 'cloutie-trees', decorated with scraps of rags and ribbons, sometimes in honour of the tree-spirit; often to ask for a blessing, or healing.

I write 'cloutie-tree' and remember my father quoting the old folk-rhyme: 'Ne'er cast a clout / till May is out' ('clout' being item of clothing; 'cloutie' in the context of tree being ribbon, scrap of fabric and the like). As children, my sisters and I used to debate this every spring: does that mean keep your clothes on till the month of May has finished, or does it mean until the May blossom is on the branches? Whichever, we very rarely took any notice – when you're a child, the shedding of clothes at the first sign of warmer weather is a big joy and freedom.

At Sancreed Holy Well

And you, solitary waykeeper hunched by this stile
and then again standing proud by the cloutie-well,
one among multitudes, and yet to each of you

your own song, here on this granite peninsula
at the land's edge where you lean to the northeast
in a slant sweep, your compactness

like the people of this land, surrendering
to wind, to seafret and rainfall, to the deep
lodestones of the ores beneath your roots.

Midsummer, and your spilt five-petalled blooms
a bouquet for Her, sparks of milky light
harvested from sun, from cloud, from the misty

rains that stroll these ancient downlands.
To you, then, hawthorn, the secrets of guardianship
of this land, the protection of her sacred

waters, the wisdom of yielding to the elements
without giving up the one place
where your roots are nourished into blossom.
Roselle Angwin

Then there's the famous Hawthorn tree on Wearyall Hill in Glastonbury; thornless, it is supposedly an offspring of the staff planted in the ground there by Joseph of Arimathea, the uncle and companion to Jesus during the latter's 'lost years' when, some say, he was seeking out the wisdom teachings of other lands and had come over with his tin-trading uncle to Britain, where he also learnt from the Druids. (This particular tree is supposed to flower around Christmas, the winter solstice, in honour of Jesus.)

If this sounds outlandish, we do know that the Phoenicians of that period and earlier traded for tin (used in making bronze in the Bronze Age) with Cornwall, and traded all the way up the Atlantic coasts of Britain. There is a tin mine, now defunct, in West Cornwall named 'Levant', which I assume is a gesture to the Levant area, or Lebanon, in the eastern Mediterranean that includes what was Phoenicia. Off Looe, in east Cornwall, is a small island where, the folk tales tell us, Jesus first set foot on British soil.

I am the most radiant among blossoms, the flower maiden

According to what's known as the 'Fourth Branch' of the *Mabinogion* in Welsh mythology, May Day is the time of the Flower Maiden Blodeuwydd, or 'Flower-Face' – a woman who takes human form at the request and with the help of the great enchanter, the Druid Gwydion, who creates a material shape for her spirit to enter (so that she may marry) from 'nine powers of nine flowers' gathered from the fields, woods and hills, of which the ninth, speculates Robert Graves, was possibly or probably Hawthorn.

The number nine is an important one in Celtic and other mythology. Often expressed as three times three in Celtic lore, it is symbolically traditionally associated with the feminine principle in the form of the ancient pagan Triple Goddess – triple in her constantly-renewing cycles of Maiden, Mother, Crone, and in the phases of the moon: new moon, full moon, dark moon. (If you come across three intertwined thorn trees, they are particularly potent.)

In the tales, Blodeuwydd is probably a shapeshifting being from the realm of Faery.

As one of the many faces of Sovereignty, as the Celts sometimes refer to the divine feminine principle, Blodeuwydd lives 'between the worlds' in the ghostly form of an owl. She takes on a flower 'body' to represent her as a wife to marry and teach Llew Llaw Gyffes, the wayward son (some say) of Gwydion, to come to his full power as the sun-god, whose time is at the height of the summer solstice. In other words, as a lunar goddess (the owl shows us that), she can initiate the new solar god to take his place in the planetary pattern of birth, death and rebirth.

This tale is, I believe, a fragment of an old pre-Christian myth, of which there is much to say: the two consummate their marriage just as the fertility of the earth and potency of the sun come towards their fullest powers of expression at Beltane, the old midsummer.

Both the thorns, Hawthorn and Blackthorn, are five-petalled, signifying as usual their connection with the pre-Christian Goddess (and you can see the pentagram on the base of the haws, too). Fertility, guardian of the wells and entrances to the Otherworld, guardian of hedges and boundaries, and the ability to endure are traits of Hawthorn.

Symbolism of Hawthorn

Hawthorn, Huath, is as full and inviting in its summer bridalwear as it's possible to be. However, it does have a darker side. The name of the tree in the tree-alphabet means something like 'fearsome' or 'terrible'. A tree with thorns; not to be messed with.

Under the protection of the realm of Faery and the old magic, Huath is not all foamy white blossom. Blossom can be a distraction; we might forget to look deeper. The heart has its own reasons and seasons; not always fair and sunny. (And then there is, too, the crown of thorns.)

Clearly, thorns are thorns – about boundaries and protection. They are also about the inextricability of life and death – to have the one you have to accept the other. Some books will give you a dark picture of malevolent trees – either or both, though most often the Blackthorn. It is true that they are not to be messed with, the latter especially. However, my experience with both has been benign – if they are approached with respect.

If one takes the view that the Blackthorn is the twin, or shadow, of Hawthorn, then we can see Blackthorn as carrying this darker side.

Writer on things Celtic R J Stewart says that the Hawthorn 'like the rose, carries blossom, thorns and fruit, showing in nature the three stages of transformation: promise, pain and fulfilment.' Hawthorn represents largely the first and third of these, with a dash of the middle one – inevitable in any process of growth. (Blackthorn, of course, reminds us of the cycles of things, and that pain comes both with the breaking-down and the cracking of skins for new growth to happen.)

A Hawthorn Story

This story was shared with me by storyteller Pat Childerhouse, participant in the first of my 'Tongues in Trees' yearlong courses in 2019, who gave me permission to share it here.

The Hawthorn Tree

Here's a story I made out of lots of local (and other) folk tales and legends. I used to tell it when leading walks over Windover Hill which is where our Long Man stands. (He may be a Long Woman actually, not being endowed as the Cerne Abbas giant is.) I used to sit my folk down by a most venerable hawthorn which was bent over to form a kind of cave. It's known that shepherds valued such good shelter in the days when the Downs had no fences and the sheep were taken up to graze on the hills in all weathers and then down to fold in the evening.

Once upon a time which was not my time, and not your time, but somebody's time, an old shepherd used to come up here with his flock and his dog. One day, when he was resting by this hawthorn, he heard music, and when he looked, he saw a small green man playing a pipe. The man stopped playing and beckoned the shepherd to follow, and led him into the shadows under the tree. Suddenly there was an opening, big enough for the shepherd to crawl through, which he did – he was curious. His dog wouldn't follow. It stayed above, in the light, and whined.

The passage opened out and the green man whispered to the shepherd, 'Quiet now, don't wake the sleepers!' The shepherd saw glints of light in a kind of cavern, and realized that the light was glinting on metal – swords, shields, helmets – that lay on the ground by sleeping men. The shepherd's hair stood on end – these were warriors. The green man led him past the sleepers to where there was more light glinting. This time it was a pile of gold and the green man gestured to his companion to take some of it. The shepherd hastily filled his pockets. He'd neither seen nor imagined such wealth. The green man led him back past the sleepers, and the shepherd, who was tense and anxious, tripped on something and made a clatter. A sleeper stirred and the green man said: 'Sleep on, it is not yet time to awaken.'

The sleeper settled back into stillness and the shepherd was led out into the light by the hawthorn tree. His companion had vanished, but the dog greeted his master ecstatically.

The sheep were taken to fold early that night and the shepherd held off from checking his pockets until he was safely home with his family. He'd heard the stories of fairy tricks. But there was no trick – what he emptied out of his pockets onto the kitchen table was gold indeed. He was a generous man and he shared that wealth with family and friends, on sworn condition that they asked him nothing about how he'd come by it. So they lived well for some time, though he carried on shepherding. He said:'What would I do with my days if I don't go up on the hill with the skylarks and the ewes?'

Eventually, the money dwindled away and the shepherd began checking out the hawthorn tree. He couldn't find any opening underneath it, or hear any music and after a while he gave up. Then, one time he was up here on Windover Hill one afternoon in November and a new moon just rising, when he looked under the hawthorn tree, he saw the opening into that dark passage.

Once again the dog refused to follow. The shepherd made his way along the passage and came to the chamber with the sleepers and the gold. He filled his pockets again, trembling with nervousness, and turned to leave. Once again, he clattered over something and a sleeper stirred. What was it the green man had said? The shepherd couldn't remember. He tried desperately to remember but no words came. He pressed on, but the sleeper was now standing, sword in hand and a fearsome expression on his shadow of a face. The shepherd staggered up the passage and out onto the hillside, the sleeper stumbling after him.

The next thing the shepherd knew, it was dawn on the cold hill and he was lying wet and shivering with his dog nuzzling him. He staggered home, and into his bed, but never rose from it again. His health and his senses were gone, though there was gold in his pocket.

Sometimes, if you're up here on Windover Hill when a sea fret rolls over, you may see a ghastly figure – a warrior wandering, unable to return to his rest, and waiting out the time until the other sleepers will awaken.

D for Duir: the Oak Tree

Quercus robur
June 10th–July 7th
King of the Woods
Steadiness, enduringness, solidity, protection

I am the oak-king who sets the head aflame
I am the god who crowns the waxing year

OAK, DUIR

In the 13-tree Celtic calendar, the Oak is the pivotal tree in the year, sitting at 7th place – the centre, and the centre too of the solar year, straddling the summer solstice as it does.

The Oak presides over, and crowns, the six months of the waxing year to midsummer, and we'll explore that further below.

One of the wonders of the Western world, as far as I'm concerned, is the cluster of prehistoric painted caves known as Pech Merle. The astonishing artwork on the cave walls is somewhere between 20,000 and 30,000 years old, and yet the ochre-and-oxide-painted animals, the human handprints, on the walls, are still so alive, so recent-seeming, so full of meaning.

Pech Merle is in the Lot department of southwest France, in the area known as Quercy, from 'Quercus', Oak. Quercy is an oak-lover's dream.

The reason I'm mentioning these caves, apart from my own remembered pleasure, is that in one of the entrance caverns there is a tap root of a living Oak tree, growing long metres down from the roof like a hairy mammoth's trunk of a stalactite, a whole *half-mile* underground from where the tree's above-ground living trunk is. This has stayed with me almost as much as the cave paintings, though of course the tree is many thousands of years younger.

Oak roots, as just illustrated, can push down a long way to seek underground watercourses; this might be one of the reasons that they attract lightning as much as they do. Fred Hageneder says the Oak's own strong electrical currents may exacerbate their tendency to 'court the lightning flash'.

On Dartmoor, not far from where I live, is the amazing tiny three-copse wood known as Wistman's Wood, a fragment of ancient Oak woodland (just a few miles away, above the Dart, is another stretch of ancient woodland: Holne Chase Woods). This wood is certainly the vestiges of a mediaeval wood, and may even be a last splinter of woodland dating from the Neolithic, when most of Dartmoor, like many upland areas, was cleared for timber and for keeping livestock and growing crops by our Stone Age ancestors using stone axes. In Wistman's, trees and granite boulders are so intertwined that you can't always tell where one ends and another begins. Each tree-rock microsystem is home to a host of mosses, lichens, fungi, ferns and more. Wistman's is mysterious, feels like a Faery forest. Walking into it is like walking in on a lively if low-voiced conversation.

According to the Woodland Trust, ancient woodland is home to more threatened wildlife than any other land-based habitat in the UK. Because just two per cent of the UK's land area is now covered by ancient woodland, it is crucially important that what remains is properly protected. So far, so good for the little Wistman's, which is within the protection of the Dartmoor National Park.

As I said in Part I, I spend some of my year in a magical and otherworldly forest in Brittany. It's believed that it's a splinter of the ancient Forêt de Brocéliande beloved of the Grail legends and King Arthur stories. This wood lost a lot of its Oaks in the great storms towards the end of the last century, but new ones have sprung up, and in the heart there are still many older Oaks*, as well as Hazel, Holly, Birch, Beech and Sweet Chestnut. Oaks frame the granite ramparts of the Camp d'Artus, an enormous Iron Age encampment at the heights of the forest. Here, you breathe in story through the soles of your feet. This forest is rather like a massive version of Wistman's Wood in its energetic quality, and has the same intertwining of tree and granite boulder.

* The gardeners at Kew in London, however, have discovered that Oaks that were partly-uprooted by huge storms with the effect that their roots were aerated have grown more, and more healthily, than they would have been expected to otherwise.

> 'Our ordinary mind always tries to persuade us that we are nothing but acorns and that our greatest happiness will be to become bigger, fatter, shinier acorns; but that is of interest only to pigs. Our faith gives us knowledge of something better: that we can become oak trees.'
> E F Schumacher

Oak history and habits

Oak, of the genus Quercus, is a member of the Beech family, the Fagaceae. There are approximately 600 extant species of oaks worldwide, with about 25 native to Europe. In the UK we have pedunculate and sessile Oaks as the most common, though others, such as holm Oak and turkey Oak (from North America), have been introduced relatively recently. Pedunculate, *Quercus robur*, is the most frequently occurring Oak in the British Isles; its name 'pedunculate', from the Latin word for 'foot', refers to its acorn that is borne on a slender stalk (the sessile Oak's acorn sits directly on the twig).

Quercus robur supports a wealth of organisms which benefit from the food, support and shelter it supplies; the Oak supports more life forms than any other native tree.

A pedunculate Oak tree bears both male flowers in the form of rather lovely small decorative catkins, and smallish female flowers. These become acorns in the autumn, although a tree won't produce these fruits until it is at least 40 years old.

An old Oak will shed branches from its canopy, and gradually the high branches left will begin to look like stags' antlers. This actually strengthens the tree, and increases its longevity. (According to the ancient vegetation rituals of our lands, the fact that Oak branches look like stags' antlers adds to its status in relation to kingship and also Druidry; beyond the scope of this book, however.)

After Dutch Elm disease, and Ash dieback, there has recently been Oak trouble too. 'Acute oak decline' has recently been identified in the UK. We still don't fully understand its causes, but it kills our native Oaks, which is more than tragic.

There's also a great deal of damage done by regiments of processionary caterpillars which, along with being highly toxic to animals and humans, strip the Oak leaves.

On the other hand, Oak provides food for purple hairstreak caterpillars, common in only a few places.

Oak is imposing in a way that makes it more noticeable, at least to me, than any other broadleaf native to the British Isles. When I look across the valley, in winter the Oak stands out for its architectural skeletal huge twisted sturdy bare branches, solid and more noticeable than the neighbouring trees, with its dramatically twiggy fairy-tale 'witches fingers' at the branch-ends.

In April and May the Oak stands out among the trees because its new leaves are a golden-green sometimes edging towards red-gold. In June and July it blends in with the more uniform greens of the woodland, though its green is darker. From about late August on, the crown begins to acquire a gold again, this time tinged with russet. By autumn proper, this canopy is gently fiery.

The gifts from Oak

OAK

these hundred thousand sun-hammered leaves
this weight of light
Chris Powici, This Weight of Light, *Red Squirrel Press, 2015*

The Oak is almost invariably a robust and solid tree, frequently as wide as, or wider than, it is tall, with no-nonsense, if gnarled, trunk and branches. (Often it seems to grow alongside an ash and their divergent characteristics are very apparent.) Its timber has long been used for ships and buildings; it becomes ever harder as it ages.

Acorns feed many creatures. Once upon a time in the UK, there were pannage rights for local peasants: pigs would have been turned out to feed on the proliferation of acorns (of which only one in 10,000, astonishingly, is likely to germinate and mature into a tree, what with pigs, squirrels and jays and general ill-luck in where the acorns fall, and fluctuating climatic conditions).

Equally astonishingly, a jay can collect and bury up to 5000 acorns in a single season, for its winter food – carrying up to nine at a time in its gullet to disgorge. Although jays have excellent memories and possibly also use landmarks for locating their trove, they do forget some – so help enormously in the increase of the Oak population. An acquaintance with land used for ceremony in Devon told me that he'd built a stone circle. He was mystified by the springing up of a number of Oaks close to each of the stones. The 'landmark' theory makes sense of this, though clearly it didn't work as well for the jays as it might have.

You can make, and I have made, a coffee substitute from acorns. My memory (it's a long time ago) is that you have to bury the acorns for some while first to remove the worst of the bitter alkaloids. I wouldn't bother – it's disgusting.

Oak, of course, because of its high tannin content, has always been associated with tanning hide. In the days when I was a shoemaker, I used to travel to the two remaining Oak tanneries in Devon and Cornwall to handpick the leather I would use for the custom-made shoes, often painted, that I'd make. I still remember with nostalgia the pungent and unique odour of Oak bark tanning.

The Oak has a high resistance to both insect and fungal attack, courtesy of the high tannin levels. And it's the tannin that gives such a distinctive flavour to wines and spirits such as whisky, matured in barrels made of its wood.

The bark of the white Oak is used in some medical preparations, and Oak is also one of Edward Bach's healer-essences: for Oak people who fight on, never give up, despite the odds. They can be over-responsible: 'They are discontented with themselves if illness interferes with their duties or helping others. They are brave people, fighting against great difficulties, without loss of hope or effort.'

It's from the Latin name for Oak, *quercus robur*, that we get our word 'robust'.

In continental Europe, certain species of highly-prized truffles grow under oaks in the symbiotic relationship that occurs in the mycorrhizal networks in tree roots. These are in sufficient demand that they generate a great deal of skullduggery as well as income for those fortunate enough as to know where to find them (or their hounds or pigs). The prices they reach can outstrip some black-market hard drugs.

So many gifts from Oak for humans (and other species), and here's another: the Oak gall, those hard round wooden-bead-like excrescences made by a wasp, used to provide us with ink for writing on vellum manuscripts.

The poem below was written nearly 200 years ago. Prescient.

The Oak

. . . It is the last survivor of a race
Strong in their forest-pride when I was young.
I can remember when, for miles around,
In place of those smooth meadows and corn-fields,
There stood ten thousand tall and stately trees,
Such as had braved the winds of March, the bolt
Sent by the summer lightning, and the snow
Heaping for weeks their boughs. Even in the depth
Of hot July the glades were cool; the grass,
Yellow and parched elsewhere, grew long and fresh,
Shading wild strawberries and violets,
Or the lark's nest; and overhead the dove
Had her lone dwelling, paying for her home
With melancholy songs; and scarce a beech
Was there without a honeysuckle linked
Around, with its red tendrils and pink flowers;
Or girdled by a brier-rose, whose buds
Yield fragrant harvest for the honey-bee;
There dwelt the last red deer, those antler'd kings . . .
But this is as dream, — the plough has pass'd
Where the stag bounded, and the day has looked
On the green twilight of the forest-trees.
This oak has no companion! . . .
Letitia Elizabeth Landon

Its mythology

Time was, we worshipped here
under the changing moons that marked
the cycle of the year...
Sheena Odle

The kingly Oak

There is a great deal to say mythologically and symbolically about Oak, and I'm going to restrict myself to the aspects that interest me personally the most. Firstly, though, its association with England and English History:

The great Oak, the kingly Oak, is perhaps the most iconic of trees, and very much an English symbol, one might say England's 'World Tree'; by which I mean its characteristics seem to have so much in common with the archetypal English character. Oak is the strongest and toughest of woods. The tree endures; is stoic, we could say, has a kind of robust magnificence to it; is deep-rooted and, Graves asserts, a tree of triumph. It's not showy or poetically romantic, and yet it acts as a kind of anchor in the landscape. It's not a coincidence that Oak and kingship are intimately linked in tree-lore.

As a royal tree it's emblematic of both chief gods and thunder-gods in European myths. Interestingly, many other European nations have also taken the Oak as their national emblem.

I suspect Oak has always been seen as a royal tree though, in Britain at least, its status was no doubt underlined by the story that the future King Charles 11, fleeing Parliamentary forces during the English Civil War, hid in what's become known as the Boscobel Oak in Shropshire to escape the Parliamentarians, following the Battle of Worcester in September 1651. What has happened since is that there is a swathe of Royal Oaks, often with a nearby inn also named that, where Charles was supposed to have taken shelter, across southern and southwestern England.

The tree standing on the Boscobel site today is not the original Royal Oak, which is recorded as having been destroyed during the seventeenth and eighteenth centuries by tourists who cut off branches and chunks as souvenirs. (The same thing is happening currently to the Fortingall Yew in Perthshire, which is anywhere between 2000 and 9000 years old.) The present-day Oak is believed to be a two or three-hundred-year-old descendant of that original, and is known as the 'Son of Royal Oak'. In the year 2000, Son of Royal Oak was badly injured during a violent storm and lost many branches. In September 2010, it was found to have developed large and dangerous cracks. Since 2011 the tree has been surrounded by a fence to ensure the safety of visitors.

Not far from Glastonbury there is a pair of ancient royal Oaks, known as Gog and Magog (named after the last British giants, who also crop up as guarding the old gates to the city of London, and again in the East Anglian hills). These 'Oaks of Avalon' are said to be ancient remnants of an oak-lined processional route to Glastonbury Tor.

Other associations

In the Bible, too, the Oak was seen as a significant tree; one that the Angel of the Lord (in 'Judges') was willing to visit and sit beneath. In Genesis, an Oak grove was seen as a fit place to worship God: 'Then Abram moved his tent and came and dwelt by the oaks of Mamre, which are in Hebron, and there he built an altar to the LORD' [original capitals].

Still in the Old Testament, the 'Book of Samuel' has a humorous little description that might not have been funny for poor Absalom, the butt of the joke: 'Now Absalom happened to meet the servants of David. For Absalom was riding on his mule, and the mule went under the thick branches of a great oak. And his head caught fast in the oak, so he was left hanging between heaven and earth, while the mule that was under him kept going.' (This reminds me of pre-Christian initiation rituals, to do with transformation to a new level of consciousness, as in the Hanged Man in the Tarot, or Odin hanging from the World Tree.)

In a more secular context, some old Oaks were 'dancing trees': platforms were built in earlier times in the spread of their lower limbs for feasting and indeed dancing. (In the village of Moretonhampstead, close to where I used to live on Dartmoor, the Cross Tree in the heart of the village was reputedly the old dancing tree.)

Perhaps more than any other tree, the Oak is associated with the Green Man foliate heads, and more of that below.

Celtic mysteries

In the ancient 'Cad Goddeu' poem Gwion calls the Oak 'Stout Guardian of the door / His name in every tongue.' Door to the mysteries, maybe. The Oak is the 'god who sets the head afire with smoke', according to the 'Song of Amergin'.

'Duir', one of the Irish names for Oak, is an interesting word. Its Sanskrit root is 'dwr', which means 'door'. Here, 'Duir' probably means both Oak and 'door'.

Standing at the heart, the apex, of the year, Duir is indeed a doorway both on past and on future. 'Door' in this context, too, most likely has a shamanic meaning: the Oak can open the portals for us to 'travel between the worlds'. It's not for nothing that the Druids are recorded as having met in Oak groves: we know it was a sacred tree to them (in fact, as I mentioned in the Introduction, the word 'Druid' may come from a variant on Duir, 'dru', coupled with words such as 'vid' or 'wiss'; in various Indo-European languages these words have a connection with seeing, as in wisdom – 'wit', 'wise', 'wizard' – as well as 'vision', and so forth). As a Druid, one is adopted by the Oak.

Above, I spoke of Wistman's Wood. There's much to say about its name, but for our purposes here there are two possible interpretations, both connected: one is 'Wisht Maen': roughly 'Wise' (or 'Sacred') 'Stone', as in standing stone, of which there are many in the immediate area ('maen' or 'men' is the old Brythonic Celtic word for stone, as in 'dolmen' or 'menhir'). Near Wistman's Wood are several Bronze Age hut circles and burial mounds.

Others say its name suggests this wood was the meeting place of wise men ('wisht' men, or Druids), so in this case 'wissman' could mean 'Place of the Wise Man'.

Graves associates Oak, Duir, with Janus. Janus, guardian of the door and more usually associated with January, looks both ways – to the past, and to the future. This is apposite, too, for the Oak at its midsummer post. Some say it's a tree dedicated to Jupiter, and faces both its own waxing past and its own waning future (more in a moment).

Oak as the 'royal tree', solar deity, is representative of the masculine principle at the height of his powers, who ascends to his zenith – that is also the beginning of his death, in mythology – at the midsummer solstice. Oak takes us through the midsummer solstice and on into early July, if you follow Graves' ascriptions.

I am the oak-king who sets the head aflame
I am the god who crowns the waxing year

NB: The summer solstice is when the Oak King who, in addition to 'his' month, *also rules the first half of the year, the waxing half,* is 'sacrificed' in the handover to the evergreen Holly *who rules the other half of the year.* Holly takes us through to midwinter, when the old battle starts again. Both Oak and Holly, note, are guardians of Sovereignty, the Goddess of the Land.*

Of course, Oak and Holly are two faces of the same principle, representing the waxing and waning cycles of everything.

Guardian of the Greenwood

There is a strong connection between the Oak King and the Green Man, or foliate head, which appears carved in stone, on wooden pews, or on roof bosses in so many of our churches. Sometimes he accompanies a Sheela Na Gig, the ancient and primal image of womanhood. You will know what he looks like: a human-type face surrounded by foliage, and with leaves spilling out of his mouth. The leaves are almost always Oak leaves, though sometimes they're Hawthorn. Sometimes the

148

leaves are intertwined with both flowers and berries.

Closely associated with Jack of the Green (and also Robin Hood), this is a truly ancient archetype of positive masculine earth energy, a fitting companion to/server and protector of the Earth Goddess, and possibly dates from matriarchal times.

It would seem that the Green Man archetype and its vital energy is being awoken again for our time, and we need him. William Anderson in his *Green Man* describes him as 'the archetype of our oneness with the earth'. He:

> 'signifies irrepressible life. Once he has come into your awareness, you will find him speaking to you wherever you go. He is an image from the depths of prehistory: he appears and seems to die and then comes again after long forgettings at many periods in the last two thousand years... In all his appearances he is an image of renewal and rebirth...'

Roger Deakin says: 'He is the spirit of the rebirth of nature. He is the chucked pebble that ripples out into every tree ring. He is a green outlaw and he is everywhere...'

Oak, like Holly, is associated not only with the ever-abundant renewing cycles of the life-death-life nature, but both are also associated with the Lord of the Greenwood, consort to the Lady of the Greenwood (the Green Chapel in the story above is probably the Greenwood or Wildwood).

As I touched on above, there is an interesting connection between the ancient 'antlered' Oaks who routinely shed part of their upper limbs and become rejuvenated as a result, and the antlered stags of the Greenwood with whom, esoterically, there is a connection with the idea of ritual sacrifice of the old god. Oak in particular is connected with Cernunnos, the Horned God who served the Goddess, commemorated also in Herne the Hunter.

Symbolism of Oak

At the old midsummer, Beltane, May 1st, fires were lit across the land and people, especially couples, jumped through them. Now, during Oak month in June, there are the fires of St John, near the summer solstice. Occasionally in Britain beacon fires are lit on hilltops at midsummer. In rural France there are still active 'feux de la Saint Jean' in many villages. I remember their being spectacular, mythical, particularly in the mountaintops of French Catalonia on Mont Canigou, our nearest peak during the time I spent there.

There are two distinct ways of relating to the image of the fire of the midsummer king, or god, who sets the head aflame, symbolically speaking.

Remember how Oak 'courts the lightning flash' – which will of course set its own head afire. As a conductor of electricity between heaven and earth, and with its love of water, too, esoterically it is a conduit for transmissions of energy, perhaps both ways: from the subtler planes of being symbolised by its upper branches and canopy (the crown chakra), to the underworld of its roots (the base chakra). Think of the Tree of Life, and how the energy flows from upper through middle to lower to upper again in a cycle; a circling fountain of energy, solar fire, so no wonder the 'head', canopy, might seem 'aflame'.

However, symbolically there's an extra meaning to the idea of setting the head 'afire with smoke' (or 'aflame', as I've chosen to phrase it).

I took the name of my programme of courses, Fire In The Head, from W B Yeats' poem 'The Song of Wandering Aengus'. Aengus is magician, lover and poet, and as a god can bring the 'fire in the head', as it is known in Celtic circles, the 'Awen', to a human. In other words, inspiration – for that is what both the phrase 'fire in the head' and the word ('Awen') mean.

Who'd have thought it? Oak as tree that transmits inspiration: not the poet's Birch, the dreamer's Rowan, the magical Hazel more commonly associated in Celtic mythology with the nuts of inspiration, but Oak as bringer-of-fire.

Oak by the Brook

When the great oak fell in the woods
the valley shuddered and we felt
the aftershock in our feet for weeks.
When the great oak fell, fifty families
of mice fled, and the pairs of woodpeckers.

Nuthatches went into exile, and a hundred
thousand insects. The heron and winter's
white egrets no longer have a lookout
over the minnow brook; no perch
for summer's turtle doves. Last week

a thousand bees hummed in its canopy;
this winter, the jays will scavenge for
five thousand fewer acorns. The valley
is a wound. The valley is a mouth with
a missing front tooth. The valley is Munch's

mouth, open and forever a silent scream.
When we walk where the oak stood we too
are now silent. The great oak fell; the valley
shuddered; we feel its echoes still.
Roselle Angwin

*Addendum
NB Both Graves' version of the calendar and the later versions of the Arthurian mythic cycle follow a midwinter solstice to midsummer solstice progression. In earlier times Oak's waxing half-year cycle possibly began at Samhain, the old midwinter

on November 1st and the beginning of the Celtic new year, and continued to Beltane, the old midsummer on May 1st, with Beltane to Samhain Holly's time. This would change the beginning date of the calendar which in our version begins at the midwinter solstice, with Birch.

Many contemporary Beltane festivals (for instance, 'Obby Oss' in Padstow) still enact, in one way or another, a fight between summer and winter, Oak and Holly, where Oak, representing the early-now-become-old half of the year, having reached its peak and released its powers for the good of all and for maximum fertility, has to let go so that the next part of the cycle can begin.

This is the time when the King would claim his sovereignty to 'husband' the land in his commitment to and sacred marriage (the 'hieros gamos') with the Great Goddess. The gift of sovereignty was always more than the right to rule over a country and its clan. It was a divine power, bestowed by the Goddess of the Land through her representative in the guise of a particular living woman, a queen, on the king, who thereafter acted as her earthy and earthly masculine representative to ensure the interests, and fertility, of land and community.

In his symbolic marrying of the Goddess he was also marrying the land. It was only through such a union – either a recognised marriage or ritualised sexual encounter, usually outdoors, but always in the spirit of the Sacred Marriage – with her that the king could rule. By joining with the goddess of the land, he in turn became profoundly connected both to the land and to its people.

T for Tinne: the Holly Tree

Ilex aquifolium
July 8th–August 4th
The Winter King
Power, resilience, protection, directness

I am the battle, the spear and the god who wields the spear
I am the god of the waning year

HOLLY, TINNE

We've passed the summer solstice now, and the outward time of Oak has segued into the inward half of the year with Holly.

Like a threshold guardian, at the top of our path linking the house and courtyard with the meadow where the orchard and veg garden are, lives a Holly tree. Most years, it bears us a fine crop of berries, much welcomed by the migrating flocks of thrushes, blackbirds and redwings who roost in the woodland margins and also in the Holly tree itself, which of course offers fine protection from predators. The local mice, too, are nourished by our Holly berries.

I spend part of my year in a Brittany forest, as I've mentioned. Close by is a slender and beautiful tall Holly, presiding over the entrance to a 'chemin creux', holloway or sunken lane, used for centuries or more as a pedestrian track. All around are megalithic monuments from the Iron and Bronze Ages, with one or two from the late Stone Age, the Neolithic. I love to imagine that ancestors of this Holly have watched over our comings and goings for perhaps millennia. This one, as so many, is twin-trunked.

When I'm out walking, I notice with pleasure the slender straight shiny pale grey trunks topping the banks that signal Holly. I used to have a neighbour who was a woodturner, and when I see Holly I remember the bowls he turned from its dense close-grained smooth silvery wood.

Graves tells us that the word Holly comes from an older word meaning 'holy', and says that in Christian times 'some property of the tree is equated with the birth or Passion of Jesus: the whiteness of the flower, the redness of the berry, the sharpness of the prickles, the bitterness of the bark'.

Holly needs no description; I imagine everyone is familiar with its leathery prickly-toothed leaves and its winter red berries.

Beautiful it may be, but let us not forget that this is a warrior tree, as its keynote tells us committed to protection, the just exercise of power, and directness.

Holly history and habits

A truly mature Holly can reach twenty-five metres. Almost all the Hollies I see, and probably you too, are relatively young, short, slender. The Holly is slow-growing, patiently waiting out its time in the understorey for the other taller trees to start to die back, allowing it to grow higher towards the light. For a long time, the trees remain slender-stemmed. They can sit it out, so to speak, for hundreds of years, according to Glennie Kindred.

The Holly tree, Tinne for T in the old alphabet, produces its little pinky-white flowers, both male and female blossom though generally (not always) on separate trees, in May or June. Only the female flowers, once pollinated, become berries. Holly's time according to the Celtic calendar is this of the eighth lunar month, July into early August. This is when we start first to perceive that autumn might be on the heels of summer.

As an evergreen, however, and symbol therefore of eternal life, Holly's true season is midwinter, when its red berries, also symbolising the vital energy of the life-force, brighten the hedges.

We decorate our houses with these leaves and berries at the winter solstice or Christmas; a reminder in the dark times that the life force hasn't gone; is merely dormant, awaiting its season for awakening again (and even red passion needs hibernatory times). In such ceremonies Holly has traditionally been combined with Mistletoe, with its white berries, and the black Ivy berries – all three colours being associated both with alchemy and with the Goddess of Sovereignty, among other things.

If in myth the Oak King rules the waxing year from the midwinter solstice to midsummer, the Holly King, his twin, in addition to ruling this eighth month, also oversees the waning year, beginning now, back to the midwinter solstice. It's for that reason that we celebrate Holly month now and not at the more obvious midwinter, as the 'twins' vie with each other once again for the hand of the Goddess.

Graves tells us that once it might have been that this half of the year was presided over not by the native Holly that we all know, but rather by the evergreen Holly Oak, also known as the Holm Oak, or Scarlet Oak, the natural twin to Quercus robur, and sharing the names of both Oak and Holly: Quercus ilex. This would make sense – except that the Holm Oak wasn't introduced to Britain until the 16th century, so would be much too late for our Irish/Welsh calendar.

The gifts from Holly

Because of Holly's straight trunk, its commonest use in times past would be to make spears and lances; and to make the smouldering charcoal in which to forge and temper swords and axes. Being a dense-grained wood, it's long been valued for turning.

It used to be hung above doorways and other entrances as a plant of protection. It's also good as a protective hedge, to keep unwanted visitors out and livestock in – and to offer shelter to vulnerable birds and animals, as do the Thorns.

As I mentioned above, it's an excellent food source for overwintering birds, as well as small rodents.

Once upon a time, Holly wands were valued for their bestowing of strength on the carrier.

Graves tells us that its name, Tinne, is closely connected with alternative European names such as Tannus, a Gaulish thunder god, and Tan or Tann, which in the Celtic tongue means any sacred tree, though in German it means the Fir. It's from Tan that we get the verb 'to tan' as, along with the better-known Oak bark, Holly bark has been used historically to tan leather (I can't help wondering if this refers really to the Holly Oak which will have a higher tannin content than Holly). We also have the evolution of the word 'tinder' from Tinne.

Midsummer is of course the time of high fire, solar power in its true sense. Ian Siddons Heginworth tells us that Holly represents the 'outward manifestation of the power that has been gathered inwardly by Oak. In this respect, these two masculine trees stand side by side in direct relationship with each other in this the most masculine time of year'[28] (as deep midwinter is the most feminine time, the inward time of the wisewoman elder, the Cailleach).

We might go to Holly if our own fire, our inner fire, is hard to access, or has been quenched; or alternatively if we express it too easily. Fire can of course express itself as fury, rage, aggression, especially when it's been pent up; but it's also the power *to*. Holly, like the spear made from its wood, is about balanced directness.

Then there are the other subtle gifts: those of the cycling seasons and their qualities, and their reverberations too, in our lives. How might it be to realign our lives to work in harmony with these deep currents?

Its mythology

I am the battle, the spear and the god who wields the spear
I am the god of the waning year

Even as a small child, hearing the Holly Tree Carol would always send shivers up and down my spine. I didn't know why but it was something to do with the Wildwood:

> 'The rising of the sun, and the running of the deer...
> Of all the trees that are in the greenwood,
> It's the holly bears the crown.'

Holly appears in the story of Gawain and the Green Knight, where the Green Knight, an immortal giant of a man who carries a club of Holly, challenges Gawain to a fight that will involve a beheading, which will be reciprocated at the next meeting. (In fact, the Green Knight's head is a magical speaking head, rather like that of Brân, and can regenerate after an execution, being evergreen; and the Knight spares the younger knight's life after a warning, having tested him to see that he might be fit to be 'reborn' as the new Oak King, waxing consort of the Goddess as she grows from Maiden towards Mother.) In Holly time, the Oak King's star is on the wane.

In the later versions of this story, this beheading of the Green Knight, the Holly King, happens at the midwinter solstice, that day out-of-time – a battle between the dying year and the new; between the Holly King and the Oak King.

However, this would not be the first time in the year these two have fought; the midsummer solstice is another occasion when they would have fought over and for the Goddess (in some Welsh myths She occurs as Creiddylad, whom Graves tells us was the predecessor of King Lear's daughter Cordelia). The one would be ritually 'sacrificed' to and for wellbeing of the land, and then six months later the other would take his place to rule a half year. Now, in Holly month, it's the turn of the Holly King to take the throne.

Once upon a time, probably the dates would have been more likely to be Samhain, November 1st, for the midwinter sacrifice of the Holly King (the old midwinter and Celtic New Year), and Beltane, May 1st, six months later at the then high midsummer, for the sacrifice of the Oak King (see the note above under Oak).

Gawain & the Green Knight

From the Arthurian cycle comes this tale that embodies the idea of the young Oak King now battling it out with the Holly King – and/or vice versa. In most later versions, the ritual handover was yearly, but I'm sure that it would have been six-monthly. (I'm currently researching this.) I place it here because it's Holly Month and because the Holly King's reign over a half-year, beginning now, will finish at midwinter. I see Gawain as representing the Oak King. Below is my retelling of the version that survived to be recorded in mediaeval times:

Feasting and merriment are just about to begin to celebrate the midwinter fires and the New Year in King Arthur's banqueting hall, where King and Queen and the King's knights are all seated round the great table, when a giant of a man rides right into the hall. From head to foot he is green – not just dressed in green, though he is, but everything about him: skin, hair, beard, even horse, though braided within the green are strands of gold, pointing to a regal or at least knightly status. In one hand he carries a Holly bush; in the other a sharp green axe. The hounds by the hearth rise and growl.

The Green Knight rides up to Arthur, dismounts and roars his challenge. Step forward, King, he says, you or one of your knights. Come and meet Sir Bertilak. My challenge to you is to take my axe and behead me. Yes, you heard. The bargain is that, if I let you behead me, you will return to the Green Chapel in the wildwood in a sixmonth to let me return the favour. He lifts the great green axe towards the assembly.

Of course, there's a shocked silence. Arthur stands up and opens his mouth to accept the challenge, but Gawain gets up first and steps forward. Gawain is the foremost of Arthur's knights-in-training, young and courageous, and needs just such an adventure to prove his manhood. Besides, he loves his uncle the King (who secretly favours Gawain as his heir).

There's just one thing, the Green Knight continues. Woe betide you if you mess with my wife.

The Green Knight hands Gawain the axe. With much fear and trepidation but with courage nonetheless Gawain lifts the axe as the giant kneels before him. With a single blow, the Green Knight is beheaded, blood spilling everywhere. His headless body bends down and lifts the head. The Green Knight tucks it under his arm and remounts his green horse. The head turns its eyes to Gawain. Remember, the Green Knight's voice continues, meet me at the Green Chapel in a sixmonth. Thus follows a sixmonth of adventure for Gawain become, for this time anyway, the hero of the court, and King Arthur's deputy. Those who love him, and his enemies too, can see the way he grows in dignity and honour in such a time. He lives, however, with the continual awareness of the date of his death – for he can see no way out of this – looming ever closer.

On the eve of the appointed day, just before midsummer, Gawain rides to the Green Chapel, where first he arrives at a castle that is close by. He is surprised to be met at the door of the castle by the most beautiful woman he has ever seen. Graciously, she invites him in. After supper, she invites him to accompany her to her chamber 'for my husband is dead', she says. Gawain, who has barely seen a woman all year, is at first sorely tempted.

Fortunately for him, though, he is not only single-minded in his quest, but he is also impeccable in his ability to be true, and willing to listen to his own inner guidance, which suggests that this wouldn't be a good idea. Although he fears angering and offending the beautiful woman who is hosting him, he gently declines.

The next day he arrives early at the Green Chapel. There, he encounters not only the Green Knight, fully-mended and with his head back where it belongs, but also the woman, who turns out to be the Green Knight's wife, Lady Bertilak. Gawain, despite his fear, feels some slight relief that at least he hadn't broken the Green Knight's injunction.

The Green Knight is leaning on his axe. Gawain, he roars. My wife tells me that you rejected her. Good. That is good. She was asked to test you. Had you failed the test, this – he gestures to his axe – would bring your world to a close in a moment. Because you were true, I can spare your life – this time.

Go home, and remember that this is my time, now.

The Holly King, and before him the Oak King, in 'their' half-year each rule the forest as Lord of the Greenwood, consort to the Lady of the Greenwood. Yet another face of Cernunnos, the Green Man, Herne the Hunter, and Lord of the Wild Hunt, the Lord of the Greenwood is a god of fertility, growth, death, and rebirth.

Jacqueline Memory Paterson says that the Holly King and the Oak King:

'become dual counterparts of the Nature god in his earth-protecting cycle and role. As such they are the god of darkness and the god of light within the solar year, who guard the transitional points of that year (midwinter and midsummer), when an interchange occurs in the natural world as all life responds to the solar tides of ebb and flow. In this context the holly king reigns over the time of the waning tide... when the sun declines in the heavens as the harvest is gathered and the earth withdraws her energy as life moves into its dormant period. The oak king reigns over the waxing tide... when the energy of the earth is outpouring into the season of growth and fecundity as the light and warmth of the sun grow. As such, both kings represent the god of Nature who protects, courts and loves the earth-goddess, ensuring fruitfulness of the land.'[29]

The traditional story of John Barleycorn (the barley from which comes meal, malt for beer, grain for whisky), and his sacrifice to the land at the early harvest approximately six weeks after the midsummer solstice, at Lugnasadh or Lammas during the time of Holly, continues this theme. From this sacrifice the land will be kept abundant so that, according to (and as a result of) this ancient ritual, humans might continue to eat, drink and procreate.

John Barleycorn Must Die

There were three men came out of the west
Their fortunes for to try
And these three men made a solemn vow
John Barleycorn must die.

They've ploughed, they've sown, they've harrowed him in
Threw clods upon his head
And these three men made a solemn vow
John Barleycorn was dead.

They've let him lie for a very long time
Till the rains from heaven did fall
And little Sir John sprang up his head
And so amazed them all.

They've let him stand till Lammas Day
Till he no longer looked pale and wan

And little Sir John's grown a long long beard
And so become a man.

They've hired men with scythes so sharp
To cut him off at the knee
They've rolled him and tied him by the way
Served him most barbarously.

They've hired men with sharpened pitchforks
Who've pricked him to the heart
And the loader's served him worse than that
For he's bound him to the cart.

They've wheeled him around and around the field
Till they've come unto a pond
And there they've made a solemn oath
On poor John Barleycorn.

They've hired men with crabtree sticks
To cut him skin from bone
And the miller has served him worse than that
For he's ground him between two stones.

And little Sir John and the nut brown bowl
And the whisky in the glass
And little Sir John and the nut brown bowl
Proved the strongest man at last.

The Wildman

If Oak is the Green Man, the vegetation god, then Holly is the related archetypal 'Wild Man of the Woods', perhaps the Wodwose, the original, more primal and atavistic and deeply powerful version of the Green Man. Mythically speaking, his predecessor was perhaps the guardian giant of Britain, one

Gogmagog (also known as the two giants mentioned above, Gog and Magog; the prefix 'Ma' being the primal universal word for Mother).

In addition to being huge, the Wildman was covered in both hair and in foliage. Protector of all, he also represented the truly fierce aspects of the instinctual life and of wild nature, fecund, abundant and not given to being tamed by humans. Carrying aloft his Holly club, and symbol of unfettered sexuality, he may well have been the inspiration behind the Cerne Abbas Giant.

Jacqueline Memory Paterson has something interesting to say about this:

'The earliest Druidic rites possibly evolved when certain people enveloped themselves in vegetation, wherein they felt an innate presence of the Great Spirit. This produced ecstatic states in which it was possible to witness and experience the powerful energy which continually replenishes life upon earth. This power filled the Druid until he radiated and lit up his dress of leaves from within, making it tremble and rustle and resemble a power-filled "vegetation man", the "wildman"... Thus we see that the Wildman expressed the procreative essence of Nature, the Godhead. And from his primal beginnings and through translations of his manifold energy he came to personify specific aspects of the energies of Nature, from which forms like the holly and oak kings evolved, embodiments *par excellence* of the seasonal forces associated with the dark and light periods of the year.'[30]

The Wildman is the subject of the wonderful, poignant, long poem by Dartmoor-based Tom Hirons called 'Sometimes a Wild God'; a kind of homage to our lost inner wild nature. You can find it online.

Symbolism of Holly

Holly is a tree of strength, protection and responsibility. It's often described as a tree of sacrifice, which makes perfect sense in the context of the Gawain story, as each goes to battle at the midwinter (or midsummer) turning willing to die for whatever needs to be reborn. Blood has to be shed, at least symbolically (the red berries), before the new can be born.

This prickly protector-tree, like Hawthorn, opens the heart, though in a different way from Hawthorn (which reminds us of the importance of trust). Some say that Holly deflects lightning (you'll remember perhaps that the oak seems to attract it); it may be fruitful to reflect on that in the context of one's emotional life.

Holly can also represent whatever needs to be restored, including a sense of direction and focus. It can also guide us towards wise action through balancing body, mind and emotional states. There is a quiet strength in Holly, allowing one to move beyond 'prickliness' into the maturity of the inner warrior (as we have now entered the beginning of the more inward time of year).

Glennie Kindred says that its energy can help one understand both one's own pain and the pain of others, and it helps enable directed thought, which can in turn be used to cut psychic or emotional ties which 'have been formed by a draining relationship'. Kindred goes on to say: 'Holly will bring you great balanced power which will guide your actions towards unconditional love and compassion, and an increased detachment from emotional turmoil' (see below).[31]

It's also worth noting here that the mature Holly King, the Green Knight, could have beheaded Gawain-the-seeker, but chose not to.

Back in the 1930s, a young man called Dr Edward Bach, recovering from being severely ill, started to take an interest in holistic approaches to medicine, specifically, initially, homeopathy. Using himself as a guinea pig by monitoring his emotional states, he realised the immense power of flower essences if he steeped specific plants and flowers in sunlight in spring water, and then preserved the results half and half in neat alcohol (usually brandy). He discovered that these flower essences worked as subtle but potent medicines on various psychological states. The idea was to bring one's emotions back into a state of balance.

Although Bach was originally an allopathic doctor, he became uncomfortable with the fact that a patient wasn't treated generally as a whole person. His own views became increasingly holistic, and he became passionate about the gentle remedies he developed to heal emotional states, which many complementary practitioners, and some more orthodox ones, see as underlying many if not most diseases.

His work is rooted in the fact that he perceived dew on a flower (the flower being the ultimate potent expression of the essence of the plant) to retain a 'memory' of the healing qualities of that plant. (Recent work with water does indeed suggest that water bears an imprint of substances immersed or carried in it.) Of Holly, Bach says it 'protects us from anything which is not universal (or unconditional) love'.

Well, Bach's words on unconditional love seem apposite; for all of us, for all the time. Who couldn't do with a hefty dose of the balanced power, emotional detachment and freedom from inner turmoil that Holly promises?

This is one of the meanings of directing power skilfully.

C for Coll: the Hazel Tree

Corylus avallana
August 5th–September 1st
The Otherworld Tree
Creative inspiration, intuition, divination, concentrated wisdom

I am a salmon's wisdom in the pool of inspiration

HAZEL, COLL

August, even in its heat, brings intimations of autumn, and the Hazelnuts are ripening. Here in Devon it seems as if the Hazel doesn't ever sleep. Just after the last nuts have fallen or been gathered the catkins appear: tight, closed and dull in colour but quite visible. By mid-January they are dusty golden.

One summer long ago I spent a week or two in early July gathering green Hazelnuts in the foothills of the Pyrenees to supply a local wholesaler. It was hard to imagine that the green nuts would be ripe enough as to eat within a few short weeks; and blissful working outdoors in the fields in early sun, even with the shield bugs dropping down the front of my thin blouse.

I remember that summer as a kind of Garden-of-Eden time. Just before the nuts we'd been picking cherries to sell in the market. After them it was peaches and apricots, and then, dreamlike, for a week or two taking a herd of brown and black goats with bells up the mountain in the morning and back down again in the late afternoon, and learning to milk them and make cheese.

Hazel history and habits

The Hazel barely needs describing, so common a tree it is, and yet one that is easily overlooked except when its golden catkins, or lambs' tails, emerge to light a grey winter, or when its nuts appear in early autumn. The catkins are male; the Hazel also produces tiny upright reddish bristley flowers that are the female parts.

Community-oriented and 'friendly', Hazels very rarely grow alone as freestanding trees. More commonly they appear in the company of other Hazels, and generally on a bank or in a hedge. They're really a large shrub, growing to something like 12 to 20 feet, though given enough water, sun, drainage and space they can grow bigger.

Their largeish lime-green leaves appear early in the spring and are favourites of browsing animals like horses. The leaves are toughish roughish ovals, veined and very slightly pointed at the tip, and toothed at the edges. Some trees have a deep red-brown spot in the middle of the leaf; pleasingly, this ties them in further to the Salmon of Wisdom with which they are associated (see below).

The gifts from Hazel

I guess most of us, in our childhood or as adults, will have found and eaten Hazelnuts. It's a joy, finding such a freely-given treat as fallen ripe Hazelnuts. They're a highly-concentrated form of nutrition, just as poetically they represent a highly-concentrated form of wisdom ('in a nutshell'). In their physical form, in addition to protein they provide vitamin E, and various minerals like magnesium, calcium and potassium.

I used to make a sugar-free hedgerow jam (which was fairly disgusting – I think I've mentioned it earlier): blackberries, rowan berries, haws, rosehips, sloes, crab apples, or any combination of these – and Hazelnuts, for crunch. Toasted and crushed, however, they make a great addition to a fruit crumble topping or scattered on vegetable dishes and pasta, especially if made into a spicy dukkah. You can also roast them, on their own or in combination with other seeds and nuts, briefly over a high heat in a little olive oil with Tamari soy sauce and lemon juice thrown in at the last minute for a tasty and nutritious snack. They can also help lower blood pressure and reduce 'bad' cholesterol.

Hazelnuts provide a very important food source for birds and some mammals in winter. Although many nuts are poisonous to dogs, Hazels are not. I had a collie who was extremely fond of Hazelnuts, and would patrol the Hazel-lined track on which our house was sited every morning for a couple of months during nut season, collecting, cracking and eating them, and our two new pups have discovered that joy, too.

Well-preserved Hazelnuts that are centuries or even millennia old have been found in bogs, and in the stomachs of so-called Bog People.

Hazel, like Willow, has an affinity with water, and a flexibility that has made it useful for millennia for making stock fences, hurdles and panels (including for house structures, like the wattle part of wattle-and-daub houses), shelters (and benders), the frames of baskets, and coracles. Like Willow, the branches can be bent and tied while living to make garden structures and furniture.

They're unsurpassable as pea sticks, and traditionally have also been used as beanpoles. People have used them for fishing rods, and also to make clogs. However, the Hazel staff, or a magical wand, is one of our most traditional uses for this tree. It was used as a pilgrim staff, or famously as a divining rod. It is the best material for dowsing for water, and a forked Hazel twig held in tension between both hands can give the bearer quite a kick, as I've discovered.

Some have described Hazel as having snakes wrapped around its roots, metaphorically, and as a tree dedicated to Mercury/ Hermes, the psychopomp who carried messages between gods and mortals, it may also represent Mercury's caduceus rod, the rod wrapped in a pair of snakes, that symbolises healing and medicine (as well as esoterically being connected with the vital energy, prana, that in mysticism sits coiled like a snake at the base of the spine awaiting the awakening that comes with enlightenment – in the Eastern tradition known as kundalini).

Hazel has a particular and welcoming 'aura': open, benevolent, embracing; that of white magic. Of all the trees we've looked at, Hazel is perhaps the one the most connected with the enchantment of the Otherworld; a true faery tree.

Its mythology

There is so much to say about this aspect of the Hazel tree that it's been hard to know where to start. What ties together much of the mythology and what I'm exploring in this module, though, is the idea of Connla's Well (Hazels are very often found next to holy wells, and are often 'cloutie' trees, bearing the votive offerings of ribbons, rags, feathers and whatever people wish to offer to these healing wells). So we'll start there.

Connla's Well

Hazelnuts, to the Celts, represented concentrated wisdom and poetic inspiration. (In Irish Gaelic the word for a Hazelnut is 'cno', and the word for wisdom 'cnocach'.) There are several versions of an ancient Irish tale concerning nine (for the nine muses, and the Triple Goddess – Maiden, Mother, Crone – multiplied by herself) Hazel trees that sheltered a sacred pool, often known as Connla's Well, and seen as the original spring from which flowed, for eternity, all the rivers of Ireland (though in some versions it's the River Boyne, presided over by the goddess Boann; and in others it's the Shannon. In some tales there are seven rivers.)

The tales of place in ancient Ireland are known as the 'dindsenchas', or 'dinnsenchas', and were a body of knowledge that the *filidh/fili*, the Irish Bards, needed to learn by heart. This body of mythology, recorded in written form between the 11th and 15th centuries, is likely to have sprung from oral sources, a detailed analysis of which points to a pre-Christian origin for most of the tales. Many place-names appear, for instance, which had fallen out of use by the 5th century A.D., when Irish written records began to appear in any quantity. What's relevant here is that the mythology gives the physical origins, and etymological sources, of several bodies of water – usually issuing from magical wells.

So Connla's Well is one of a number of wells in the Irish vision of the Celtic Otherworld, but is perhaps the Ur-well. It is also named 'The Well of Wisdom', or 'The Well of Knowledge'; sometimes 'The Secret Well'.

This Otherworldly well could be found, variously, at the heart of the world, through the Hollow Hills, or even under the sea. A fragment from an ancient tale preserved in written form some time between the 11th and 15th centuries reads like this (tr. Edward Gwynn 1913):

Connla's well, loud was its sound,
was beneath the blue-skirted ocean:
six streams, unequal in fame,
rise from it, the seventh was Sinann [Shannon].

The nine Hazels all dropped their nuts into the water of this most sacred pool, where they were eaten by the Salmon of Wisdom (according to Druidry the salmon is the most ancient animal, and very much revered).

In so doing, the salmon absorbed the wisdom given by Hazel, and anyone spiritually prepared who cooked and ate the salmon would thereby absorb its wisdom, be given inspiration, and have insight into the true mysteries of the world.

There are various stories in the Celtic corpus about young men being initiated by tasting, apparently accidentally, just a little of the roasted skin of such magical salmon, caught and cooked by an elder for his own consumption – but maybe this was intended to happen. Finn MacCool (whose name originally was MacCuill, later MacColl, 'Son of Hazel'), and Taliesin in his earlier incarnation as Gwion Bach had a not dissimilar initiation by being splashed with three drops of a brew from Ceridwen's Cauldron, cognate really with sacred springs and wells, such as Connla's Well.

The legendary Fintan the White, or Holy, was a Druid-shaman associated with Connla's Well who could transform himself into a, or the, salmon in the Well. I'm certain that in earlier times Connla's Well was associated with women, specifically Ceridwen, the Great Goddess, and her cauldron of life, healing and rebirth, but later tales are not very kind about women associated with this well.

The number of red spots on the salmon supposedly indicate how many nuts they have eaten, and therefore how much wisdom they might impart.

I am a salmon's wisdom in the pool of inspiration

Connla's Well is a common motif in Irish poetry. The mystic George William Russell, also known as AE, wrote a poem called 'The Nuts of Knowledge', or 'Connla's Well', around 100 years ago:

> And when the sun sets dimmed in eve, and purple fills the
> air,
> I think the sacred hazel-tree is dropping berries there,
> From starry fruitage, waved aloft where Connla's Well
> o'erflows,
> For sure, the immortal waters run through every wind that
> . blows.

The poet W B Yeats described the well, which he encountered in a trance, as being full of the 'waters of emotion and passion, in which all purified souls are entangled'. His most magical poem, which I read as being an account of a mystical or shamanic transformation, is 'The Song of Wandering Aengus' (Aengus is the god of both love and poetry, and bore a Hazel staff). All roads lead back to this poem, for me, it seems: you might remember that I spoke of having taken the title for my course programme, Fire in the Head, from this poem; and it's the only poem I know by heart. It's full of esoteric symbolism. Note that the 'silver trout' may well actually be the salmon of wisdom (which is why I mention it here), as they are sometimes used interchangeably, but 'salmon' wouldn't have scanned. I see the whole poem as speaking of a vision related to Connla's Well.

The Song of Wandering Aengus

I went out to the hazel wood,
Because a fire was in my head,
And cut and peeled a hazel wand,
And hooked a berry to a thread;
And when white moths were on the wing,
And moth-like stars were flickering out,
I dropped the berry in a stream
And caught a little silver trout.

When I had laid it on the floor
I went to blow the fire a-flame,
But something rustled on the floor,
And someone called me by my name:
It had become a glimmering girl
With apple blossom in her hair
Who called me by my name and ran
And faded through the brightening air.

Though I am old with wandering

Through hollow lands and hilly lands,
I will find out where she has gone,
And kiss her lips and take her hands;
And walk among long dappled grass,
And pluck till time and times are done,
The silver apples of the moon,
The golden apples of the sun.
W B Yeats

Below is a story of mine, first published on my blog and then later on the website of the Order of Bards, Ovates and Druids. It's relevant here to mention that recent research has uncovered that in a body of water such as a salmon river, or even a stream, there is a narrow current of water that flows counter to the main channel. A salmon can nose out this current and use it to return home to her birth pool for her own spawning.

The Salmon of Wisdom – *Bradán Feasa*

Like calls to like, and the Salmon of Wisdom leaps from her saltwater home to her freshwater home, and then into air. Over and over she leaps the falls, bruised, battered, bleeding, until finally she is there – the Sacred Pool at the heart of the world, the Sacred Pool of the Secrets, the Sacred Pool where she was born.

Home. Water to water to air to water.

Celts know Salmon as the oldest being. Salmon lives now in the Sacred Pool, eating the nuts of inspiration from the nine hazel trees, the poets' trees. Salmon is wise; knows how to live in two elements and the three worlds, knows when it's time to return. Salmon now is charged with keeping counsel for those who are ready to seek it out, who are ready to give away their old life for the sake of the new.

Those who approach Salmon at the right time in the right manner will be given the ability to see through the veils between this world and the other.

Those, on the other hand, who arrive too young, too unformed, or who have hungered for the wrong thing or grown fat on that which belongs to others will not make it up the falls; not this time. Or if they do, they will find their fingers burned – so close, so far away; the itch of the search for wisdom never quite assuaged.

Like calls to like and the woman hears the call.

The woman has been travelling a long time. All her life, in fact. All her life she has struggled against the current, feeling in her blood the pull of the Sacred Pool. Her long skirts are ripped, her hair dishevelled, her feet torn and muddy. She is alone, apart from the old grey mare with whom she has travelled so far.

The woman is no longer young. Like calls to like. The woman is no longer beautiful to the eye. The woman does not care for adoration. Now, at last, she is free. She can glide through the shadows without being noticed. She can watch, she can learn.

She knows what it is to be betrayed by those she trusted. She has had her words and her dreams stolen, the lifelong work of her heart. She knows what it is to be loved, then to be cut off for not fulfilling another's dream.

She no longer cares about false friends, false promises. She does not care. What she cares about is the call of the Well, the Sacred Pool. She knows the songs of the birds; she can speak with trees and plants and animals. She knows how the planets move and the way the tide sings just so on the shore.

And she knows what it is to be truly loved; deeply loved. More, she knows how to love; and the cost of an open heart. She knows this is all.

She is no one's servant, though she will serve the true of heart. The pony mare is her sister; the morning mist her friend; dusk a cloak she can wrap around her. Rain does not trouble her, nor hunger of the ordinary sort.

Like calls to like, and she can be true to the calling, only to the calling, which means she is true to herself, to everything and nothing. In her freedom she can smile into everybody's eyes, through to their core.

Salmon has been waiting all winter, feasting on the fat of the hazel nuts. Visitors are few.

The woman kneels in the rushes and mud at the edge of the pond. A breeze whispers in the willows. The woman maybe sheds one tear. It's been a long hard journey. She can barely breathe for the shock and joy of arriving here at the heart of the world.

Salmon swims slowly over. She is huge, magnificent, a queen of all waters.

The woman kneels, asks permission of the waters' guardian to be here.

Salmon disgorges a nut, soaked in inspiration: Awen, the eternal fire in the head.

The woman lifts the nut from the water, holds it as if it were gold, gazes into Salmon's eyes.

In that moment she learns what will finally change her life: there is a current beneath the current; a reverse current that will always take her, without struggle, to where she needs to be. All she need do is surrender, relinquish control. Water will find her, take her.

Then she will have brought her life into balance: the perfect tension between the path of least resistance and the path of the will; the path that will take her beyond need, beyond striving, to the heart at the heart of it all, which is Love.

Symbolism of Hazel

Salmon is a most royal fish, one of the truly ancient and most sacred animals to the Druids. Insight, vision and enlightenment have long been associated, in myth, with eating its flesh. Combined in particular with the concentrated knowledge and wisdom of the Hazel nut, its gifts to humans are immense.

Given that Connla's Well is surrounded by the nine Hazel

trees associated with the Triple Goddess, the Nine Muses and so on, there is a divine feminine aspect to this pool, and a long journey to be had to find home beside it.

My own experience of Hazel is that it is a joyful and benign presence that will help begin, or confirm, an inner journey, and that a little of its essence goes a long way. Never insistent, it is still a constant companion, if you ask that of it.

M for Muin: Bramble (or Vine)

Rubus fruticosus (rose family); Vitis vinifera
September 2nd–September 29th
The Tree of Poetry, Prophecy & Vision
Speaking in tongues

I am a hill of poetry

The vine, the prime tree of Dionysus, is everywhere associated with poetic inspiration. Wine is the "poets' proper drink" (Robert Graves), and in times past, or at least after Laureate Ben Johnson requested it, the Poet Laureate's fee was paid in wine.

BRAMBLE, VINE, MUIN

It would be easy to argue that these two are not trees. It would also be true. In addition, some writers on the Celtic tree alphabet don't 'do' Bramble. However, either or both have been significant plants in Britain and Europe for, probably, millennia; and in the wilder rocky uplands or the windswept westerly coasts where the Celtic tree alphabet was born, Bramble is perfectly at home, being hardy and determined.

When I was first working with this tree calendar, I too resisted going with this plant. But it happens that there's quite a bit of significance attached to brambles and blackberries, and vines and grapes, too, especially mythologically. They are also approximately cognate, for my purposes here certainly. Read on.

Bramble history and habits

The Bramble needs no introduction. Every child knows the pleasure of cramming the free hedgerow food, stumbled upon, juicy and dripping, into their mouths. It's perhaps this plant that reminds us most of the abundance of the natural world, not least because Bramble's fruiting season is so long. I've seen flowers as early as March and as late as December here in Devon, with berries coming from May till November or so.

An equinox-month plant, it is said here in the Westcountry that it's not good to eat after St Michael's Day, Michaelmas, the 25th September, as after that the Devil has peed on the fruit. It's true that around that time the fruit becomes overly sweet, lacking the tartness that gives it its earlier edge. A high sugar content, though, makes it good for wine – on which more below.

Very frequently you will find flowers, green drupes, red drupes and fully-ripe blackberries all in the same cluster. The colours green, red and black in the berries are said to represent the Goddess in her maiden, mother and crone aspect (though Her maiden form is often represented by white, and therefore the flowers, instead of green, in Celtic iconography).

The Bramble is an iconic symbol of the harvest, gathering-in, and celebrations.

Brambles don't stand upright like 'real' trees. Although it's not really a climber in that it has no tendrils or suckers, it does elbow itself upwards on other shrubs, and then when it becomes over-top-heavy it will arch downwards, and can take root. It's not long before Bramble has leaped a colonising distance over fields and meadows – very hard to eradicate.

Some people say that this month should belong to the Vine. We associate Vine with the Roman invasion. Although it isn't a native British plant, it has certainly been known and propagated here in Britain for a very long time – it appears on various Bronze Age artefacts, and we also know that the climate during part of the Bronze Age was gentler than ours; for instance, grains and vines were probably grown on the heights of Dartmoor in that era, where we wouldn't find them now (although we find plenty of both on the lower margins).

Robert Graves suggests that the Danaans/the Tuatha dé

Danaan ('Children of the Goddess Danu'), early invaders of Ireland, a race of gods and the earliest inhabitants of Ireland, *or* the descendants of the Trojans (take your pick), brought the grapevine with them. Graves also points out that M for Muin is the initial of the Roman goddess of wisdom, Minerva; of Mnemosyne, the mother of the muses, as well as of the muses themselves; and, too, of the Moirae, or the three Fates, who according to some invented the alphabet.

The gifts from Bramble

Blackberries and the preceding flowers are welcomed food for insects such as butterflies and bees, and for animals and birds – particularly loved by blackbirds and mice.

Humans have probably been gathering Bramble fruit for millennia. Apart from its deliciousness raw or cooked in a variety of ways, and the joy of foraging for it, it contains a range of nutrients with health benefits. Blackberries contain important nutrients such as potassium, magnesium and calcium, as well as vitamins A, C, E and most of our B vitamins. They are also a rich source of anthocyanins, powerful antioxidants that give blackberries their deep purple colour, so are good for eradicating free radicals, and may prevent and/or slow the growth of cancer. Blackberries are great for the skin; can help regulate menstrual cycles and function; contain antibacterial and also antiviral properties. They can help against infection and inflammation, and can boost the immune system. The blackberry can improve and maintain brain function, and is good for the cardiovascular system: like grape juice, it's good for the heart.

There is another gift, hinted at in the sub-title: 'I am a hill of poetry'. Both the Bramble and the Vine are associated with eloquence, imagination, and prophecy. Bramble is a plant of inspiration.

This may be partly due to the idea of 'in vino veritas': we speak more truly, perhaps when our inhibitions are loosened.

Its mythology

Bramble wine, or of course what we think of as the 'true' wine, from grapes, is a potent drink, and was probably used as a sacred intoxicant in our ancestors' ceremonies.

This is not the same as the way in which alcohol is generally used in Western culture: getting blasted and passing out (although I'm sure that happened too). It would have been taken in relatively small quantities in a ritual context, and I can vouch for the fact that, used in this way, it can indeed aid shamanic entry into the Otherworld: a shift of consciousness in which inspired poetry may be written, or words uttered; even prophecies. This is visionquest; entry into the spiritual dimensions, the Otherworld.

Such a state of consciousness will also include a sense of a psychic opening, and an ability (as Elen Sentier expresses it) to walk between the worlds while intertwining your consciousness with that of another, human or other-than-human.

Such interweaving lies behind the shapeshifting expressed by the 6th century magician, Bard and seer Taliesin, as he journeys between the worlds in the form of different creatures of earth, water, air and fire (see my book *Riding the Dragon – myth & the inner journey*), and also in the words uttered by Amergin in his Song: 'I have been' or 'I am', from which the keynotes of each lunar month in my calendar have been taken, you will remember.

This is the ability to walk truly in the hooves or paws of, fly in the wings of, swim with the fins of, breathe with the breath of, break with the waves of, another.

It is also associated with the ability to loosen inhibitions and give expression to different facets of yourself.

In Greco-Roman culture, the Vine was sacred to Dionysus or Bacchus, the gods of intoxication, where letting one's hair down was a perfectly permissible and necessary part of the celebrations at certain times of year. Bacchus in some images resembles a Green Man – he too stands for untrammelled pleasures and shaking off the bonds of 'civilization' in the famous Bacchanalian revels.

In Celtic lore, the Bramble is dedicated to the Goddess of joy, exhilaration, intoxication in its many forms – and, if necessary, anger.

According to Celtic Irish mythology feminine Sovereignty, probably a memory of earlier times (more in a minute), was at one time vested in a goddess or semi-mythical priestess and queen known as Medb. In her original form, she was an intoxicating warrior-queen who ruled this time of harvest with its fruits, including and especially the Bramble and possibly the Vine which might well have been brought over from the Mediterranean or Asia Minor. As a representative of the land She was probably also an initiator for the new king into his duties of husbandry of the earth.

This archetype manifests almost as two different women. Medb/Maev/Mebh later became known as Queen Mab/Mabh. In this latter shape, she seems to have lost much of her original power, degenerating into a more biddable figure, associated with the fay.

Queen Mab appears as mostly benign and sometimes gently mischievous in Shakespeare. Mab as portrayed by Arthur Rackham as Queen of the Garden and its sensual delights clearly smells only of roses. She's the 'soft' face of the Goddess, innocent and still a girl. Mab is light-hearted.

However, in other images we see the warrior-queen seductress, undoubtedly closer to the ancient Goddess of Sovereignty, offering erotic pleasures and verbal swordplay, and not someone you would expect to roll over and have her tummy tickled; rather a queen of initiation and intoxication (also addiction), two aspects of the original Medb. An empowered woman, she is strong-willed and determined (think Boudicca meets Aphrodite).

This one knows that it doesn't always work to be a Good Girl, and that innocent pleasures are wonderful but that the deeps are more complex and ultimately rewarding. In the ancient texts, this Medb is described as a 'fair haired wolf queen, whose form was so beautiful that it robbed men of two-thirds of their valour upon seeing her' (that is, she was intoxicating).

Her name (Medb is pronounced approximately 'Mave') is said to mean 'she who intoxicates', and has etymological connections with the English word 'mead'. It is likely that the sacred marriage ceremony between the king and the goddess, in this case Medb, would involve a shared drink (mead was an ancient favourite, made from honey).

One of the most significant ancient texts from Ireland is a collection of legends known as the *Táin Bó Cuailnge**, or 'The Cattle Raid of Cooley' (more significant than it sounds. It was my misfortune to have to attempt to translate that from its original language during my degree course; all I remember now is how I never really grasped the literary concept of paradigms and glosses.)

The main story was kicked off by Medb's successful attempt to steal a white bull – very significant to the Celts and pre-Celtic peoples – by leading a raid on what is now Ulster from Connacht (though the raid itself was repulsed by the Ulstermen). In this story, we meet the famous Celtic hero Cú Chulainn.

Medb is sometimes connected with the Morrigan (often portrayed in threesomes, a memory of the old Triple Goddess of the pagan peoples: maiden, mother, crone; certainly Mab is reminiscent of the Maiden, and Medb might represent aspects of both of the latter two), and is a goddess associated with the land and its species, wild and domestic. Though she can be fiercely defensive at times as a protector-goddess, her primary role is to oversee the tending of the land, its animals and plants, and humans too. She is another shapeshifter, and some have commented that this ability is an expression of her affinity with the whole living universe. Goddess of the Harvest – and abundance, including sexual abundance. And then there's the intoxication of poetry.

Medb has at times been associated with Morgan le Fay – another powerful queen, intelligent, proud, kind, and schooled in the arts of magic, as well as representing both dark and light, and only later diminished into the better-known spiteful woman as she appears in the Arthurian legends in their written form.

It's my view that Queen Mab, as well as the Three Witches in Macbeth and alongside Morgan le Fay, are all degenerated images of women in Christian patriarchal times; women who held sovereign powers in pre-Christian society.

We know that it's likely that in late Neolithic times, and in the early Bronze Age, a Goddess-cult favoured the feminine principle as the bringer of all life. It is also the case that probably, until the Bronze Age warrior culture really took hold, Gaulish and British culture recognised a matrilineal succession, and that the Queen, representative of the Goddess, was expected to initiate the new King into becoming husband of the land in the sacred marriage, the *hieros gamos*, mentioned above, through sex.

Although this seemed to continue in the Celtic Iron Age despite the spread of the Judeo-Christian patriarchy, little by little the liberty of Celtic and proto-Celtic women to choose their own sexual partners and remain free of marriage ties if they wished subtly began to be portrayed as promiscuity. Medb of course acquired that label too.

I am a hill of poetry

Intoxication, in small doses, can certainly help with both visions and poetry...

Brambles are sacred to the faery realm, and supposedly drinking the sacred wine of the Bramble would help the person journey into the faery realm to communicate with them. This is a plant considered to protect entry into the hollow hills, the realm of the faeries, unless one is prepared, just as it protects entry into the places of shelter of small animals and birds.

Both Bramble and Vine were considered sacred in the worship of many pagan deities in ancient Europe, and temples and altars in honour of the deities would have carvings of one or the other to represent growth and the abundance of harvest.

There is also the altered state – the hundred-year-dreaming – vision? Prophecy? – that shows up in some of our fairy tales, such as Sleeping Beauty, via the 'princess' being pricked by, perhaps, a thorny Bramble.

Symbolism of Bramble and Vine

I think this has been covered above, one way or another. To recap, both fruits are symbols of abundance, intoxication, especially with sacred intent, prophecy, far-sightedness (metaphorically), vision, poetry and dreaming.

* The oldest manuscript of the *Táin*, known as *The Book of the Dun Cow* was compiled in the 12th century and contains language dated to the 8th century. However, it is assumed by most scholars that the story originated as an oral tale several centuries previously and that it includes descriptions of practices current in Celtic society in Ireland or Britain or in continental Europe as much as several centuries before the birth of Christ. (The *Táin* remains an invaluable source for Irish early history.)

Q for Quert: the Apple Tree

Malus sylvestris
September 30th–October 27th
The Otherworld Tree
Magic, and the land through the mists

I am the island of apples and eternal life

APPLE, QUERT/APFAL

When I was an undergraduate at Cambridge, uprooted from the beaches, cliffs, woods, and fields of my childhood and adolescence as I believe I said in relation to Willow, I often felt intensely lonely for wilder landscapes and fewer houses and people.

One of my consolations was to visit the Fitzwilliam Museum, where I would spend much time transfixed in front of a little painting, 'The Magic Apple Tree' by Samuel Palmer, painted almost 200 years ago now. I bought a postcard of it, and have it still – more than forty years later.

As a child growing up in rural Devon, my parents' walled garden (not as grand as it sounds – modest in size, bounded by ancient cob walls topped with slate slowly, and after heavy rain sometimes somewhat swiftly, subsiding back to soil) boasted four Apple trees of different varieties. We four children 'adopted' a tree each, gave it a name, had conversations with it perched in its boughs, told it our secrets, waited for the blossom in spring, collected the autumn fruit, buried our cats, when the time came, beneath the trees. I remember summer nights when I slept out beneath 'my' tree, listening to the hedgehogs revelling in the dishes of cat food we'd put out for them.

I know now that my tree was a Russet – as it happens, my favourite variety of Apple, though I hadn't put that together with my childhood tree at the time.

Now, I spend part of my year in Brittany. Brittany, like Devon and Somerset, has always been an Apple-growing region, and cider is one of its main products.

In and around the local forest the little Crab Apples (Crab Apple, *malus sylvestris*, being the ancestor of all our cultivated varieties and pollinator to all, too), gleam like small suns, or Christmas tree baubles. Once, when the forest hosted pigs (and wild boar), Apples would have been a much-relished part of the pigs' autumn diet, along with acorns, as would have happened in Britain too.

Once upon a time I used to look forward to the celebratory process of making the first Crab Apple jelly of the year; the jars would carry their warm deep amber cheer right through the winter.

As I mentioned in the introduction, Apple is not included in the Brythonic, or 'P' Celtic, alphabet that Graves uses (the Brythonic tongues are Welsh, Cornish, Breton and originally Manx), even though the Apple is hugely significant in so many of our Brythonic Celtic myths and legends. It does occur in the Goidelic, or 'Q Celtic, tongue of Ireland and Scotland, hence Quert for Apple.

No Celtic tree alphabet is complete without Apple, that most magical and sacred of trees, even though in this case it does of course throw Graves' alphabet, if not calendar, out of whack. (But how could late September/early October *not* belong to Apple?)

In the Brythonic Celtic tongue apple is apfal, aval, abhal, apfallen and many other recognisable versions of this word, all beginning with A, occur in other Indo-European languages. It's easy to see how Avalon developed out of these words. I've also found an older Irish Gaelic word for Apple than Quert: abhlach. Now we're talking. You will remember that the dying King Arthur was ferried by priestesses to the island through the mists, the Isle of Avalon, Avellenau, the Otherworld across the waters, whose very name means 'Apples'.

'A' would be the obvious Ogham letter, then; but it's a vowel, and in Graves' version, the vowel A is carried by Ailm, usually seen as Silver Fir (or by some sources Wych Elm).

This confusion notwithstanding, my version of this calendar allows Apple to carry Q for Quert as per the Irish Ogham, and Apple replaces Gort, Ivy, for this lunar month.

But I am galloping ahead of myself. (Apple is such an exciting tree it deserves a whole book.)

Apple history and habits

The Apple is a hardy, deciduous woody perennial tree that grows in all temperate zones. Apple trees like sun with a little shelter from frost, do well in coldish winters, and need reasonably high humidity. A full-size Apple tree cultivar can grow to about 30 feet (and can almost rival its height in its width), increasing by up to a foot a year, though its growth will slow with age. Apple trees can live for 100 years or more, and cultivated ones reward pruning with healthy crops.

Behind all our cultivated Apple trees – and we now have approximately 20,000 varieties worldwide, with about 6000 in Britain alone – stands the beautiful wild Crab Apple. As I said above, the Crab Apple, *Malus sylvestris*, is an ancestor of them all, and is also a pollinator for every variety.

But there is an older variety altogether, behind the Crab Apple. Who better to learn from about the history of Apple than Roger Deakin, in his inspiring book *Wildwood*?

'I am travelling to Kazakhstan, propelled by a story told to me by [Oxford don] Barrie Juniper... I had heard of Juniper's pioneering work in tracking down the origins of the domestic apple to the Tien Shan Mountains of Kazakhstan and had come to sit at his feet and learn more. Over lunch, he outlined the long journey of the domestic apple from the wild fruit forests of the Tien Shan along the so-called Silk Road to the west. In the course of that journey, Juniper has discovered, the wild apple of the Tien Shan, *Malus sieversus,* evolved into the domestic apple, *Malus domesticus,* and eventually found its way to Britain with the Romans.'

'By which time, it was already many thousands of years old.' Deakin continues that according to Barrie Juniper *Malus,* the botanical family to which all Apples belong, first evolved roughly an unthinkable twelve million years ago. Its journey west came via the guts of birds, bears, horses, through which the pips travelled unscathed and undigested. Luckily for us, the livestock naturally enough selected the juiciest and sweetest Apples they could find.

The Romans, Deakin continues, grafted this older *Malus sieversus* onto the Crab Apple, *Malus sylvestris,* stock. And helped to create the many hundreds of varieties the modern world knows.

The new kinds of Apples we know are in part due to the fact that you can plant, Deakin tells us, the pips of a hundred Apples from the same tree and the new generation of trees can differ, often dramatically, from their parents as well as from each other. Clearly, people taking cuttings and grafting the shoots continues this process. Deakin goes on:

'All Bramley seedlings are descended from a single tree in someone's back garden in Northampton. And so on, down thousands of years, so every single kind of eating apple in the world is a direct descendant of the apples that evolved in the forests of the Tien Shan.'

Deakin speaks of Kazakhstan's two great gifts to the world: 'the cultivated apple and the tamed horse'. How different life would be, and have been, without either of those.

On a different note, the Apple flower, like the Hawthorn and Blackthorn as well as the Rose to whose family these all belong, is five-petalled; and you can clearly see the five-pointed star on its base, as well as in the arrangement of pips if you cut an Apple around its waist. This pentangle, at the risk of excessive repetition, is associated with the Goddess, and sometimes identified with the five vowels. It is seen in some pagan teachings as representing the five 'stations' of the Goddess' year: Birth, Initiation, Love/Consummation, Repose, and Death (at the midwinter solstice).

The gifts from Apple

Throughout history, Apple has often been associated with the Tree of Life in various paradise gardens. It is indeed a tree of great beauty, with its blossom and fruits. Apple is the Fruit of Love, which may be why the Bible was so hard on it and Eve (see below).

Medicinally speaking, the Apple is indeed the fruit of the Tree of Life: scientifically it appears to be true that an Apple a day keeps the doctor away. For instance, studies have shown that Apples are full of vitamins, antioxidants and more, making them one of the best fruits for your health; and regularly eating whole Apples including the peel (preferably organic) has been linked to a lower risk of chronic diseases including type 2 diabetes, cancer, heart disease, and dementia. One study links Apple consumption with decreased levels of asthma.

In some country areas of the UK, wassailing ceremonies celebrating the Apple tree have been reinstated (they usually happen on January 17th), to wake the tree up and encourage its abundance. At home we too have observed this practice, pouring a small libation of cider or Apple juice onto the roots of each tree in our little orchard, or onto toast then lodged in a fork of the branches, and thanking the tree for its last harvest, telling it we're looking forward to the next.

Apple wood burns sweetly, and has a distinctive and for me at least very evocative scent (if you can bear to burn it at all – as one of the 'Noble' trees in Irish mythology it shouldn't be cut down).

Its mythology

In legend and folklore, the Apple (usually a Crab Apple), like the Hazel and Hawthorn, is a tree often found at the threshold between the worlds where magical things may happen. It is a tree of the Otherworld. The shaman's Silver Bough was hung with nine silver Apples; or sometimes it was the Golden Bough and golden Apples. W B Yeats brings the two together in 'Song of the Wandering Aengus', where at the very end Aengus says that he will 'pluck till time and times are done / the silver apples of the moon, / the golden apples of the sun', so synthesising the lunar – feminine, and solar – masculine, energies.

Apples, especially golden Apples, are significant in many cultures, and of course there was (or is) much migration of myth and legend to and from different shores. What we have now in the British culture is a rich fusion of many other cultures and their stories.

However, my own interest and speciality is the Celtic, hence my focus on the Celtic Ogham calendar and native British mythology.

I am the island of apples and eternal life

Apples are very much associated in Celtic myth with Avalon of the Otherworld, sometimes known as the Blessed, or Fortunate, Isles, or the Summerlands, with their Apple orchards, bees, birds and gentle sunshine.

The ancient Celtic Otherworld is generally seen as being on

a horizontal plane (rather than vertically upwards from this plane, like the Christian heaven): outward from the land mass. It is associated strongly with the sea and islands, or sometimes as a realm below the surface of the water.

The Otherworld is a happy place of peace and harmony, a perfect mirror image of this world, but one in which where there is no pain, sickness or ageing; the Otherworld in myth generally confers immortality on its inhabitants.

Geoffrey of Monmouth in his *Vita Merlini* says:

'The island of apples which men call "The Fortunate Isle" gets its name from the fact that it produces all things of itself; the fields there have no need of the ploughs of the farmers and all cultivation is lacking except what nature provides. Of its own accord it produces grain and grapes, and apple trees grow in its woods from the close-clipped grass. The ground of its own accord produces everything instead of merely grass, and people live there a hundred years or more.'

In the early texts, many individuals make journeys to the Fortunate Isles, this Garden of Eden in the western ocean (including Brân, or Fearn, the Alder god).

The Apple is an archetypal tree with deep connections to the Isle of Avalon, whose name means just that, as I've said. As the 'island through the mists', Avalon was the resting-place in the Otherworld to which Morgan le Fay, healer, seer, Druid priestess, poet, shape-shifter and one-time Queen of Avalon, and a Lady of the Lake, with her eight sister priestesses ferried the dying Arthur.

Avalon has been traditionally associated with Ynys Witrin, the Glass Isle arising from the misty waters of the ancient Summer Country that once surrounded what we now know as Glastonbury Tor (a place noted for its Apple orchards, previously but also now). For the Celts, Avalon was known for its abundance of orchards of golden (solar) Apples (though silver, lunar, Apples – as in Yeats' poem – were also associated with Avalon and/or the Otherworld).

The Isles of the Blessed are the Hesperides in Greek mythology, the Isles of Hesper (Aphrodite, goddess of love), or Venus in the Roman culture, the evening star. (Possibly, the Hesperides were once identified with what we now know as the Hebrides – 'Bride's Islands', Bride, or Brighid, as will be more than clear by now, being one manifestation of the Great Goddess in Britain.)

The Hesperides, like Avalon, were governed by nine wise women, and the orchard was host to a particularly special Apple tree, around whose roots coiled a guardian serpent of wisdom.

Esoterically it's said that, if you cut an Apple in half, one half is dedicated to Venus, the other to Lucifer, the Light-Bringer, Son of the Morning (Lugh, a fire-god, by another name; you'll remember he is an ancient solar god whom as 'Llew', as I mentioned in Hawthorn, marries a representative of this same Goddess, the Flower-Face, Blodeuwydd. Robert Graves tells us that Olwen, too, is a further face of Venus: 'the laughing Aphrodite of Welsh legend', associated both with Hawthorn and Blodeuwydd, and with Apple.)

This offers an altogether different take from the Christian one on Lucifer, doesn't it? Lucifer is simply the other, and necessary, pole to Venus, and our task according to spiritual psychology is to bring them both together.

This is another reason why I think the Apple is a suitable equinox tree: at the equinox the apparent opposites are held in balance, as are day and night at this time. What's more, the sign of Libra begins here at the equinox, and Libra is ruled by Venus.

One last little esoteric detail: Venus the planet, our nearest neighbour, in her eight-year journey around our earth scribes a trajectory that forms a beautiful geometric fivefold rosette.

Wise women: Morgan le Fay

We spoke of Morgan le Fay in relation to Bramble/Vine, but she is also very relevant in relation to the Apple. Morgan was probably to the Celts originally a goddess, then a member of the Faery Folk (as her old name, 'le Fay', announces), and queen. It is Morgan who rightly presides over the Isle of Avalon with its Apple orchards and its intrinsic gifts of healing into immortality.

Known to be skilled in the arts, especially music and poetry, in magic, in healing and in law, she'd have been quite some queen. She exemplified the kind of power that women were able to hold in pre-Celtic and Celtic (Iron Age) British and European society. It is no doubt because of this that the misogynistic Roman Christian religion denigrated and demoted her into the cunning malicious sorceress of the later legends who still appears as such in our contemporary films, artworks and writings.

In Geoffrey of Monmouth's *Vita Merlini*, where she is called Morgen, she is the most powerful Lady of Avalon. She is both healer and leader, and the mystical Isle of Apples is alive and fertile under her rule. Geoffrey describes her and her sister-priestesses thus:

'There, nine sisters administer genial rule over those who come to them from our homelands, and the first of them is the more learned in the art of healing, and her beauty exceeds that of her sisters. Her name is Morgen and she had learned the use of every kind of plant in curing the sicknesses of the body. She also knows the art of changing her appearance and of flying, like Daedalus, through the air on curious wings. As she wills it, she can be at Brest or at Chartres or at Pavia; and as she wills, she comes from the skies to your shores. They say she taught mathematica to her sisters Monrone, Mazoe, Gliten, Glitonea, Gliton, Tyronoe, Thiten – Thiten is famous for her lyre. It was there that we took Arthur after the battle of Camlann where he was wounded... we came there with the prince, and Morgen received us with honour, as was fitting, and placed the king in her chamber on a golden bed, and with her hand she unwrapped his wound and looked at it for a while, and then said that it would be possible to return him to health if he were to stay with her for a long time and place himself in her hands. Rejoicing, therefore, we committed the king to her...'

Gerald of Wales (Giraldus Cambrensis) also makes Morgan a queen and healer, in his description of Avalon/Glastonbury in the *De instructione principum*:

'It was here, to this island which is now called Glastonbury, that Morgan, a noble matron and the ruler/leader and patron [dominatrix atque patrona] of those parts, and also close in blood to King Arthur, took Arthur after the battle of Camlann for the healing of his wounds...'

Marion Zimmer Bradley opens her iconic 'feminist' portrayal of the women, and also of the conflict between the old goddess-based earth religions rooted in paganism and Druidry and the new religion of Christianity, in Arthurian myth in her novel *The Mists of Avalon* with this passage:

'MORGAINE SPEAKS...

In my time I have been called many things: sister, lover, priestess, wise-woman, queen. Now in truth I have come to be wise-woman, and a time may come when these things may need to be known. But in sober truth, I think it is the Christians who will tell the last tale. For ever the world of Fairy drifts further from the world in which the Christ holds sway. I have no quarrel with the Christ, only with his priests, who call the Great Goddess a demon and deny that she ever held power in this world. At best, they say that her power was of Satan. Or else they clothe her in the blue robe of the Lady of Nazareth – who indeed had power in her way, too – and say that she was ever virgin. But what can a virgin know of the sorrows and travail of mankind?

'And now, when the world has changed, and Arthur – my brother, my lover, king who was and king who shall be – lies dead (the common folk say sleeping) in the Holy Isle of Avalon, the tale should be told as it was before the priests of the White Christ came to cover it all with their saints and legends.'

Wise women: paradise and Eve

So to recap, the Apple tree is associated with Paradise – of which the fabled Avalon is a reflection and a version – in which the Goddess nurtured and protected all beings.

I'm interested in what happened to this original 'Garden of Eden' under Christianity. In the earlier pagan tradition, Paradise was a land in which the first human being, whom we know as 'Adam' from the Bible, was blessed by the Great Goddess with her sacred fruit, which gave everlasting life as well as knowledge.

Here's an alternative. The Goddess here is perhaps in her incarnation known as Sophia, the Goddess of Wisdom, and she and the serpent worked together to further the evolution of human consciousness. The serpent, sometimes depicted as a dragon, was previously identified in pagan times as a bringer of knowledge and wisdom. It was a formidable but predominantly benevolent force associated with the earth and earth's electrical currents mapped out as ley lines or dragon lines.

Very different from orthodox Christianity's view of humans in the Garden as having succumbed to wicked ways by being tempted by an 'evil' serpent. The serpent's being reviled began to happen probably only when Roman Christianity started to separate matter and spirit and enforce a dualistic view. (It's also the case that the probable matriarchy, or at least matrilineal descent, and female sexual freedoms of Neolithic and early Bronze Age times were also being forcibly phased out, little by little, though they hung on, just, into the Iron Age. This was despite the continuing positions of power held by women before the Christian era, and the warrior spirit that infused the Bronze and Iron Ages was also partly responsible, ushering in our continuing climate of patriarchy.)

How different would it be if we had seen Eve as a bringer-of-wisdom, her ally the snake, rather than an ignorant and shameful woman deserving only of our blame for bringing about, singlehandedly but with the snake complicit, in effect, the downfall of the whole human race?

In fact, some aspects of the Garden of Eden myth as we now know it were scribed by Cyprianus Gallus in 425 CE, though he was not the first to rewrite the myth: at various times before, it had been recorded by male monotheists in forms that blamed woman and serpent (though earlier versions – for the myth recurs throughout history – didn't), presumably as a way of keeping women in check, and making sure the human race knew just how sinful it was.

It's interesting, too, that the Latin Apple genus is 'malus', or 'malum', a word carrying shades of evil in its etymology. ('Malum' also refers to the pomegranate, another fruit dedicated to the Goddess. 'Apple' in the Latin Bible may have been a mistranslation; some say it should be neither apple nor pomegranate, but fig.)

Cyprianus was a poet, and who knows whether he was deliberately making a play on the word 'malum' to mean both 'apple' and 'evil' since the word carries both meanings.

Symbolism of Apple

Apple is a tree associated with increased poetic inspiration (building on the gifts from Bramble or Vine), abundance, generosity, open-heartedness (once again), and sensitivity. It's a portal tree into the realms of the Otherworld, and especially given to aiding those who seek a glimpse of the Blessed Isles.

In the Bach flower remedies, the Crab Apple is a potent cleanser on a psychological or emotional level.

My own experience is that it's a tree of vision/s. I see it as a most Otherworldly presence, and it is a 'threshold' tree, as I mentioned above. I've had unexpected visions or lucid dreams beneath or near a Crab Apple tree. If you have ever seen the way a wild Crab Apple deep in the woods hung with golden globes of small fruit in the autumn glows like a tree decked with lanterns, you will also know just how magical it is. Up the lane from me there is one right now, radiant in the rather drab autumn hedgerows.

Apple Tree

Wassail night has passed and winter's
blue flames have retreated for now.
In the orchard, a thrush stabs the last
soft apple, and another calls from the tallest
tree. If you were to come by here, come
and stand by me here, I would hold
your palm to the trunk, tell you how to open
the eyes and ears of your hand so you
could feel how again the xylem and phloem
are waking, making their long slow
streaming journey between earth and star,
if you were to come here, to come by here again.
Roselle Angwin

S for Straif (also St, Z) the Blackthorn Tree

Prunus spinosa
October 28th–November 24th
The Old One: guardian of secrets and the inner world
Protectorship; hibernation; rest; renewal; will

I am the black bough, the Cailleach (Crone)

BLACKTHORN, STRAIF

If Hawthorn is the portal to midsummer, then Blackthorn heralds the approach of the depths of winter. Where Hawthorn represents the May Queen, the Flower Maiden, Blodeuwydd in Welsh myth, Blackthorn is the fierce face of the Great Goddess Ceridwen, the Old One who tends the cauldron of life, death and rebirth: Crone and Cailleach.

You will remember that Hawthorn and Blackthorn, according to my calendar, sit each at the month diametrically opposite the other, and have to be considered as a pair – Hawthorn the light face, the Blackthorn the darker aspect.

As sister trees, the Whitethorn (another name for Hawthorn) symbolises the peak of the light time, and the Blackthorn the dark: faces of the same principle, and between them they map the journey of the Maiden of Imbolc in early spring (2nd February) to the Mother of midsummer, followed by the Cailleach, the wise crone, who ushers in winter at Samhain, 1st November, which used to be the old Celtic new year – after which the Maiden is once again reborn.

Blackthorn history and habits

Blackthorn is most noticeable through the late autumn and winter months, with its sloes and then its early new blossom. In rain, its stems are black. Blackthorn symbolises the entry into the dark at midwinter with its ink-blue sloes, and also the emergence into early spring when it often blossoms before there are any leaves, Blackthorn or otherwise, or any flowers other than snowdrops, anywhere in the hedgerows.

In part because of this, the thorns are easily told apart, since Blackthorn's blossom will be on the trees before either has leafed (though Hawthorn will leaf before Blackthorn and before she herself flowers). Unlike the lobed leaves of Hawthorn, Blackthorn leaves are slender, slightly pointed and oval.

The wood of Blackthorn is very hard, very durable. It has been used for cudgels and shillelaghs, and for witches' and wizards' magical staves, or 'black rods'.

Blackthorn's thorns were used in domestic magic of the more malign sort for sticking into 'poppets': wax dolls made to represent a specific person to whom one, or one's client, wished ill.

The gifts from Blackthorn

We all know about sloes: those bitter tongue-squinching relatives of our damsons and plums. They used to be used as powerful purgatives for cleansing the stomach; and are also an ingredient in that infamous hedgerow jam. The berries make a dye, though it's hard to make it light-fast.

Once used to make walking sticks and the teeth of wooden rakes, especially hay-rakes, they're now best known for gin: made at Samhain, or later, once the berries have a good 'bloom' on them, this is best stored and drunk at the following Samhain (recipes are easily found). Sloes are also a favourite in wine-making. And her thorns can be made into sewing needles and natural pins or nails.

Like the Hawthorn, Blackthorn is an excellent hedging shrub, and long rows of the two thorns were planted during the dark time of the Enclosures in the 18th century onwards, to keep the country people out and the landowners' stock in.

Like haws, the sloe berries help feed over-wintering birds, and the bushes protect the homes and passage of many small mammals and birds.

The Blackthorn, however, has a secret weapon against those who stray too far towards her: her thorns are known for their ability to cause septicaemia.

Blackthorn

I fell in love that late winter
and in the January she flowered
so dramatically, so early –
the hedge at the bottom of the field
lit like a snowfield – white bells
on all the black branches.

Early, the Cailleach gave way
to the Maiden, and I
was almost blinded by her
abundance, as if she'd come out
to celebrate, as if youth, as if
love, would always triumph.
Roselle Angwin

Its mythology

I am the black bough, the Cailleach (Crone)

As the tree of the Cailleach, or Crone, Blackthorn is dedicated to Ceridwen, the great Old One of Celtic tradition, as Hawthorn symbolises the Maiden ready to become the Mother, Blodeuwydd.

Ceridwen, Keeper of the Cauldron of life, death and rebirth (you may remember we met such a cauldron in the story about Brân, Fearn, in Alder month), is an initiatrix, inducting young men into the mysteries of life.

Another way of looking at such a cauldron is as the womb from which all beings emerge, eventually to return as they soften back into the earth. Ceridwen stirs the Cauldron, the magical Cauldron, even as she guards and protects the watery places of the earth, and in Welsh mythology her cauldron was boiling away by a lake, and was the cause of Gwion Bach becoming the great seer-Bard Taliesin.

The Cauldron preceded, and probably was an earlier form of, the Grail.

I think it might be important to remember that the Crone, known in the Celtic tradition as the Cailleach, although fierce, is not necessarily the traditional repulsive old hag, known only for being grim, in fairy tale, but actually someone who is on the way to being the wise elder (coming to full maturity in the next month, Elder month). She is someone who knows her own boundaries and is not afraid to enforce them in whatever way seems fit at the time. She is also someone who is not constrained by what people think of her.

Not all fairy tales, of course, do paint the Crone in a repulsive wicked light; for instance, many of the Arthurian tales, while hardly being flattering in relation to the Crone, still have it that it is she who will offer the young knight the crucial wisdom that he seeks so urgently – *if* he will listen, rather than simply passing by in disgust. Sometimes this wisdom comes at a price – I'm reminded of the spiny spiky nature of Blackthorn.

Blackthorn's Old Irish name of Droigion (and the Welsh Draenenwen) are probably cognate with the Irish names for a wizard, Draoi, and a Druid, Draí.

Symbolism of Blackthorn

Both the thorns are guardian trees, and Blackthorn has the task both of allowing us and protecting our journey into the Underworld for healing. Simultaneously, Blackthorn can promise emergence into light while we're in the darkness, like her blossom.

Where Hawthorn is all midsummer showiness and 'out there', my sense of Blackthorn is its privacy: its secretiveness, its quiet inwardness. Its fruits point into the dark, into which we all need to enter sometimes as part of the perennial cycle: to see, clear and shed our past, our burdens and our pain; to rest; to be reborn with the simple, spare, five-petalled flowers on the dark spiny boughs towards the waning of the dark times, at the time of the spring maiden – altogether less extraverted than Hawthorn.

Clearly, thorns are thorns – about boundaries and protection. Blackthorn in particular can teach us about the skilful development and use of willpower and intention. Thorns are also about the inextricability of life and death – to have the one you have to accept the other. Some books will give you a dark picture of malevolent trees – either or both Blackthorn and Hawthorn, though most often the Blackthorn. It is true that they are not to be messed with, the latter especially. However, my experience with both has been benign – if they are approached with respect.

If Hawthorn, Huath, is as full and inviting in its summer bridalwear as it's possible to be, Blackthorn's blossom is early and less showy, and for most of the year she is easily passed by. However, even Hawthorn has a darker side. The name of the tree in the tree-alphabet means something like 'fearsome' or 'terrible'. A tree with thorns; not to be messed with. Blossom can be a distraction; we might forget to look deeper. The heart has its own reasons and seasons; not always fair and sunny. (And then there is, too, the crown of thorns.)

Sweetness and light always have a shadow. 'Straif', the Celtic name for Blackthorn, means 'strife', more challenging again. If one takes the view that the Blackthorn is the twin, or shadow, of Hawthorn, then we can see Blackthorn as carrying this darker side for both thorns. Blackthorn lies in the hedges secretly; unless you are there to gather its sloes it's easy to pass it by. Guarding its secrets, it can cause serious damage with its thorns. However, although there is a 'keep-off' quality to Blackthorn, my experience is also that, if one stops to notice it at a respectful distance, it welcomes the connection.

Often blossoming before spring has really begun to arrive, hanging her flowers on bare branches in February when all else is bleak, Blackthorn remains a particular favourite of mine. Blackthorn offers the way into darkness – and the way back out into the light.

In our extraverted culture, I wonder if we tend to find introversion, privacy and inwardness a bit 'dark', whereas actually it's an essential counterpart to fully living in the outer world? Blackthorn offers us a chance to remedy this. Actually, it will happen whether we go willingly or not – that is how it is in this world, which appears to cycle between the poles.

Blackthorn at its Cailleach sloe-time of Samhain, October 31st/ November 1st, the old midwinter festival, offers us healing and inspiration as we enter the dark time of the cycle. But Blackthorn *is also* the young maiden emerging at Imbolc, February 1st/2nd: hope arising from darkness. (We see this motif of the Old One, once embraced, once again becoming her spring self in various Celtic myths.)

In Hawthorn month I mentioned the idea of promise, pain, fulfilment. Here's a recap: Writer on things Celtic R J Stewart says that the Hawthorn 'like the rose, carries blossom, thorns and fruit, showing in nature the three stages of transformation: promise, pain and fulfilment.' I asked you to look at fulfilment in relation to Hawthorn, during the year's zenith of maximum light and fruition. Blackthorn may seem to offer more of the pain side (followed by the promise of spring). It's pain that is the impetus, often, for evolution. I said:

This triad is worth considering in the light of our own lives. New beginnings, whether in a job, or a relationship, or a house or area, seem to hold out such promise at the beginning.

Later, rose-tinted spectacles slipping down our noses a bit, we see the worm in the heart of the rose, the frog-warts on the prince, the frown lines on the princess. We think we might be happier elsewhere (or at least, we do when we're younger). We try and avoid the pain.

But actually, of course, we can't – it's through the struggles associated with pain that we learn and grow, after which transformation might be possible.

The two thorns taken together epitomise the understanding of this twin-nature, as well as the threefold cycle of death>birth>maturity (Crone or Cailleach, Maiden, Mother). Even in the depths of winter, light, spring and summer are all in waiting, just as even at the height of summer, darkness and winter are in the slipstream.

The wheel of the year
turns through its spheres and seasons
the spikes of growth, the cycles of decay

shallow times
and deeper times
fallow times
and full –

and here's the rub: creatures
of night and day both

we mislay ourselves somewhere
maybe forever

in the siren strait between the two

all seems lost

and then
all is not lost
but waiting to return

(lines from 'Entering the Wood' in *Bardo*, by Roselle Angwin, Shearsman 2011)

Remember that I wrote of the right use of the will. It has been suggested that Blackthorn also offers the possibility both of retribution (it's not a coincidence that the fester-making thorns of Blackthorn were traditionally used to stick into poppets, wax dolls representing someone to whom one wishes harm) – and redemption. Which route we will take will depend on many factors, not least our own level of personal development.

This is a Celtic recognition of the laws of give and take, and also cause and effect. What you put out will return to you. It's wise to use this power skilfully.

R for Ruis: the Elder Tree

Sambucus nigra
November 25th–December 22nd
The Faery Tree
Endings & beginnings; sacrifice & regeneration

I am the faery tree, and I am a wave of the sea

ELDER, RUIS

Making an Elder Whistle
for my father

You taught me the names of birds,
their patterns of flight; got me up
at first light for the dawn chorus.

Before I was five I knew how to catch
sticklebacks, up to my childish knees
in the Vellator streams. You taught me

which species of waterbirds roosted
in the marshes in winter; how to spell
the tides and the movements of the moon.

It was you who took me to the holy wells
and stone circles of our land; you who
showed me how to strip the pith

from a neat-cut twig of elder, how to
shape it, make a pipe to whistle
up the wind, or the Fair Folk.
Roselle Angwin

Elder history and habits

And we come to the thirteenth tree, the thirteenth moon, of our solar year. Elder takes us right up to and Graves would say just beyond the winter solstice, the darkest point of the year, before the tree cycle begins again with Birch.

The Elder tree, like other small but magical trees of the Celtic lands and northern Europe such as the Rowan and the Birch, seems to have been a tree of significance to our ancestors, with Elder artefacts dating back to the late Neolithic. Pollen core samples suggest that Elder was here before the last Ice Age.

Elder is a small tree, or large shrub (although it can grow to more than 30 feet, the ones we commonly see are rarely more than five to seven metres in height) with a deeply fissured trunk. It thrives on waste ground, especially if the latter is nitrogen-rich from, say, waste-heaps or middens of organic matter from human cultivation or settlements. Throughout western Europe it's a common shrub of hedgerows, in gardens, or by footpaths, although because of surrounding superstitions it was often grubbed out of hedgerows by farmers.

It is distinctive by virtue of its wide extravagant creamy blooms in early summer, which perfume the air around it; and distinctive in late autumn on account of its dark red-black berries (which I now remember were also a vital component of my so-so-hedgerow-jam-making days) on bright red stems.

The heads of blossom can grow up to 20 cm or so across as spreading umbels. Formerly Elder was classified as a member of the honeysuckle family, Caprifoliaceae, and there is a similarity between the two fragrances. Now, however (though the fragrance remains the same!) it has been reclassified as belonging in the Adoxaceae family. Elder's tiny flowers making up a spreading head of blossom are – guess what – five-petalled, each with five yellow stamens, and each flower nestles in a minute star of five green sepals.

The gifts from Elder

Elder's name probably originated from the Anglo-Saxon *aeld* and *eldrun*, meaning 'fire' and 'furnace' respectively. It's had many names in northern and western Europe, many of them connecting the tree with the Lady of the Woods, Elen of the Ways, the Old One.

The wood of the Elder has rarely, if ever, been used for timber, building or firewood (and in fact, the Elder being a sacred shrub, it was considered taboo and disrespectful in the extreme to the spirit of the wood, the Elder Lady, to cut down or burn an Elder). However, twigs and small branches were often gathered or even cut and turned or carved for simple household utensils such as pegs or combs, or hollowed out (the pith is spongey and easily pushed out) and used to blow on a fire to increase the flame.

In addition to a kind of bellows, they were used in earlier generations to make peashooters. Short straight lengths of the young green wood also were also cut to make whistles – best cut in winter when their sap is low. I can still remember their tone from when my father used to make them for me, and my sense of excitement that something so wonderful came from such a small length of twig. (There is some connection here with Alder, both in name and in the fact that both make whistles or pipes and/or are connected with music.) Whistles, pipes or flutes made from Elder wood have a reputation for aiding enchantment, and contact with the Fair Folk, the faery. The chanters of Welsh bagpipes are traditionally made from Elder wood.

An infusion of the flowers is an excellent tonic to drink through the summer, and good for the skin of the face, too. And almost everyone will know of Elderflower cordial, drink of the goddess – best with sparkling water to dilute it, and a little ice and twist of lemon – and sparkling Elderflower pressé is a drink almost to rival champagne (try it in a gin instead of tonic water). Here's the recipe I use for **Elderflower cordial**:

take 25 heads of elderflowers
use the pared strips of 2 lemons
remove the ends and pith of those lemons, slice and put with
elderflowers in large bowl

Gently bring to the boil, stirring all the time:
1.2 litres of water with
1.8 kgs of sugar

When the sugar has dissolved pour on the flowers and
lemons. Stir in
75 gms of citric or tartaric acid

Cover and leave to steep overnight. Strain through muslin
the next day, and bottle – it makes two litres and should keep
a few months; sterilise the bottle/s first (after washing) in a
hottish oven. Dilute to taste.

Elder has been an invaluable source of food and, more, medicine
to humans from ancestral times. Elder bark, leaves, flowers and
berries all treat many ailments including bruises, wounds, colds,
inflammation, hay fever, respiratory illness and fevers (though
the bark, leaves and roots can be toxic if ingested in quantity).

The berries are rich in vitamin C, and I remember my mother
(and later I myself, too) making elderberry cordial for the winter
to help with colds and to boost the immune system.

Its berries are particularly potent, and it is said that the Druids
viewed any that remained on the tree in December as a gift from
the Earth Goddess (or the Moon Goddess, who was seen as the
spirit of the Elder). The December berries would be gathered
and made into a sacred wine, said to enable clairvoyance.

The berries also offer rich nutrition to all manner of small
creatures and birds in the early winter; and in human use various
colours can be obtained as dyes from the leaves and berries,

though it's hard to make the colours light-fast.

Elder trees are very often found near homes, where in the past they were seen to protect the home and family against both negative influences and lightning; and despite the fact that it's a tree of enchantment, a witch's tree and a faery tree itself (see below), it's said it protects against bewitching and the black arts.

It is other

in this inextricable thicket where winter Elder holds life and death
an urge to separation pulls right now when my heart's strung out
and there's no closure for the family madness   only endless overlapping

trees let twigs and branches fall   let their dead leaves turn to nourishment
this is how they live   a single bracken frond waggles like an admonishing finger
says don't ask the green for answers   the grove is not a mirror where you'll see yourself
Pat Childerhouse, participant on the first (2019) course; first draft

Its mythology

I am the faery tree and I am a wave of the sea

Elder, the faery tree in its low-growing many-trunked habits, doesn't succumb to winter storms very easily.

Death & rebirth
In the Celtic Tree Calendar, Elder marks the darkest time of year and so is associated with death and the Cailleach, the Crone

aspect of the triple Goddess. She guards the entrance to the Underworld and the cauldron of life/death/rebirth, and what are also known as the inner mysteries.

Robert Graves tells us that Ruis' month is when 'the wave returns to the sea, and the end of the year to its watery beginning'. A cycle is complete. What adds potency to this is that it foretells the roebuck in the thicket: 'A wave of the sea in Irish and Welsh poetry is a "sea-stag": so that the year begins and ends with the white roebuck.'

So Elder marks endings, associated first with death (a cycle, a habit, the fullness of a season, the completion of a relationship, a project, a job, a home, or a phase of life), and then with regeneration – the transition from Crone to Maiden, which happens at Imbolc, February 2nd. The cycle never finishes, and life hands over to death, which hands over to new life, and on and on.

As we go into the dark time of the year, we meet a kind of death, and symbolically we often need to sacrifice something of our previous life, no matter how small. Elder frequently sacrifices small branches; just as frequently it regenerates with more, sprouting shoots from any part of its trunk or branches (or roots).

There is something in us, naturally enough, that resists endings and the idea of death. Making peace with endings is a key to liberation. Nothing new can begin without the passing of the old. And we could say that every day, every moment, is a new beginning – this is simply the natural order of things. Elder symbolises this.

We can learn from Elder. Elder in my experience has the unusual quality of being kind, friendly, self-contained; 'tame' by virtue of growing so frequently near human habitation but 'wild' because, although flexible, Elder bows to no-one, and commands respect.

To do this as a human without emotional reactivity,

posturing or defensiveness (Elder is not big enough to posture, and has no thorns for self-defence; simply gives freely of leaves – some caterpillars need them – flowers and fruit) requires a degree of the kind of wisdom that comes with maturity. It's a fine art, that of individuation in a human; a prerequisite, psychotherapeutically speaking, of Elderhood. It requires giving up some of our younger ways and living with a wise and self-determining generosity.

John Matthews and Will Worthington in their *Green Man Tree Oracle* deck say this about Elder:

'FROM SACRIFICE COMES RESTORATION
Sacrifice requires us to set aside something we value, in a specifically sacred way. We give what is worthy, honouring our most holy ones and acknowledging the reality of the unseen side of life, which is too often ignored or neglected. We do not give out of fear or in appeasement, but to make space in our daily lives for the Divine, for we believe that if we do so the Divine will make way for us. Sacrifice is a way of generous and unselfish giving to the whole of the universe, without something being lost.'

They also have this interesting little snippet: 'Witches were rather fond of turning themselves into Elders.'

Witches & faery

The Elder is very much associated with the Fair Folk, and witchcraft in the sense of white-witchery and healing (though this was of course later demonised by the Christian Church so that the Elder became a negative symbol. It's for this reason too that it has been rumoured that Judas Iscariot hanged himself from an Elder tree – however, this motif first occurs only in the mediaeval text of Langland's *Piers Plowman* – and that the cross on which Jesus Christ was crucified was supposedly in part made of Elder. Both stories are extremely unlikely, for many reasons, not least the fact that if you really look at an Elder tree it's almost impossible to see how anyone could be hanged from its dense, raggedy and slender branches (it grows many trunks rather than one, generally); and it doesn't have the strength to be turned into structures.

Music-making, & the moon

I've said already that Elder makes fine pipes and whistles; it seems that it may have been used also to make stringed instruments, not dissimilar to harps and lyres (the etymology of 'sambucus' suggests this). This, of course, adds an extra dimension to its being a singing tree, a tree of 'enchantment' - 'en-chant-ment' ('chant' meaning 'incantation' as much as song or plainsong).

The Tarot card in 'Das Baum Tarot', 'The Tree Tarot', a relatively recent German deck, shows the Elder Lady, identified by many mythologians including and notably Robert Graves with the White Goddess, as also the Moon Queen, which is apposite for the end of our yearlong cycle of lunar months.

Symbolism of Elder

An Elder person is wise, generous and loves freely. They can thrive anywhere, and know that they are both resilient and resourceful, and, just as an Elder branch might take root and the Elder tree can drop and replace its limbs easily, they too can shed the past, regenerate, and rejuvenate.

Elder knows deep truths that many people prefer not to look at, thereby remaining unconscious.

Elder invites us to review our past year, and to consider what doors we may need to close before the midwinter solstice offers new ones to open as we turn back towards the light.

Even more than Blackthorn, a particular, and challenging, gift of Elder is its invitation to think about death and deaths.

Endings

So we have come to the end of the solar year and this 13-month cycle; and Birch at midwinter with her pioneering ways will take on the task of regeneration that is the promise of the Elder tree (its name, Elder, is apposite for the culmination of a cycle, and the symbolism of the Crone).

And we're back at the winter solstice, a 'thin veil' time when, with the aid of Elder, we may walk between the worlds with the faery folk.

I am going to close with a very different poem about Elder written by another participant on the first of my 'Tongues in Trees' online course in 2019.

Elder, Ruis
(Sambucus nigra)

We are the elders now ~
blossoms blown
cordial crushed
leaves loosened
berries bitten
bark bare.
Beautiful!
Sabah Raphael Reed

An extra tree for the midwinter solstice

Y or I for Iolo: the Yew Tree

Taxus Baccata

December 23rd (properly the 21st, the winter solstice, in my view)

The Time of No Time

Longevity; regeneration; birth, death & rebirth

> *I am the waves' eternal return*
> *The grave of every vain yearning*
> *I know the secret of the three moons*
> *And the secret path*
> *And my dwelling place is the wind on the sea, the dolmen on the*
> *hillside, the rock in the river.*

Now we've come to the end of the 13-moon Ogham tree calendar. Or – not quite, as there is still the hiatus between the very end of Ruis and the beginning with Beth. In my calendar, Yew straddles this gap; so here is an outline for Yew, Iolo, Y, I, astride the winter solstice and the following couple of days (in Graves' reckoning it's 23rd December).

Winter solstice

> First you need to shed all you know
> or can name
> then you need to step out of
> your shoes, your shadow, your own
> light, and your home. Strip
> naked as the four winds
> and forget being upright

215

unless you want to dance, and then
dance the stone row to the stone circle
and allow the sky to take your voice.

This is the season of yew and periwinkle
of Persephone's descent
to the winter god.
Watch for the barn owl
and Hecate at the crossroads
and prepare to hang from the World Tree
until you are sobered by silence
and stillness, and the great
white unending song of the spheres.

Kneel on the earth until
you become a reed, a snail, a fox,
another word for truth.
Be the berry in the midnight stream
that the water bears away.

Transformed into all
you may be, step forward and cross
the threshold, gateway to gods
and ancestors, to what will endure
beyond all that you can imagine
of the play of particle, of wave –
take the hand that's offered, step through
this gateway to the light that burns within
which now you'll never lose again.
Roselle Angwin

YEW, Y or I for IOLO, TAXUS BACCATA

The Yew tree, representing the vowel 'Y' or 'I', probably stood
at one of the five gates of the Goddess year. Some place Yew

at Samhain, including the more common Celtic ascriptions; for me, its natural position as guardian of the doorway between life and death is at the darkest time, the longest night, of the winter solstice (which is also when the old Germanic calendar has it).

In many Ogham calendars there is an evergreen, a conifer, at the winter solstice. Yew, not bearing cones as we normally recognise them, used to be classified between the broadleaves and the conifers, but it is certainly evergreen. However, in taxonomy, it has now been reclassified as a conifer.

As I've written elsewhere, in fact the solstice, the 'sun's standstill', appears to take place over three days, and in the Celtic Ogham calendar, according anyway to Robert Graves, Yew/Iolo's day is the day-out-of-time of December 23rd. Let's say it keeps watch over the 21st, 22nd and 23rd of December.

There's much to say about Yew: it's one of the trees that is most compelling in our calendar, both revered and feared and sometimes both. As it probably guarded, symbolically as well as actually, the doorways between life and death of our ancestors (often found by prehistoric megaliths, especially barrows and tombs), so it was also adopted by the Christians, to do the same thing in graveyards. It has long been seen as a protector tree. The Christians took over the ancient sacred sites of the pagans, and there is reason to suppose that some of the Yew trees, especially in very old small churchyards that are on raised, and maybe circular, ground, could date back to the Celtic Iron Age and its earthworks.

Yew was significant enough to give its name to the Iberian peninsula, from 'ibe' meaning Yew; and the Gaulish Celts had at least two significant tribes named for Yew: the Eurobones and Eburovices. The old name for what is now Ireland was Ierne, or Ibar, 'Yew Island'. It is said that the Druidic Isle of Iona may well have actually once been Iolo, Iola or Ioha, or more probably derived from Ioua, the Pictish word for Yew, and that 'Iona' was a monk's mistranscription.

In a previous life, I was a shoemaker working out of the old ox-yard at Buckland Abbey: once a Cistercian monastery, then owned after the Reformation by, variously, Francis Drake, Richard Grenville and in the twentieth century the National Trust.

From the window of my workshop I could look out and see the great line of ancient Yew trees. During a violent storm in the late 1990s the one nearest my workshop came down. It was shocking, much more than I would have expected: it took a long time to fall, with a great deal of woody groaning as the roots were pulled out of their hold. After, I went and stared and stared, feeling shaken and helpless. It looked like some great felled mammal, roots waving slightly in the aftershock. It wasn't by a long way the first time I'd related to a tree, obviously; but it was the first time I'd felt such a heart shock, akin to seeing an animal die.

We don't know how old the Yews were, but a thousand years plus was mooted.

Later my neighbour, a woodturner, made me a set of four claves, and a beautiful wide shallow bowl from the wood.

Yew history and habits

While Yews are very slow-growing, and often spread more laterally than they gain in height, British Yew trees rarely exceed 15 metres in height.

Most people have probably heard of the Fortingall Yew in Scotland, one of the known oldest Yews in Britain, estimated to be anything from 2,000 to 9,000 years old.

Estimates of the longevity of Yews in general vary enormously, from a few hundred years to several thousand. For various reasons it's hard to date them, and an ancient one we see may not be the original 'body' of that particular tree, as once the heartwood has died down (with age), the tree can regenerate from the outside-in with shoots of new life – or a shoot will begin in the inside and take the place of the old trunk. One of the reasons it's hard to age Yew trees is because the trunks of almost all old yew trees end up hollow – a good survival strategy to resist wind and storm – and therefore leave no growth rings.

Birds, who eat the seeds, are the primary form of Yew distribution. They also reproduce themselves by internal roots, suckering, when branches touch the ground and take root, and layering. In this way they can form groves.

Fred Hageneder, who has written several informative books about trees, suggests that it might be Yew rather than Ash that is 'The World Tree', the Tree of Life. He says: 'The Nordic Tree of Life, Yggdrasil, not only represents the central pole, the foundation and the unity of the universe, but is also intimately connected with the spiritual search for divine knowledge. In the Eddas, the Icelandic scriptures, Yggdrasil is described as "winter-green needle-ash". Unfortunately, this has been understood as an Ash tree over the past few hundred years. But the Ash is not evergreen, nor has it needles. And anyway, Nordic 'ask' can mean Ash, but also simply "sharp, pointed".' Was it, in fact, the Yew?

Hageneder also reminds us:

'In [Norse] myth, Odin, the god of wisdom, hangs himself from Yggdrasil's branches for nine days and nights, on a vision quest from which he brings back the runes, i e the magical alphabet, to share with humankind. Odin climbing the Universal Tree is the prototype of the truth-searching shaman, a tradition we find right across Eurasia.'

The gifts from Yew

Another name for the Yew is 'ironwood' – so called because it can endure longer than even metal. Still extant is a spear which has been dated at least as far back as 150,000 years; some speculate that the 'Clacton spear tip' might have been made in the Hoxnian interglacial period, 200,000–300,000 years BCE.

When some of the original Yew foundations on which Venice was built were removed, they were good enough to be sold off for contemporary building!

We know from the preserved Alpine Iceman that Yew longbows were being used in the Neolithic, at least 5,300 years ago. Later, British archers using longbows made from Yew were significant in crucial battles during the Hundred Years War, and in later centuries too. It is because there was such demand for Yew wood in the Middle Ages that we have so few stands of Yew today.

'Yew that is old in churchyard mould, He breedeth a mighty bow' says Rudyard Kipling in 'Puck of Pook's Hill'.

Every part of the Yew is highly toxic to animals and humans – except for the flesh of the berries (see my poem below). However, for 50 years or more medicine has been researching, trialling and, since the 1990s, using an extract from the Yew tree to treat certain tumours.

Yew trees provide food (in the form of the berries, known as 'arils'), and shelter for birds and small mammals. The scarce goldcrests and firecrests seem to seek out Yew trees.

Its mythology

There is much to find online if you search for Yew. All I'm going to say here is that for the ancient Greeks, the Yew was a guardian of the soul as it went into the Underworld, aiding it in finding its right path. In Druidry, Yew adopts the Ovate.

Yew

the falling of light
and the place where it pooled
between us

if you were to come back now
I would eat your red berries
Roselle Angwin

Symbolism of Yew

Yew can help us to understand the life-death-life nature, and how it plays out on a small scale, every day, every moment.

Sitting as it does between the endings of Ruis, Elder, and the beginnings of Beth, Birch, we can see Yew as offering a concentrated dose of both – not unconnected, perhaps, symbolically, with the fact that it can target and kill cancer cells but leave the living organism healthier.

I am the waves' eternal return
The grave of every vain yearning
I know the secret of the three moons
And the secret path
And my dwelling place is the wind on the sea, the dolmen on the
    hillside, the rock in the river.

In the cycle of the year, 'the wave of the sea' that we met in in Elder is now joined to the many waves that 'eternally return'; subsumed into Ocean. In order to begin, to move forward, to be transformed, we have to be willing to let go of our desires and attachments, at least in the forms in which we crave them, over and over. The Triple Goddess in her three phases of the moon is illustrative of this endless cycling. The secret path can be known – to one who is willing to walk these hidden ways.

And, finally, eventually, we find that we are simultaneously here, there, and everywhere. Everywhere.

Part III

Practical

A Spell in the Forest

Working with the Trees & The Symbolism of 13 Trees in Practice

(a workbook and practice guide)

The way you'll work with the yearlong course of 13 moon-months in this book is like this:

DATES FOR EACH TREE MOON MONTH
Dec 24; Jan. 21; Feb. 18; Mar. 18; Apr. 15; May 13; Jun. 10; July 8; Aug. 5; Sept. 2; Sept. 30; Oct. 28; Nov. 25.

There is a day 'out of time', sometimes dedicated to the Yew tree, on 23rd December (probably originally 21st, during the winter solstice in the northern hemisphere; the word 'solstice' literally means 'sun standstill' – as it appears to do so over three days at this time).

During the first part of each tree 'chapter', above, you will have found a tree description for the tree of that month, in which we explore some or all of:

- that tree as a botanical being
- its habits, properties and qualities
- its place in the ecosystem
- its gifts to us
- its mythological aspects, including a story or poem for most of the months
- and then its symbolism, its wisdom teachings, predominantly in the Celtic Tree Calendar/Alphabet tradition.

Please buy a big hard-covered notebook – one you'll enjoy working with. Decorate the cover with an image or poem that seems to you to fit the work. Into this will go all your notes, associations, creative tasks, photos, sketches or images, fallen leaves, bark/leaf rubbings, quotes, any poems or stories you write or find in relation to that tree and its month, and aspects of the reflective process of working with the tree-months.

When you have some clear time to yourself close to the beginning of that tree-month, read the notes through. If you are not familiar with the tree of the month, look its image up online or in a book; maybe photocopy/print it out and stick into your notebook. Take a little while to see if you can remember/picture any individual trees of this species, and if you have personal associations with such a tree from your past or in your present. Write about this in any way you want.

Set aside a day or half-day within this tree's month to go out and find a tree of that particular species. Towards the bottom of this document will be instructions for the way that time is spent; you might want to print this out and paste it into the front of your notebook, as these tasks will be involved each month.

Outdoors by your tree you will be making a number of notes, prompted by my guidelines, directly into your notebook (or take paper for a rough copy). Hopefully you will also have creative responses in the shape of pieces of prose, little stories, or poems (but if not, don't worry – they may arrive later), and perhaps a small piece of land art.

As you go about your daily life over the rest of that tree-month be aware of images, thoughts, memories, feelings, associations that arise in connection with the tree or past trees, and be sure to write them down. If you can, visit that tree again.

Each month, you will be heading out to observe the trees wherever you are, and then wandering until you experience the sense that a particular tree of the month's species is 'speaking' to you – in other words, you'll be drawn to it. (This sounds flaky but it does happen, if one can be receptive enough.) I'll give you *guidance on the process of engaging*, and I'll give you some *preliminary writing suggestions,* and then *a writing task in three parts* designed to deepen a sense of connectivity.

You'll be sitting by or on or leaning against that tree, being as open as you can, until you feel a kind of connection, or reciprocity, arising. (People ask whether they're 'simply' imagining it. It doesn't matter whether this is a measurable and objective event, or whether it is an imagining. What matters is that it happens; and people do experience that it does.)

I will ask you to sustain this relationship until you are moved to write something from or about the experience. I encourage people to voice some words to the tree, though some people won't as it feels 'silly'.

At the end, you will make an offering to the tree in the shape of a small piece of land art, or a kind of shrine, to reflect respect and gratitude.

You might choose instead or also to leave a small offering – a feather, a crumb of home-made bread, a pinch of herbs, a tiny libation of fruit juice, cider or brandy, a note, a poem – whatever feels right to you.

You will need to write up some reflective notes on the whole experience afterwards.

After forming such a conscious relationship to one tree, and through it to its species, personal attachments are made, and a kind of 'spirit medicine' lodges in one.

I relate differently and more deeply to the tree realm in general and certain species in particular, often unexpected ones, each time I do this work.

Bit by bit it becomes more and more a felt experience that we are truly all in this together, held in a vast web of interrelationship.

SUGGESTIONS FOR YOUR TREE VISIT (you might want to photocopy this and glue it into the front of your workbook). You might also want to prepare a 'Tree Bag' to take out each time.

BEFORE
- take a small offering with you, each time time, as above
- take a notebook and pen; penknife; pencil or crayon and sheet of paper; camera perhaps
- general rule: don't cut living wood (unless there are no shed twigs; if you have to cut one, ask the tree first; be aware that 'barking' the tree can let disease in)

MEETING
- if you have enough trees to have a choice, wander until you feel pulled by a particular individual
- ask permission of each tree to work with it
- notice the tree's environment: sun, shade, dry, wet, company
- notice e.g. leaves, twigs, fruit in comparison with a different tree (e.g. Oak/Ash)
- notice its pattern of growth, very different in shape for each tree (e.g. Oak/Ash)

ENGAGING
- enter 'dreamtime' by leaning against the tree. Be aware this is a co-creative experience. Simply on a physical level you are exchanging your carbon dioxide for the tree's oxygen in a mutual accord. What does this feel like? What are you aware of? Perceptions, thoughts, feelings, memories?
- now let all other thoughts evaporate. Breathe deeply and slowly until you can in some way perceive the tree's being. This might take five minutes or it might take thirty. Listen deeply with your inward ears
- if you would like to, try the TREE MEDITATION on the

next page
- when you are ready, write about this experience

RESPONDING

This is quite a focused bit of writing, and will possibly be the most significant. Please follow the three suggestions (a paragraph or verse from each perspective) closely:

Firstly: draw back from the tree and observe it again, in close detail. Write ABOUT it – as 'it' – with careful near-scientific precision, and no fancy ideas(!)

Secondly: now write TO the tree, addressing it as 'you'. Write what you like; questions too, if they arise. NB this is a monologue, not a dialogue

Thirdly: write AS, or FROM, the tree, so in the first person, 'I'. Allow whatever lyricism presents itself

- make a piece of land art. It can be lovely to make a subtle wheel-like mandala at the foot of the tree, from its own fallen parts: leaves, twigs, fruits, catkins, nuts, seeds. You might want to photograph this
- write a few lines in response to your land art: whatever presents itself. A poem?
- ask the tree what it needs from you
- find a small twig, as straight as possible, shed by the tree. If there really isn't one, cut a small one once you are sure the tree is OK with this action. Bring it back and let it dry naturally
- take a bark and/or leaf rubbing with a crayon or soft (B+) pencil
- thank tree and make an offering when you leave

CLOSING

- at home: recall as much as you can about the tree, and

revisit the keynote' phrase for this tree-month
- write up anything you haven't, reflect on the process, and glue anything you need to in your notebook
- You may want to shape or redraft the 3-step process in RESPONDING into something more worked.

MOST IMPORTANTLY: What commitment can you give this tree, and all trees, in terms of your attention, your tending, your speaking up on behalf of trees? Write about this in a single sentence, if possible.

Things that might be useful:

- a magnifying glass
- a tree identification book (with photos)
- a knife and/or secateurs, to collect a fallen twig/piece of bark and maybe make an Ogham 'fidh', or 'letter'
- a flower press
- a small container to bring back twigs, seeds, berries, fallen leaves for your notebook, or you might wish to make a shrine.

Tree Meditation

I'm hesitant to include this as it will either seem like playschool, or you might have done something similar if you have in the past attended New Age-type groups or courses. However, it can be very powerful, so I don't want to omit it.

This is best done right beside, perhaps leaning against, the tree that has chosen you for each month; if you do it elsewhere, you'll need to be able to conjure an image of that tree.

Breathe in and out a few times, with an emphasis on a firm exhalation, letting go of thought. When you feel you have slowed to tree-time, picture the way the tree seems to touch the sky with its uppermost branches and canopy of leaves.

Then picture the tree's roots extending just as far into the soil as its upper parts extend heavenwards.

Imagine how those roots intertwine with each other and with the mycelial – fungal – network that supports them and transfers nutrients and messages.

Picture the xylem and phloem, circulating as your own blood circulates, a 'tree pulse'.

Next, bring to mind what you know that this tree symbolises, according to its month and the materials I have shared. Hold together in your mind and heart both the 'properties' and symbolic qualities of the tree, and also the line from 'The Song of Amergin' that is associated with that tree.

Now picture yourself as the tree. See how the crown of your head, your mind, your thoughts extend far beyond your skull. Imagine how your body, too, is rooted in this earth.

Bring your attention to breathing slowly in and out. See if you can harmonise with the tree's 'pulse'.

Is there something you can learn in relation to your own life from the tree's being and its symbolic properties?

SYMBOLIC 'MEANINGS' FOR EACH TREE MONTH

This is work you do *in addition* to the general outline above. What I offer is my perception; you may experience it differently. If so, follow that.

Each time, consider the 'keynote' and what it might suggest to you.

The dates again for each Tree Month

Dec 24; Jan. 21; Feb. 18; Mar. 18; Apr. 15; May 13; Jun. 10; July 8; Aug. 5; Sept. 2; Sept. 30; Oct. 28; Nov. 25.

BETH/BIRCH (December 24th)

I am a stag of seven tines in the midwinter Birchwood

Meditate on, or beside, Birch if there are situations in your life that need renewal or regeneration; or if there are toxic situations, or patterns of being, that you need to be free of. Birch can also symbolise clarity, courage, boundaries and the importance of solitude.

You might also want to consider if you are over-stretching yourself in some areas, or have isolated yourself; perhaps you are too proud to ask for and receive help?

On the other hand, if you feel stuck in a stale job or an overly claustrophobic or codependent situation or relationship, perhaps you need to find new ways to move forward, forging your own path, risking being on the edge a little.

- Do you need a new beginning?
- What might this beginning look like?
- Are you ready to step over the threshold?

Bear in mind, too, Birch's signification in relation to initiation (which of course can take many forms).

LUIS/ROWAN (January 21st)

I am the mist over a wide river-valley

As a powerful talisman, we could see Rowan as a guide when we journey into the unknown.

With its roots in the Otherworld and branches in this, so to speak, Rowan can help us draw back the veils of unknowing so that we might see more clearly, and understand the purpose of our journey here from a subtler perspective. Rowan can help us reconnect to our higher knowing and purpose.

Rowan protects, guards, guides and cleanses us on many levels, and links us too to sources of inspiration. Remember its connection with Bards, music, poetry (via its link with Brigid) and divination.

We can also contemplate and request guidance of Rowan when we are straying a little in the dark.

Do you have any memories in relation to this iconic tree? If you meditate beside it, can you feel the protecting quality of its spirit? Do you need guidance; or have secrets to tell Rowan?

NION/ASH (February 18th)

I am the wind on deep waters and the returning tide

I've always had the sense that Ash is a boundary tree, symbolising 'right relationship', 'right connectedness', and so on – not too distant, not too close. (I personally experience an Ash boundary through the fact that I find Ash a little slippery to engage with: slightly aloof, almost; impersonal. It might be different for you.)

This a good time to consider your connections, the state of your relationships: with yourself and your soul-life, with each other, with the other-than-human.

How is the balance of masculine and feminine in your own inner life?

You might want to *meditate on*, or beside, an Ash tree for insight into your connectedness, and whether/how you might be neglecting or blocking that – or indeed over-emphasising it.

Ash is also an opener tree: into the realms of inspiration.

FEARN/ALDER (March 18th)

I am the song of a shining tear of the sun

As we come up for the equinox, you might want to consider how much time you give to 'out there' activities, and how much time you offer to the more reflective inward needs of your psyche (and body).

We can call on the power of Brân, Alder King, when we need to cross an ocean, metaphorically, and feel overwhelmed by it. He will carry us.

This is also the perfect time to look at the way in which your life is in balance; or more probably out of balance, since that seems to be our common state on this plane. How is the balance between your head and your heart? What might need to change for greater equilibrium?

'The battle-witch tree.' Are there ways in which you are letting conflict ride on, when actually an understanding of complementarity might be more helpful? On the other hand, do you need to take action to right a wrong, inner or outer? Can you do this while still rooted in the feminine (water) aspect of being? The Tao Te Ching counsels: 'Know the masculine but cleave to the feminine.' You can call on Alder/Brân to champion the feminine.

And might you need the protection of a psychic shield in any part of your life?

You might also want to consider what in you needs transformation. Is there a gateway you need to go through? Can Alder with its otherworldly powers help here?

SAILLE/WILLOW (April 15th)

I am the Hawk of May, balanced above the cliff

Meditate on, or beside, Willow to have easier access to your dream life, your intuition, your unconscious imaginal and emotional life.

- Are there ways in which you exclude the above qualities from your life?
- What is your relationship to the deep feminine?
- Do you place too much value on the reasoning mind?
- Alternatively, do you need 'hawk medicine' to lift you above emotional 'swampiness' and superstition? Do you tend to passivity and being overly-yielding?
- Or are there areas in your life in which you are somewhat inflexible, unbending?
- Have you been neglecting your intuition or your dream life?
- Do you keep yourself too small? Willow can help you expand.

HUATH/HAWTHORN (May 13th)

I am the most radiant among blossoms, the flower maiden

In Hawthorn month, we might consider what promises, in which areas of our lives, might come towards their peak of fulfilment with this early summer.

It's also worth looking at the state of our 'inner marriage', and considering whether we have forgotten or neglected the vitality of that youthful inner 'maiden' who brings joy and fertility to our lives.

Do you remember how to bloom?

We could also consider the cycles of things: how summer is inevitably followed by winter, inwardly as well as outwardly, and how comfortable or otherwise we are with this transition.

DUIR/OAK (June 10th)

I am the oak-king who sets the head aflame
I am the god who crowns the waxing year

Someone once said that if it's a poet's job to transmit lightning, then s/he should stand out in as many storms as possible, or words to that effect. Whether or not you're a poet, inspiration is an important part of feeling alive. How often do you – and I stress that this is metaphorical! – 'court the lightning flash' that will fire your mind with ideas? How could you improve on this?

'Oak' people are stoic, keeping on keeping on, through all difficulties, and often at personal cost, keeping everything together. Do you, perhaps, need to recognise your limits, say no sometimes, let things drop, learn to delegate?

Think of that Green Man. In Oak month, the earth's vitality and fecundity is peaking now, in the northern hemisphere. This month, head out and find some Green Man carvings (they're often to be found in churches), and seek out your inner Green Man. Be outdoors as much as you can.

TINNE/HOLLY (July 8th)

I am the battle, the spear and the god who wields the spear
I am the god of the waning year

Holly represents the ability to act with assertion and kindness, together. That's quite some skill.

Meditate on or beside this tree if:

- you have lost your sense of Wild
- you feel yourself to have problems accessing your inner fire and power-to
- you find yourself over-sensitive and prickly
- you are not good at recognising your own rightful anger
- you feel yourself full of rage or anger but keep expressing it less than skilfully
- you feel yourself held back or disempowered by the repression of such pent-up energy
- you feel overly vulnerable, or your energies are scattered (Holly is good for directing energy, remember)
- you have ties to cut to separate you from people or situations that drain
- you could do with practising unconditional love.

COLL/HAZEL (August 5th)

I am a salmon's wisdom in the pool of inspiration

Meditate on, or beside, Hazel:

- for accessing the deep wisdom of the long-lived Salmon of Knowledge
- for finding concentrated insight and inspiration (the nut kernel)
- to divine the truth of something
- to experience the patience to wait for the nuts to fall in their season
- to discern where you belong; where home is.

MUIN/BRAMBLE (September 2nd)

I am a hill of poetry

Bramble offers the gifts of joy, exhilaration, intoxication in its many forms – and, if necessary, a fierceness. How are you doing with these expressions of yourself? Can you let yourself, when appropriate, be uninhibited?

How and how often do you let your creativity out? Can you easily move beyond the rational and literal mind into something freer?

What place do you make for the arts, and for poetry – however you understand that – in your life?

Do you recognise within yourself the two different faces of the feminine aspect of being as detailed under Muin? Is there the quiet biddable woman who is counterbalanced by the altogether wilder and fiercer woman? (This is true whatever your biological gender, as we all have this contrasexual aspect to our psyche.)

QUERT/APPLE (September 30th)

I am the island of apples and eternal life

Meditate on or beside Apple to increase poetic inspiration, abundance, generosity, open-heartedness, and sensitivity.

Where are your own 'Blessed Isles', literal or metaphorical? My own experience is that Apple a tree of vision/s. Try this out, with your back to an Apple tree trunk and your eyes closed.

In the Bach flower remedies, the Crab Apple is a potent cleanser on a psychological or emotional level, helping you if you are low in self-esteem, or go through phases of self-loathing or shame. It can lift one out of mild depression, too.

And bear in mind the fact that the old adage of 'an Apple a day keeps the doctor away' seems to be rooted in verifiable fact.

Try to include one in your diet every day during Apple season.

STRAIF/BLACKTHORN (October 28th)

I am the black bough, the Cailleach (Crone)

On a psychological level, Blackthorn reminds us of our periodic need to 'go into the dark'. This way, we can meet the things in us that have festered or not healed, and that need our attention. In its inwardness, it can aid our meditation in relation to courage to walk into the dark, the unknown and unfamiliar, trusting that we will emerge again.

Do you let yourself go into the dark, psychologically, and if not, why not? What are your fears? Do you pay attention to your need for rest, retreat, hibernation? Can you simply take time out, with no agenda?

How is your will? Blackthorn too is about developing strong boundaries, not being afraid of anger – one's own or others' – and effective use of the will and intention. Blackthorn can help if one is not good at keeping one's own counsel, or one feels that everything should be shared, nothing should be private, no one should have secrets (while this might be admirable, it is also unbalanced, and can be the mark of the co-dependent).

How do you deal with the fact that life is inevitably followed by death? Blackthorn can remind us of the natural laws of the opposites that together make a whole (e.g. day and night); of the laws of mutual exchange (give and take); of cause and effect.

RUIS/ELDER (November 25th)

I am the faery tree, and I am a wave of the sea

Meditate on, or beside, Elder to access your own deep wisdom.

An Elder person is wise, generous, and loves freely. They can thrive anywhere, and know that they are both resilient and resourceful, and, just as an Elder branch might take root and the Elder tree can replace its limbs easily, they too can regenerate, and rejuvenate.

What might it mean, to be an elder, in our culture? How are you tending your own move towards elderhood, or at least through the different phases of your life?

What deep truths do you know?

A particular, and challenging, gift of Elder is its invitation to think about death and deaths. Do you/have you had to face this?

Now is a good time to review your year, in order to step forward into the earth's turning back towards the light at the midwinter solstice. What doors are you closing this year, and what might you need to let go of as you do so?

Similarly, it's helpful to consider, as we move towards new beginnings, whether there is a situation or relationship that is holding you back, in which closure might be needed.

And we come to the end of the 13-moon cycle that sits within the solar year. But not quite: at that time out of time, the solstice, sits the Yew, in my calendar. Here's a kind of bonus Tree:

IOLO/YEW (December 21st)

I am the waves' eternal return
The grave of every vain yearning
I know the secret of the three moons
And the secret path
And my dwelling place is the wind on the sea, the dolmen on the
*   hillside, the rock in the river.*

After leading us through the possibility of death as symbolised by Blackthorn to the representation of death offered by the ageing solar year and Elder, Yew brings us face-to-face with the inescapability of death at the time, in the northern hemisphere, of maximum darkness and minimal light. Now we have no choice. And yet, like the waves, the Yew also promises us eternal return, and nurtures the young shoots, sometimes within the corpus of its own hollowed-out body, of new life.

If you have read this far, I consider that you are now equipped to work out the deeper meaning of the Yew's keynote, above, without my help. And perhaps in the belly of darkness, the womb of the Yew tree, are the shoots of new poems or stories, books or ideas to blaze a trail for you.

The Intertwinement

'Saving the remaining rainforests and other rich ecosystems, while restoring those we have lost, is not just a nice idea: our lives may depend on it.'
George Monbiot[32]

It's all very well taking a poet's look at trees, and the wonder of them. It is of course right to celebrate the miraculous whole that is Wildwood, Forest, and the tree realm. But it is no longer possible to write a book about trees – about any aspect of the whole miraculous natural world of which we're an integral part – without addressing the climate crisis, and the extinction crisis, and the looming food and water crises, each of which has happened at our hands and in each of which trees play a part, major or minor.

The mainstream prevailing belief is still less than joined-up thinking, but if we turn, as I do frequently in my thinking, living and writing, to the Hindu and Buddhist image of Indra's Net in which every single being exists as a kind of diamond-bright 'node' at the junction of countless utterly interconnected filaments, a very helpful image for our 'interdependent co-arising', as Buddhism would say, then it becomes very clear that every action affecting one node, no matter how small, has a consequent effect on the whole web of life, and clearly applies as much to positive actions as to negative. (This is a more useful definition of 'karma' than the more common and somewhat facile interpretation.)

I find this a useful way of looking at an ecosystem. Try as we might, we can't live outside of the natural ecosystem, despite the fact that we so routinely and destructively (albeit usually unthinkingly) damage our home. Each species, each individual, has a place in the ecosystem that contributes to the healthy – or otherwise – functioning of the whole. Remove any one species, but especially a key species, and the whole is threatened with collapse. Trees are nothing if not a key species.

Currently, the world is losing an area of forest the size of the UK every year.[33] In Brazil, an area the size of three football fields is cleared *every minute* for cattle-ranching, monoculture cropping (around 90 per cent of all arable crops, largely grain and soya beans, are grown to feed said cattle, which are most often reared in intensive farming conditions, i.e. indoors or penned in vast grassless shadeless feedlots) and timber. Mining for minerals to feed our industrial and technological economies only too frequently also depends on clearing rare old-growth forest.

Ironically, the act of deforestation itself releases carbon dioxide emissions into the atmosphere that account for about ten per cent of the total.[34]

As I type this, there's a report in today's *Guardian* that informs us that in the 1990s, 46 billion tonnes of CO_2 produced by human activity was removed by tropical forests. Now, in the last ten years, the second decade of the 21st century, only 25 billion tonnes was sequestered by tropical forests – that's just 6% of global human emissions. If this trend continues, the typical tropical forest 'could become a carbon source' instead of carbon sink by the 2060s, says an author of the research, Simon Lewis, a professor at the school of geography at Leeds University.[35]

At the very least, we should be angry – at the industries and multinationals that perpetrate it, at the governments that allow this, at the capitalist markets that demand it.

Britain is one of the most deforested lands in the world, shockingly. We have between 10% and 13% per cent tree cover only, the greater part of which is plantation conifer. As I write, we are debating the future of HS2, the high-speed rail link between London and northern cities. If it goes ahead, we will be losing even more ancient woodland.

There is now an accelerating movement to plant more trees. Clearly, this has to be a good thing.

But there is another more effective way of addressing runaway climate change, loss of habitat and biodiversity and restoring healthy ecosystems, and that is succession: natural regeneration, natural restoration, of existing woodland or embryonic woodland without human interference; otherwise known as rewilding. Leaving trees to seed and spread themselves can be faster, more effective for growth and tree-health, and richer in relation to ecosystems than replanting.

So surprisingly, perhaps, in general terms new planting of woodland is a less effective solution, at least in the short- and medium-term. That doesn't mean, though, that planting trees is useless: very far from it. We need as much tree-cover as possible, and in Britain we are falling far behind our current target, estimated by the Committee on Climate Change as 1.5 billion trees needed (which equates to approximately 30,000 hectares, or 74,000 acres, planted each year) if we are to achieve carbon zero by 2050. This would mean increasing our current forest cover from 13% (at best) to 19%.[36]

Clearly a solution has to incorporate both natural regeneration and helping this process with careful replanting where necessary (for instance, where trees are struggling to establish themselves, and in this case, it might mean clearing some of the competing vegetation). Clearly, we need far more broadleaf trees, as well as the habitat they offer. However, given our reliance on timber for building, we will also still need some faster-growing conifers, it seems, who may also sequester carbon more swiftly than their slower-growing neighbours.

While I don't intend to address this issue in this book (I'm writing another about sustainable plant-based lifestyles), one of the most effective things we can do to help the planet and her other-than-human species as well as our own is to reduce or eliminate animal products from our diet. Given that it takes in excess of ten times more land to feed our current population on a meat-based diet that inevitably includes clearing forest, one step, that of switching to a plant-based diet, would free up land to make the regeneration of woodland more immediately possible, simultaneously with drastically reducing pollution of air and water, and the reduction of animal suffering on an almost unbelievable scale, given that each year we eat around 77 billion land animals (and rising) and over 2.7 trillion marine animals.[37] It would also start to address the social inequality that exists as a result of our current consumption: the affluent countries' individual diets typically consist of at least one meat meal a day and plenty of dairy, while billions of people starve from lack of basic less land-hungry staple crops.

At a time when ancient woodlands and old-growth forests have shrunk to a tiny percentage of their original blanketing of much of the globe, current natural woodlands (as opposed, of course, to coniferous timber plantations, which on the whole are by comparison disastrous for anyone and anything other than those who profit from their logging, despite what I said above) are establishing what will become the old-growth forests of tomorrow.

Of course, depending on the site and its current tree cover or lack of, it can take time for scrubland to develop via the pioneer species such as birch into mature forests. Arguably, we don't have that time, but it's a question of preserving what we do have while simultaneously replanting for new growth. The latter needs to be done with sensitivity: native trees, ones that flourish in the particular planting site and not imported, ones that mimic as much as possible the natural mix of species found in the area. There is an argument that climate change may require us to plant non-native fast-growing trees including various conifers as well; I'm not qualified to speak on this.

It goes without saying that such replanting should be done without clear-felling, and preferably without weeding out species such as birch, hazel and thorn, and certainly without herbicides such as glyphosates.

Reciprocity

If we are to address climate change and stop both loss of forests and the consequent disastrous global impacts, plus the terrifying acceleration of species' extinction what we need, and I hope that this is implicit if not explicit in this book, is a transformed relationship to everything that is other-than-human: a conscious relationship rooted in understanding and awareness of our inter-connectedness.

As a species we have tended, probably for millennia and certainly during the Christian era, towards a mindset that assumes that everything on earth has been put here for our benefit as a so-called apex species; that everything is a 'resource' for us. Quite apart from any moral issues, on a finite planet we cannot expect to be sustained by a one-way relationship. It's imperative that we wake up, shake off our complacency and apathy, recognise not simply the relevance but the essential and urgent need for a relationship of mutual giving.

Our hope now lies in a relationship that might best be described as one of 'reciprocal affinity'. Clare Dubois, co-founder and CEO of Tree Sisters, says: 'We have to make it as natural to give back to nature as it is to take nature for granted.' We need to 'shift from a consumer species to a restorer species'.[38]

What we can do as individuals

This is necessarily a partial and simplistic attempt at summarising a huge picture, but here are some suggestions. I'm uncomfortably aware that they are small gestures. The more of us who commit to doing *something*, the better the outcome will be, however, clearly. And you will feel better, too.

Get to know tree species If you don't already, then get to know your local trees. Make a species' count in your garden, hedgerow, street, road, lanes, fields. Make a tree-map.

Plant one, or ten, or a hundred native trees, and pledge to do this at least once a year. While one tree might not make much difference, a million of us planting one or more a year would. In Britain, the Committee on Climate Change reported that while the European average of woodland in relation to land area is 35%, the UK's is currently (2019) around 13% (Monbiot says more like 10%). Source local whips or seedlings and saplings, or collect your own seeds. Collect acorns, beechmast, hazelnuts, conkers, sweet chestnut, apple pips, rowan berries. You can plant any of these in your own garden, but be aware of their potential final height, and the fact that they can impede drains, affect house foundations, block your neighbour's light, interfere with telephone wires and electricity supplies, and so on, so choose your spot, and tree, carefully. It's less easy to plant on wasteland or common land or in parks without permission (but try the council), and in towns you might ask about planting in local school grounds, around municipal buildings, in hospital and library grounds. Trees are beneficial for so many reasons in towns.

But tree planting doesn't go far enough, as I said above. Here's George Monbiot in *The Guardian* of 25th September 2019:

'We urgently need more trees, but we appear to believe that the only means of restoring them is planting. We have a national obsession with tree planting, which is in danger of becoming as tokenistic as bamboo toothbrushes and cotton tote bags. In many places rewilding, or natural regeneration – allowing trees to seed and spread themselves – is much faster and more effective, and tends to produce far richer habitat.'

So if you are a landowner consider **setting aside land for natural**

regeneration, planting only where it might help, and don't be too hasty to clear too much scrubland, such as brambles, gorse and thorn, that might protect the young trees from deer or rabbit damage (better and more effective than plastic tubing).

Campaign to stop local trees being cut down (some are being removed in cities for 5G) and consider getting a group together. Consider taking out tree preservation orders on old or significant trees.

Lobby. Protest. Write letters to MPs, your council, various bodies, the Prime Minister. Speak to friends, family, neighbours about all this.

Become a tree guardian or tree warden – ask your parish council if they have a scheme. 'Tree Wardens' are part of a national network of volunteers co-ordinated by the Tree Council. They help protect trees in their area.

Volunteer for tree-planting days in your local community or through one of the charities such as Trees For Life, Trees For Cities or The Woodland Trust. Check out or set up a local community orchard scheme – they're on the rise.

Grow your own food and do it sustainably. Going vegan or, if you prefer, plant-based is a major contributor to this thriving future scenario, given that it takes ten to fourteen times less land to feed people on a plant-based diet than to raise animals to eat or for dairy, whether it's grazing land or land used to grow monocrops to feed intensively-farmed livestock. It's also healthy, and it feels good to minimise suffering. (Some will say that our upland regions are perfect for sheep-rearing; they're even more perfect for natural regeneration.)

Taking up a great deal less space to feed the people of

the world means that our current population could co-exist alongside a serious and diverse regreening of our planet and a restoration of habitat, tree cover and species without people going hungry as far as production is concerned – the political reasons incorporating unequal wealth and distribution are a different matter.

I recommend watching George Monbiot's film *Apocalypse Cow*; and also seek out *Demain,* or *Tomorrow* (a 'feelgood' film – there's more happening that's positive than you might be aware of).

Plant a forest garden. I mentioned in the Introduction the swift-growing worldwide initiatives for forest gardens, which would transform our currently-devastating agricultural practices. Forest gardens allow us to replicate successful and biodiverse ecosystems that produce perennial food crops in symbiotic or at least synergistic 'vertical' systems (which thrive on several 'planes' from canopy to understorey) that will not only act as carbon sinks and habitat but also have a much lighter footprint than annual cropping (which has many destructive side-effects, such as depletion of soil health, disturbance of mycorrhizal networks, increasing soil erosion, diminishing habitat and biodiversity).

Related to this, look into **permaculture**, a different, arguably less labour-intensive and certainly more sustainable method of growing food crops.

Minimise your consumption altogether. Only buy **recycled paper products** where possible, including obviously toilet tissue. The FSC certification is better than nothing but doesn't go anything like far enough as it justifies the continued planting of softwood forests, mostly sitka spruce, which contributes to sterility and acidification of the soil, plus the planting of coniferous trees in straight rows and logging them young doesn't do the soil and the mycorrhizal networks, the trees or the habitat any favours: no biodiversity, no understorey, nowhere to encourage the return of wildlife, devastation caused by clear-felling, and so on.

Help cut emissions by stopping **flying**. Cut back on all your **personal fossil fuel use** and lobby your council to provide cycle lanes and more public transport, preferably powered with renewables. In your home, retrofit insulation and consider solar thermal power and photovoltaics, and ground, water or air source heat pumps. Change to a renewable energy provider.

Instead of lawn, create a **wildflower meadow**, which will of course benefit pollinator insects and the birds who eat them. Or plant a shrubbery, fruit bushes or a vegetable garden.

Don't build super-trendy **decking**.

We don't, at this point in history, know whether we can turn it all around in time. But whatever we individually believe, I feel that there is no ethical justification for not doing anything. What we can each contribute might only be a leaf in the forest, but then the forest is made of leaves.

None of us is truly separate; we are one another, we are part of an endless whole, unceasingly changing and reinventing itself. There's some consolation in that, don't you think?

Endnotes and References

1 Ferguson, David, 2016, Trees Make Our Lives Better in Unquantifiable Ways, The Guardian, 24 April 2016 [online]. Available at https://www.theguardian.com/commentisfree/2016/apr/24/trees-make-our-lives-better-in-unquantifiable-ways (accessed March 2020)

2 Livni, Ephrat, 2016, The Japanese practice of 'forest bathing' is scientifically proven to improve your health, Quartz, 12 October 2016 [online]. Available at http://qz.com/804022/health-benefits-japanese-forest-bathing/ (accessed March 2020)

3 This chain might have its origins in truly ancient times: the abri I mention, a shelter known to have been used in the Mesolithic period, dates back several thousand years BCE. Marchand, Grégor; Monnier, Jean-Laurent; Pustoc'h, François and Quesnel, Laurent, 2014, An original settlement during the Tardiglacial in Brittany: the rock shelter of Kerbizien in Huelgoat, PALEO revue d'archéologie préhistorique, Issue 25 2014 [online]. Available at https://journals.openedition.org/paleo/3012 (accessed March 2020)

4 Deakin, Roger, *Wildwood – A Journey Through Trees* (Penguin, London 2008)

5 Lee, Laurie *As I Walked Out One Midsummer Morning* (Penguin, London 1973)

6 Anathaswamy, Anil, 2014, Roots of consciousness, *New Scientist* issue 2998, 6 December 2014

7 Wohlleben, Peter, *The Hidden Life of Trees* (tr. Jane Billinghurst, Greystone Books Vancouver, Canada 2016)

8 Keim, Brandon, 2019, Never Underestimate the Intelligence of Trees, Nautilus, 31 October 2019 [online]. Available at http://nautil.us/issue/77/underworldsnbsp/never-underestimate-the-intelligence-of-trees?fbclid=IwAR3w0EC5LtRZh

xLQeitVxWkT4vWpfpmDx2stowDH9SxRo8QVOU3Kc3U-
WHc8 (accessed March 2020)

9   Simard, S., Perry, D., Jones, M. et al. 1997, Net transfer of
carbon between ectomycorrhizal tree species in the field.
Nature 388, pp579–582 7 August 1997 [online]. Available at
https://doi.org/10.1038/41557 (accessed March 2020)

10 MacFarlane, Robert, 2016, The Secrets of the Wood Wide
Web, New Yorker, August 7, 2016 [online]. Available at
http://www.newyorker.com/tech/elements/the-secrets-of-
the-wood-wide-web (accessed March 2020)

11 Montgomery, Pam, *Plant Spirit Healing – A Guide to Working
with Plant Consciousness* (Bear & Company, Vermont 2008)

12 Fowles, John, *The Tree* (Vintage Classics, London 2000)

13 O'Connor, M R, 2019, A Day in the Life of a Tree, New Yorker, 27 August 2019 [online]. Available at https://www.new-
yorker.com/science/elements/a-day-in-the-life-of-a-tree (accessed March 2020)

14 New Yorker, ibid

15 Poetry Wales 55.2, January 2020

16 Hageneder, Fred, *The Heritage of Trees* (Floris Books, Edinburgh 2001); see also *The Spirit of Trees* (Floris Books, Edinburgh; Continuum, New York 2000/2006/2017) and *The Living Wisdom of Trees* (Duncan Baird, London, 2005/2020)

17 For an excellent overview and much detailed information
on modern Druidry, go to www.Druidry.org

18 Matthews, Paul, *The Ground that Love Seeks* (Five Seasons
Press, Hereford 1996)

19 Matthews, Paul, ibid

20 Matthews, John, *The Song of Taliesin – stories and poems from
the books of Brocéliande*, (Aquarian Press, London 1991)

21 Pennick, Nigel, *Ogham and Coelbren: keys to the Celtic Mysteries* (Capall Bann, Chieveley 2000)

22 Hageneder, Fred, *The Heritage of Trees* (Floris Books, Edinburgh 2001)

23 Stewart, R J, *Earthlight* (Element Books, Shaftesbury, 1992)

24 It seems from early Irish chronicles that the daughter, Meritaten, of the exceptionally metaphysically-enlightened pharaonic/priestly couple, Akhenaten and Nefertiti, may have been buried at Tara and her descendants, it has been suggested, might therefore have been the high kings of Ireland, whose seat was at Tara. Certainly, a necklace of Egyptian faïence beads found around the neck of a female skeleton at the sacred mound of Tara have been carbon-dated to Akhenaten's time, 1350BCE. Again, the chronicles also record the arrival of an Egyptian woman, a pharaoh's daughter this time called Scota, into what is now Ireland at around the time in question.

25 Matthews, John, *The Song of Taliesin: stories and poems from the Books of Brocéliande* (Aquarian Press, London 1991)

26 According to scholar Graham Robb, Herakles was a significant god in ancient Gaul, possibly the inspiration for some pre-Roman long-distance sunrise to sunset straight roads right across the land – upon which, according to Robb, the Romans then built the straight roads for which they are, possibly unjustifiably, famous. See *The Ancient Paths: Discovering the Lost Map of Celtic Europe* (Picador, London 2014)

27 Matthews, John, ibid

28 Heginworth, Ian Siddons, *Environmental Arts Therapy and the Tree of Life* (Spirit's Rest Books, Exeter 2009)

29 Paterson, Jacqueline Memory, *Tree Wisdom – The definitive guidebook to the myth, folklore and healing power of Trees* (Thorsons, London 1996)

30 Ibid

31 Kindred, Glennie, *The Tree Ogham,* (Glennie Kindred, Wirksworth 1997)

32 Monbiot, George, 2019, Rewilding will make Britain a rainforest nation again, The Guardian, 25 September 2019 [online]. Available at https://www.theguardian.com/commen-

tisfree/2019/sep/25/rewilding-britains-rainforest-planting-trees (accessed March 2020)

33 Saner, Emine, 2019 Grow your own forest: how to plant trees to help save the planet. The Guardian, 4 September 2019 [online]. https://www.theguardian.com/environment/2019/sep/04/grow-your-own-forest-how-to-plant-trees-to-help-save-the-planet (accessed March 2020)

34 Saner, Emine, as above

35 Harvey, Fiona, 2020, Amazon region losing carbon sink capacity as climate crisis takes hold, *The Guardian*, 5 March 2020

36 Barkham, Patrick, Woodland and the climate crisis, *The Guardian,* 27 February 2020

37 There's an Elephant in the Room blog, 2020 Slaughter numbers jump by 2.2 billion, 10 February 2020 [online]. Available at https://theresanelephantintheroomblog.wordpress.com/2020/02/10/slaughter-numbers-jump-by-2-2-billion/ (all statistics are derived from FAOSTAT http://www.fao.org/faostat/en/#data/QL) (accessed March 2020)

38 Barkham, Patrick, 2019, Can planting billions of trees save the planet? The Guardian19 June 2019 [online]. Available at https://www.theguardian.com/world/2019/jun/19/planting-billions-trees-save-planet (accessed March 2020)

A note on my use of the word 'Faery'

I use the word 'fairy' in its common usage for e.g. fairy tales. Since I also use the word 'faery' throughout this book, I want to make an attempt to justify and explain this.

I've mentioned a parallel, more subtle, realm (one of many such possible realms). In mystical or psychical and occult language this is often known as 'the astral plane' with its devas, presiding spirits of the other-than-human, and elemental beings; to some, the realm of soul. To the Celts, this was one understanding of the Otherworld (some have called it the Land of Faery).

I see it as (also) an inner realm which requires a minute adjustment of consciousness towards the more subtle.

It's to do, for me, with this material plane being arguably the densest form of the manifestation of energy-as-matter. In other words, there are underlying shaping 'causes' of which planet earth might be an 'effect'.

I assume the existence of other planes of being, planes of consciousness, in which exist invisible intelligences – I'm not talking 'aliens' from outer space, but an enwrapping field of consciousness to the material existence of our planet – that shape the external world of nature which, in this theory, then consists of the visible effects of subtler energetic causes. Jung says something about the body inhabiting the soul (as opposed to the more usual idea of it being the other way round); this has a bearing on this idea.

At certain times, maybe, to certain people or people in certain states of consciousness, the 'nearest' of these more subtle worlds intersects more noticeably with our more familiar physical world; and in certain places, and especially in a heightened mood of sensitivity, this might happen more readily.

In times less scientifically sceptical than ours, and notably in the Celtic areas of Great Britain and in Brittany, until relatively recently the existence of entities from these planes of being – people of the 'Royal race', the 'Little Folk' (though some say they were, or are, no smaller than us), Fair Folk or Faeries – interacting with our own was commonly believed and frequently experienced.

If there is interchange between subtle planes and our own more familiar material one, there is every likelihood that the subtle plane would shape what is actually an exchange of energy into a form that might be perceived by the physical senses of the receiver or witness – (if that is required – for many people it's an intuited sense of a parallel reality rather than a physical manifestation as a distinct being).

It may require, too, a collaborative effort between a human open to the idea of the existence of planes beyond the material, and a being from such a plane for their manifestation to happen; and/or for us to witness it.

Another possibility, clearly, is that we anthropomorphically shape intuited but essentially formless experiences as entities in our own form.

Most people in our scientific era think we have simply grown out of this naïve rubbish and that such planes and entities, of course, not only don't exist but have never existed except in people's imaginations.

Others believe that the occurrence and experience of such interchanges diminishes, naturally, if people are not open to it.

However, there is a standing wave of people now turning to these ancient beliefs and ideas, and many who understand the concept of such an Otherworld and have been trained to, if you like, 'speak its language'. It's not a coincidence that, in a search for meaning and value, many are looking beyond the purely material 'answers' of our technological and industrialised times, and that there has been not only a huge resurgence of passion for the rest of the natural world, but also of interest in the metaphysical: informing and shaping forces beyond the material.

Commitment to the various Druid, pagan and panpsychism beliefs and organisations globally espousing these beliefs and practices, for instance, has grown enormously.

Author Biography

Cornish writer Roselle Angwin grew up in the rural Westcountry of Britain. This allowed her to run free as a child, befriending animals and birds, plants and trees. Later, she read Anglo-Saxon, Norse and Celtic with Mediaeval French at Cambridge, focusing on Celtic and Grail mythology in the original languages, then trained in transpersonal psychology and counselling.

Author of a number of books of poetry, novels and non-fiction, Roselle has been described as 'a poet of the bright moment... whose own sources of creative inspiration are her native Westcountry, the Scottish islands, and a highly individual blend of Celtic myth and metaphysics, psychology, shamanic and Zen Buddhist thinking'.

Working with the creative imagination, deep ecology, poetry, myth, depth psychology and the Druid way, all her work focuses on personal and collective transformation, as she believes that the best way to change the world is to change oneself. All her work too now has as its central aim the re-visioning of our relationship to the other-than-human.

Roselle leads two programmes of workshops and retreats: one with a holistic writing focus ('Fire in the Head', established in 1991), the other working largely outdoors to bring soul into the way we relate to the rest of the natural world ('The Wild Ways: ecosoul – the ecological imagination').

Her 20 years of guiding participants through her 'Islands of the Heart' annual retreat on the sacred Isle of Iona have earned her an international reputation, and in 2019 *The Telegraph* listed this retreat in their worldwide top ten creative writing holidays. Her current project is her yearlong 'Tongues in Trees' course.

From the Author

Thank you for buying A SPELL IN THE FOREST – TONGUES IN TREES. I'd like to think that you have enjoyed reading this book as much as I enjoyed writing it (but without my headache of multiple redrafts). I also hope it inspires you to look at trees differently.

If you have a few moments, I'd be delighted if you were to add your review of this book to your favourite relevant online sites – such reviews, even just a sentence or two, make such a difference to authors.

I'm currently working on Book II. If you'd like to know more about this or other books of mine, plus related courses and new projects, or read my blogs, do visit my websites and sign up for my newsletter.

Thanks and blessings

Roselle Angwin

www.roselle-angwin.co.uk
www.thewildways.co.uk
roselle-angwin.blogspot.com
Facebook: Roselle Angwin & Fire in the Head
Twitter @qualiabird
www.goodreads.com/rosellel

Bibliography & Further Reading

Adams, Max, *The Wisdom of Trees* (Head of Zeus, London 2014)

Adams, Max, *Trees of Life* (Head of Zeus, London 2019)

Anderson, William, with Hicks, Clive, *Green Man – The Archetype of our Oneness with the Earth* (COMPASSbooks, Fakenham, 1998)

Billington, Penny, *The Wisdom of Birch, Oak and Yew* (Llewellyn Publications, Woodbury 2015)

Buhner, Stephen Harrod, *Plant Intelligence and the Imaginal Realm* (Bear & Company, Vermont 2014)

Bouchardon, Patrice, *The Healing Energies of Trees* (Journey Editions, Boston, Tokyo 1999)

Criaghead, Meinrad, *The Sign of the Tree* (Artists House, Mitchell Beazley, London 1979)

Crawford, Martin, *Creating a Forest Garden* (Green Books, Totnes 2010)

Cowan, Eliot, *Plant Spirit Medicine* (Swan Raven & Co, Columbus 1999)

Deakin, Roger, *Wildwood* (Penguin, London 2008)

Graves, Robert, *The White Goddess*, (Faber, London, 1975)

Hageneder, Fred, *The Spirit of Trees – Science, Symbiosis and Inspiration* (Floris Books, Edinburgh, 2000)

Hageneder, Fred, *The Heritage of Trees – History, Culture and Symbolism* (Floris Books, Edinburgh, 2001)

Hageneder, Fred, *The Living Wisdom of Trees – Natural History, Folklore, Symbolism, Healing* (Duncan Baird Publishers, London 2005/2020)

Haskell, David George, *The Songs of Trees – stories from nature's greatest connectors* (Viking, New York 2017)

Heginworth, Ian Siddons, *Environmental Arts Therapy and the Tree of Life* (Spirits Rest, Exeter 2009)

Kindred, Glennie, *Walking With Trees* (Permanent Publications,

East Meon 2019)

Kindred, Glennie, *The Tree Ogham* (Kindred, Wirksworth 1997)

King, Angela & Clifford, Susan, *Trees Be Company – an anthology of poetry* (Common Ground/Green Books, Totnes 2001)

Maitland, Sara, *Gossip from the Forest – the tangled roots of our forests and fairytales* (Granta, London 2012)

Montgomery, Pam, *Plant Spirit Healing – A Guide to Working with Plant Consciousness* (Bear & Company, Vermont 2008)

Paterson, Jacqueline Memory, *Tree Wisdom – the definitive guidebook to the myth, folklore and healing power of trees* (London, San Francisco, 1996)

Pennick, Nigel, *Ogham and Coelbren – Keys to the Celtic Mysteries* (Capall Bann, Chieveley 2000)

Phillips, Roger, *Trees in Britain* (Pan, London 1983)

Powers, Richard, *The Overstory* (William Heinemann, London 2018)*

Sentier, Elen, *Trees of the Goddess* (Moon Books, Alresford 2014)

Swinfen, Alison, *Through Wood – Prayers and poems reconnecting with the forest* (Wild Goose Publications, Glasgow 2009)

Williamson, John, *The Oak King, The Holly King and the Unicorn* (Harper & Row, New York 1986)

Wohlleben, Peter, tr Jane Billinghurst, *The Hidden Life of Trees* (Greystone Books/David Suzuki Institute, Vancouver 2015)*

Zucchelli, Christine, *Trees of Inspiration – Sacred Trees and Bushes of Ireland* (The Collins Press, Cork 2009)

* *If you only read two of the above list, make it these two.*

**MOON
BOOKS**

PAGANISM & SHAMANISM

What is Paganism? A religion, a spirituality, an alternative belief
system, nature worship? You can find support for all these defini-
tions (and many more) in dictionaries, encyclopaedias, and text
books of religion, but subscribe to any one and the truth will evade
you. Above all Paganism is a creative pursuit, an encounter with
reality, an exploration of meaning and an expression of the soul.
Druids, Heathens, Wiccans and others, all contribute their insights
and literary riches to the Pagan tradition. Moon Books invites you
to begin or to deepen your own encounter, right here, right now.
If you have enjoyed this book, why not tell other readers by
posting a review on your preferred book site.

Medicine for the Soul
The Complete Book of Shamanic Healing
Ross Heaven
All you will ever need to know about shamanic healing and how to become your own shaman...
Paperback: 978-1-78099-419-2 ebook: 978-1-78099-420-8

Shaman Pathways – The Druid Shaman
Exploring the Celtic Otherworld
Danu Forest
A practical guide to Celtic shamanism with exercises and techniques as well as traditional lore for exploring the Celtic Otherworld.
Paperback: 978-1-78099-615-8 ebook: 978-1-78099-616-5

Traditional Witchcraft for the Woods and Forests
A Witch's Guide to the Woodland with Guided Meditations and Pathworking
Mélusine Draco
A Witch's guide to walking alone in the woods, with guided meditations and pathworking.
Paperback: 978-1-84694-803-9 ebook: 978-1-84694-804-6

Naming the Goddess
Trevor Greenfield
Naming the Goddess is written by over eighty adherents and scholars of Goddess and Goddess Spirituality.
Paperback: 978-1-78279-476-9 ebook: 978-1-78279-475-2

Shapeshifting into Higher Consciousness
Heal and Transform Yourself and Our World with Ancient
Shamanic and Modern Methods
Llyn Roberts
Ancient and modern methods that you can use every day to
transform yourself and make a positive difference in the world.
Paperback: 978-1-84694-843-5 ebook: 978-1-84694-844-2

Readers of ebooks can buy or view any of these bestsellers by
clicking on the live link in the title. Most titles are published in
paperback and as an ebook. Paperbacks are available in traditional
bookshops. Both print and ebook formats are available online.

Find more titles and sign up to our readers' newsletter at
http://www.johnhuntpublishing.com/paganism
Follow us on Facebook at https://www.facebook.com/MoonBooks
and Twitter at https://twitter.com/MoonBooksJHP

You might also like...

eds. *Paul Davies*
Caitlín Matthews

Foreword by Graham Harvey
Afterword by Ronald Hutton

This volume is an absolute treasure trove · a stunning collection of essays that offer much food for thought for every spiritual seeker'.
Philip Carr-Gomm, Order of Bards Ovates and Druids.

This Ancient Heart: Landscape, Ancestor, Self
Paul Davies & Caitlín Matthews

*This Ancient Heart brings together leading spiritual and academic thinkers in order
to explore the threefold relationship between landscape, ancestor, and self.*

978-1-78279-967-2 (Paperback)
978-1-78279-968-9 (ebook)

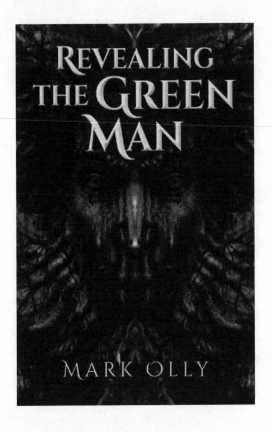

Revealing the Green Man
Mark Olly

A full history of the physical and spiritual development of the Green Man from Prehistoric origins to modern-day archaeological discoveries.

978-1-78099-336-2 (Paperback)
978-1-78099-573-1 (ebook)

Trees of the Goddess
Elen Sentier

Work with the Trees of the Goddess and the old ways of Britain.

978-1-78279-332-8 (Paperback)
978-1-78279-331-1 (ebook)